THOMAS B. LITTLEWOOD
HORNER OF ILLINOIS

The life of the man who served as Governor of Illinois from 1933 until his death in 1940, one of the most turbulent periods in the history of the state.

Horner of Illinois

Governor Henry Horner—a portrait painted by John Doctoroff.
By permission of The Standard Club, Chicago.

Thomas B. Littlewood

Horner of Illinois

NORTHWESTERN UNIVERSITY PRESS

EVANSTON

1969

Library of Congress Catalog Card Number: 70–78329
SBN: 8101–0250–1
Manufactured in the United States of America

Thomas B. Littlewood was chief of the Springfield, Illinois, Bureau of the *Chicago Sun-Times* from 1955 to 1964 and is currently on the staff of the *Sun-Times* Washington Bureau.

For Barbara

"Henry Horner was the Real Goods . . . He collaborated with men who were purchasable without becoming purchasable himself. He got to high places without selling his soul."

CARL SANDBURG
Interview with the author,
October 12, 1961, Springfield, Illinois

"An honest man's the noblest work of God."

ALEXANDER POPE
Essay on Man
Epistle IV

"When certain people meet with the slightest disappointment, such as the refusal of a post they have requested for some rascal who happens to be a relation, they turn against me; some are even ready to plot against me if I put a stop to their peculations and open pillage."

NAPOLEON BONAPARTE

Contents

Contents, *continued*

Preface

Standing at the freshly-dug grave of the governor of Illinois, the Jewish rabbi glared out at the assembled high officials of the mighty political organization all turned out in their top hats, formal mourning clothes, and properly funereal demeanor. Upon these florid-faced men of great public prominence, the rabbi proceeded at that embarrassing but appropriate moment on October 8, 1940, to attach responsibility for the death of Henry Horner. Some years later, performing the time-honored cathartic ritual of erecting public monuments as a method of cleansing the collective conscience, the state of Illinois dedicated in Horner's honor a handsome bronze and granite memorial on the Lake Michigan shore. By then the emotions had cooled, but not the memories. On the occasion of that solemn ceremony, Carl Sandburg, son of Illinois and good true friend of Henry Horner, said:

> A biography taking his measure will some day be written. It will report the cost of his devotion, his consecration of himself to the dark and complex duties of his office. . . . When circumstances and conditions would not let him have what he wanted of justice, he carried a heavy burden of tragedy.

The purpose of this book is to fulfill that assignment—to measure the person and to examine the burden of tragedy, circumstantial and man-made, that he carried through an eventful period in the history of the state that he governed.

Sandburg has spoken of Lincoln's fortuitous combination of drifting-fog softness and rock hardness. Horner was blessed with the former, but not the latter. He was a complicated individual—warm, soft in many different ways, lonely, sensitive, sentimental, wanting and needing to be liked. Not the balanced qualities that are best suited for a man in political life. He matured and persevered, nonetheless, leading his state through the 1930's in the face of a grotesque sequence of political events brought about by selfish, greedy men for whom cataclysmic economic depression inspired no compulsion to suspend their hunger for the spoils of power.

This then is a historical narrative of the experiences of the governor of one large industrial-agricultural state during the Great Depression. A special effort has been made to spell out in terms that can be understood today what a grinding, painful struggle was required to put across the New Deal in the land-locked reactionary mid-section of the nation. As an exercise in political science, Horner's story touches on some of the practical dilemmas of an era in urban politics that hopefully is nearing an end. Before television and image manipulators and volunteer workers, an army of helpers (an "organization") was absolutely essential to win elections in the big cities. The soldiers were rewarded with public jobs, and many of them expected to be turned loose to pillage the countryside like a conquering army. Furthermore, candidates in the big city "machines" were selected for and elected to office more as representatives of an ethnic constituency than as representatives of a political party. Among immigrant groups especially, the proudly installed public official then became "their fellow," whose special attention they demanded and commanded. The importance of ethnic politics is woven through the history of Chicago. There were additional reasons, traceable to events in Europe during the 1930's, why this is a specially meaningful element in the Horner story.

The sources from which this book is drawn are given in detail at the end. For the most part the work has been based on the plentiful collection of Governor Horner's official and unofficial papers that are deposited in the Illinois State Historical Library at Springfield and on occasionally contradictory interviews with his surviving contemporaries. For the errors of fact and interpretation which inevitably occur in the reconstruction of past events partly from the testimony of interested parties, the author alone is responsible. If, in the process, the author has been unfair to anyone—or to the truth—he pleads absence of malice.

I am grateful to the then state historian, Clyde Walton, and to the assistant state historian, Margaret Flint, for the privilege of browsing unhurriedly through the raw, unsorted Horner Papers that had been gathering dust in the library for twenty-one years. Special thanks are due Milburn P. Akers, the retired editor of the Chicago *Sun-Times*, who unwittingly supplied the inspiration for my project with his anecdotes of Springfield in the thirties; Dr. Nathan Rosen of Los Angeles, who offered the use of his extensive notes from diaries and other records; the late Carl Sandburg, who took the time at the end of a tiring day to chat about his old friend; Mrs. Hazel Mannheimer of Laguna Beach, California, the governor's cousin; and Barbara Littlewood, my indispensable helpmate, who supplied not only encouragement but the sorely needed services of consultant grammarian, typist, and editor.

Horner of Illinois

CHAPTER ONE

Of Thistles and Flowers: Days of Reconstruction

"Speed, die when I may," Abraham Lincoln once confided to his old friend Joshua Speed, "I want it be said of me by those who knew me best that I always plucked a thistle and planted a flower where I thought a flower would grow." From his earliest days, Henry Horner had groped for guidance in the wisdom and example of Mr. Lincoln. These words about thistles and flowers impressed him as a commendable guide.

In Illinois in the spring of 1933, the thistles were proliferating beyond control and the flowers were fast withering. National Guard troops used tear gas to disperse fifteen thousand "anti-hunger marchers" as they gathered at staging areas around the state. Prevented thus from converging on the state capital as they had intended, the angry citizens insisted on delivering their message to the governor:

> We see billions being given to the bankers, railroads and other corporations spent for war purposes and maintenance of troops to attack the workers. We workers of Illinois insist that our demands be acted upon. The situation becomes grave. We cannot wait. We declare that we will go back to our homes and organize the workers for more militant struggle and not cease until our demands are fulfilled.[1]

II

In the metropolis of Chicago a sickly pallor of coal smoke shrouded the drab tenements that were clustered about the towering St. Stanislaus Kostka Church like the houses in a European cathedral town. The Great Depression had infested the Northwest Side with poverty, hunger, and jobless despair. Down on the South Side, Negroes chanted melancholy spirituals at anti-eviction rallies. One out of two Chicagoans was out of work. In the South Chicago steel district, the Steel and Metal Workers' Industrial Union, an affiliate of the Trade Union Unity League (described in the military intelligence records as a Communist organization), launched an organizing drive. Eighty-six Communist "workers' schools" operated in Chicago alone. The Unemployed Councils, a Communist group, rallied to the defense of a father of seven starving children who had stabbed a public aid caseworker after being dropped from the relief rolls. "Graft runs in hundreds of thousands of dollars in Chicago relief stations," asserted the leaflets of the Unemployed Councils.

Downtown, a thousand Chicago public school teachers formed in Grant Park to march on the Loop banks and the Chicago Title and Trust Company. For a year the teachers had been paid in scrip and tax anticipation warrants. Three high school bands led the way down Michigan Avenue, followed by teachers singing "School Days" and carrying placards reading "Free Education, That's Us!" The teachers tried in vain to invade the office of General Abel Davis, chairman of the board of Chicago Title and Trust. "We want Davis," they shouted. "Pay your taxes. That's why we can't get paid. Real estate barons!" They were incensed by reports that $30,000,000 was being held in escrow by the company as its part of a property tax strike. Throughout Chicago the accumulation of uncollected taxes had reached $300,000,000. Repelling the onrushing teachers, two policemen wielded billies at the entrance of the building, and five women fainted in the crush. A plate glass window shattered. Finally, a woman teacher whacked a policeman on the head with the only weapon she had—a school book.

Deep in the downstate coal country at the little town of Ziegler, a more lethal object, a rock, crashed through the window of a coal miner's house. A cryptic note was attached to the rock: "You work tomorrow—maybe you die."

Elsewhere, troops manned machine guns behind sandbags piled at a church corner in Taylorville. The National Guard had been on duty for months to prevent open warfare between members of the United Mine Workers of America and the Progressive Mine Workers of America. These days when there was a knock at the door after sunset, the cautious miner darkened his lights and went for his shotgun before answering. Patrols of snipers roamed the alleys at night. Men were gunned to death while taking out the garbage. The wives of the miners eventually picked up the combative spirit of what had started as a mere organizational dispute. Some of the women were tear-gassed by guardsmen on a picket line near Taylorville. Cooperating with UMW czar John L. Lewis, the Peabody Mines would hire only UMW members as they endeavored together to starve the upstart Progressives into submission. From one of the women's auxiliaries of the Progressive union, the governor received this plea:

> [Our men] established a new union that is responsive to the wishes of the rank and file. A reign of terror resulted. A reign of terror in which officers of the old union, coal corporation, county and municipal authorities, and even the State joined—clubbing, tear-gassing, shooting, killing our people, bombing our homes, making it impossible for us to assemble or to enjoy our constitutional rights.
>
> We women see our undernourished children steadily losing weight and going to school poorly clad. In ever increasing numbers our people are losing their homes, homes that represent the meager savings of a lifetime. In this age of unlimited electrical power, we are forced to return to the dim coal lamps of a past generation. We are forced to see our sick children unattended by a doctor.[2]

Local 110 of the Progressives wired an urgent protest from the small town of Buckner: "If you cannot or will not intercede to prevent a massacre, we law-abiding citizens must take the law into our own hands."

Anxious to capitalize on this unrest, the Communist party stepped up its activities in the mine areas. "We must organize our work in such a way," the district committee advised, "that it will be in a position to give leadership to the struggles of the workers that may be developed suddenly in other industries or outside of the factories. Unity in the struggle of members of both unions against the trade union bureaucracy, coal operators, and government is an immediate task." [3]

A crop of thistles sprouted too on the fertile farms of the Corn Belt. Farmers who had purchased their land and equipment at inflated prices after the World War now faced bankruptcy. The price of corn dipped to 10 cents a bushel. Tax bills, including the levy of 50 cents per $100 valuation for the state government, could not be met. The farmers acted, however, to frustrate eviction and tax lien sales by bidding for a neighbor's farm at only a few dollars and then returning it to the original owner.

For three days Chicago area milk deliveries were stopped altogether. Dairy farmers blocked the highways and spilled milk from trucks onto the pavement. Although sheriff's deputies fortified with tear gas were able to break the blockade, a National Guard intelligence officer was prompted to submit this report to the governor:

> Much violence and lawlessness has been displayed by the milk producers. As these producers represent a cross section of the solid, substantial, law-abiding citizenry, their willingness to resort to violence and lawlessness for the purpose of gaining their personal ends without any consideration for the public at large is believed to be another ominous sign of the weakening of our civil government.[4]

From a farm near the little town of Ramsey, Carmen Welch wrote a letter to the governor:

> I have just $13 in my pocketbook—every cent I have in the whole world. The stores here have gone on a cash basis. No money—you don't eat. That wouldn't be too bad but I have four children who must eat too. All week long it's been coffee and a bacon sandwich for supper. We are farmers or have been. I read yesterday where a woman in Chicago asked the court to make her husband give her more alimony. Eighteen hundred dollars a month wasn't enough. When the bank failed last spring our employer lost all his money. You can't borrow money. Henry Ford couldn't come to this town and borrow 50 cents. Strange things have happened in this little village since the bank went busted. One garageman sent a businessman a bill for 35 cents and threatened to sue if it wasn't paid at once. Years ago we sent food to starving Belgians, but today in the heart of America children are starving.[5]

From the upper end of the ladder, the fall, being steeper and longer, hurt even more. Ernest Mayer, a real estate investment broker from Highland Park, directed a stream of letters at the governor demanding a moratorium on mortgage debts. He cited examples of North Shore businessmen who were losing their mansions. "You," he wrote, "can be the Moses to lead the overtaxed, burdened citizens of Illinois out of bondage as Moses led the children of Israel across the Red Sea."

Colonel Robert R. McCormick, the haughty editor of the *Chicago Tribune*, addressed the Bond Club of New York. "Property of every kind has been raised," he said, "as a ship on a wave, and left by the receding wave high and dry on the jagged rocks of ruinous taxation. [The nation] has drifted close to ruin—finance controlled from Washington; agriculture about to receive a dictator; the very hours of occupation to be regulated by a lady secretary of labor." [6]

III

On New Salem Hill, brooding alone in the night, pressed down by his loneliness and the weight of his problems, Henry Horner sat on the doorstep of the Lincoln-Berry store. Under the soft glow of the prairie moon, the fresh bloom of springtime masked the thistles that occupied his thoughts. Here in the ghostly community that Edgar Lee Masters called this Bethlehem of America, Lincoln had lived as a young man. And here, to this reconstructed log grocery, the governor of Illinois crept away from the barren melancholy of the Executive Mansion in search of solitude and solace in this frontier village downstream a few miles from Springfield. New Salem crumbled in decay almost as suddenly as it had been forged out of the prairie wilderness by two itinerant millwrights from the South. "Something remains," Masters had reflected, "as if the Muse of History touched the village with her hand, bringing it to sleep, and charming the log houses to fall, and the grass to grow again in front of the Rutledge Tavern." [7]

It is not uncommon for seekers of public office in Illinois, and elsewhere for that matter, to cultivate an attachment to Lincoln. But Horner had been a serious student and collector of Lincolniana for thirty years, predating by far his political career. In the study of Lincoln he found a "keen sense of the opportunities that life held forth if a man could be true to himself and concerned with the well-being of his fellows. Studied from every standpoint, he is about the most satisfactory human sample produced by modern times—the most satisfying when measured by the intellect, by the heart, by the soul."[8] At the dedication of the restored New Salem, the governor presided "as a devoted worshipper at this shrine to Illinois' greatest son." It was, he said,

> the consecration of an abode for the spirit of Lincoln that appeals to us all—the young, vigorous, studious, ambitious Lincoln, who groping blindly yet diligently and unceasingly here fitted himself for that future greatness which the whole world acknowledges and reveres. Here the Lincoln lover will come to browse and dream and hope. . . . If it is courage we need to face the future, it is courage that we shall find here. If it is inspiration we need, that too we shall find here. . . . Vast social and economic changes have occurred [since Lincoln]. . . . These are days of reconstruction, and the greatest good for the greatest number shall guide the nation in the future.[9]

CHAPTER TWO

The Levys and the Horners, Under Grandmother's Wing

The most significant single fact in the life of Henry Horner is that his name was not actually Henry Horner. The name Horner, that of his deceased maternal grandfather, was bestowed upon young Henry Levy as a vital condition for being invited to live in the home of his maternal grandmother, Hannah Dernburg Horner, following the divorce of his parents. Because this remarkable woman left such a profound imprint on his life (as well as on every life she touched), Horner's story must begin with Hannah Dernburg in the nineteenth century.

Both her parents had died when, at the age of nineteen, Hannah left her native village of Zeilhard in the state of Hessen in Germany to journey alone to America. Her family, whose roots extended far back into the intellectual, judicial, and rabbinical history of Germany, had been the only Jewish family in this small rural village near the Rhine River. Jews in Hessen then suffered little from anti-Semitism, and some owned land. The public schools, though under strict supervision of the state church, were open to all. As a girl, Hannah had dreamed of becoming a teacher. But, as the nineteenth century neared its midpoint, revolutionary forces stirred in Germany, and an anti-Semitic tide, called the Stockel movement, made it impractical for a Jew to aspire to a teaching career.[1]

Hannah's forebears, beginning with her great-grandfather, the rabbi of Hanover, had been distinguished and well-to-do citizens.

One was a professor of jurisprudence at the Sorbonne in Paris and later chief justice of Hesse-Darmstadt. A cousin, Anselm, taking a different course, went to Zeilhard and fell in love with a beautiful but poor girl. Although his brothers and sisters tried desperately to distract him with a lucrative business opportunity in Cologne, Anselm returned to Zeilhard and married his true love. Writing in a family history, a relative recalled rather sadly that "his family supplied him with all the money he wanted, for he was a student and not cut out for business."

Abnormally impatient and aggressive, Hannah traveled from the port of New York by stagecoach cross country to the pioneer town of Chicago that had risen on the "wet prairie" bounding Lake Michigan. As one of the first Jewish women settlers in the West, it was inevitable that Hannah soon made the acquaintance of the founder of Henry Horner and Company, Retail and Wholesale Grocery and Flour Dealers, who was a prominent young Jewish businessman.

Henry Horner I had been born in 1818, the son of a Jewish farmer, in Seyn (sometimes spelled Ckyn), Bohemia. He came to Chicago in 1840, only three years after its incorporation as a city. At twenty-four years of age, after clerking for two years in a clothing store, he established Chicago's first grocery business across the Chicago River at Randolph and Canal Streets. The city then had only six thousand residents, but warehouses, grain elevators, breweries, and packing-houses were going up everywhere. From the surrounding prairie came long lines of farm wagons laden with corn, wheat, oats, barley, beef, pork, lard, potatoes, wool, hides, and tallow.

On January 12, 1849, less than a year after her arrival in the New World, Hannah Dernburg married Henry Horner. The half-dozen or so Jewish families living in Chicago had all fled oppressive political conditions, particularly the harsh Bavarian marriage laws and commercial restrictions, in search of liberty and economic improvement. Having emigrated for the most part from neighboring communities abroad, they settled within a few blocks of each other in what is now Chicago's Loop and visited together on Friday evenings. The Horners were somewhat of an exception, however, living and operating their business nearby on what was then considered the "West Side." In their candlelighted store they sold or bartered pelts and produce brought in by the farmers who lived in the outlying area. Horner devised a "shield of quality" for his store emblem. The 1850's were boom years for a city that was already destined to become a great wholesale grocery, clothing, and hardware market.

It was, nevertheless, a swampy, disagreeable place with muddy streets, a few elevated wooden plank sidewalks, and transit by mulecar. The wind swept violently across the lake from the east and over the prairie from the west.

These first Jews observed Yom Kippur services in a small room over a store and collected $40 to buy an acre of land for a cemetery. Later, the Horners were instrumental in the organization of an orthodox congregation, Kehillath Anshe Mayriv (Congregation, Men of the West), usually called K. A. M., whose first makeshift temple was in a shanty at Clark and Jackson Streets. There was no gallery, and the women sat on the same floor with the men, but in seats at the rear.

As might have been expected, Horner and Company flourished in the rapidly-growing frontier town. It was the first wholesale grocery house to issue a price list, "Horner's Guide." Its proprietor was one of the founders of the Chicago Board of Trade and also engaged briefly in a banking partnership. From the beginning, however, the guiding force in the business, the pusher, turned out to be not Henry but Hannah. She demonstrated exceptional drive and business acumen, while her husband proved to be a gentleman of considerable intellect, a lover of books who seemed to take more pride in accumulating his library of Hebrew and English volumes than in his groceries.[2]

A daughter, Dilah, the first of eleven children born to the Horners in the next twenty years, arrived on April 15, 1851. Despite being pregnant almost half those twenty years, Hannah engaged energetically in a host of activities. She was a charter member of Johanna Lodge, the charitable and educational sisterhood of B'nai Brith. She gave promising young men a start in business. She took young German-Jewish girls into her home as domestic servants and, after they had learned the domestic skills, introduced them to nice boys of like background who worked in the store. In many cases she financed the weddings of her protégés and loaned them money to start their own store.

Chicago served as an important purveyor of food for the Union Army during the Civil War, and many of Hannah's charities benefited families of soldiers at the front. A committee once called on her to ask aid for families of wounded soldiers back from the war. She opened the cash drawer and emptied its contents of about $400.[3] Wagonloads of provisions also were donated to the thirteen thousand Confederate prisoners at Camp Douglas on the South Side.

An anecdote that has been passed down through succeeding generations tells much about Hannah. The family living quarters were above and behind the grocery. When Hannah was confined to her bedroom with a newborn baby, she moved her bed next to the frosted glass window and scratched a clear space in the glass just large enough to look down on the grocery area below. If a clerk hesitated longer than an instant while closing the money drawer, she would rap a reprimand on the window glass, thereby conditioning a crew of swift but slightly neurotic clerks.

The young couple thus fell into the traditional European Jewish family pattern. The mother had not only the burden of rearing the family but also the need to participate in the family business. Of necessity she often developed a strong, domineering personality and pushed her sons so zealously that they had great difficulty in emancipating themselves.

In Chicago the prospering grocery business soon outgrew its quarters and moved to larger ones, in 1859 to 78 West Randolph Street and in 1864 to the northwest corner of Jackson Street and Wabash Avenue. Even in those early days, Chicago's Jews formed distinct social strata according to their origin. South of the grocery store in the downtown area between Jackson and Twelfth Streets, Russian and Polish Jews inhabited the original ghetto. By 1870 the more prosperous Jews had begun drifting south into the prestigious Irish neighborhoods near the lake. With the influx of Russian migration after the pogroms, a wretched ghetto stretched across the Chicago River along Jefferson Street west to Halsted Street.

Concurrently, the Horners and other German Jews began falling away from orthodoxy. At K. A. M., services were read in German instead of in Hebrew, and the congregation eventually turned to Reform Judaism. This Americanizing process was carried a step further in 1861 when the Sinai Congregation splintered off from K. A. M. At Sinai, under the brilliant leadership of Emil G. Hirsch, son of a Hegelian philosopher and former rabbi at Dessau and Luxemburg, the old customs were discarded and services were read in English, and on Sundays.

In the meantime, keeping her wary eye all the while on the cash drawer, Hannah brought a succession of children into the world. After Dilah came Joseph in 1851, Isaac in 1854, Angel (a boy) in 1856, Minnie in 1858, Charles in 1859, Maurice in 1861, Dora in 1863, Harry in 1866, Albert in 1868, and Mattie in 1871—eleven in all.

In October of 1871, when the business and the family were both prospering, a devastating blow struck the Horners and Chicago. Fire started in a barn near Jefferson and DeKoven Streets, swept north through the wholesale district, and destroyed seventeen thousand buildings in the interior of the city. As the Great Chicago Fire bore in on Jackson and Wabash Streets, Henry Horner I sat transfixed in his magnificent library, frozen into a state of shock, stunned by indecision, unable to decide which of his precious books to try to carry out. Outside, Hannah hurriedly bartered groceries for horses and wagons, into which she loaded children and as many household items as could be salvaged. Finally, with the roof of their house ablaze, Hannah literally dragged her dazed husband out and into the wagon. They drove to the lake shore and watched the flames gut their city. In this moment of crisis the scholarly grocer had almost lost his life out of concern not for the grocery inventory but for his beloved books.

He never fully recovered from the emotional blow. With both home and store destroyed, the Horners had to build anew. They relocated at Randolph Street near Clinton, living for a time above the store and then moving into a new house at 14 Park Row on the fashionable near South Side. Horner did not attempt to resume his banking venture after the fire, and in 1878 the retail end of the grocery business was discontinued, leaving it solely a wholesale operation. He began suffering asthmatic attacks and his health gradually declined until, on February 11, 1878, Henry Horner I died of a brain hemorrhage at the age of sixty.

Even before the death of their father, the children all worked in the store and were subjected to Hannah's educational and character development devices, including her "injunctions for a united family." [4] On May 17, 1871, only three months after the birth of the last of Hannah's children, her first-born, Dilah—whose sturdy, plain, large-boned features resembled her mother's—was married to Solomon Levy.

Solomon Abraham Levy had been born in 1839 in Verder, near Landau, in Bavaria. He was brought to America in 1850, with two brothers, two sisters, and a grandmother, by his uncle, Frederick

Moss, who lived in Louisville, Kentucky. His uncle put him in charge of a clothing store in Frankfort, Kentucky, when Solomon was only thirteen years old. But the discovery of gold in California sparked a wave of excitement across the land, and in 1853 the adventurous Levy left Kentucky with the families of two Louisville friends. Their sailing vessel was shipwrecked along the Central American coast, and the party did not reach San Francisco until fifty-three days after their departure. The Schlosses, one of the families with whom he had traveled, urged him to take a job with their newly formed Alaska Fur Company, but Solomon was attracted by Sacramento and settled there instead. He opened a successful retail and wholesale cigar store and became acquainted with many of the leading families in town. Leland Stanford, a justice of the peace, occupied an office over his store at J and Seventh Streets. The young cigar merchant liked to read and mastered four languages. In 1864, when he was twenty-five, he sold the business to his brother Moses and went into the wholesale cutlery and diamond drill business with Morris Weil in San Francisco. Levy traveled abroad every year on buying expeditions to England, Sweden, France, Germany, and Russia. His long friendship with the Schloss family ripened into love for one of the daughters, and in due course they were engaged to be married. She bought her bridal gown, and Solomon arranged on one of his European buying trips to bring back her trousseau from Paris. Upon debarking in New York, however, he learned the shocking news that his fiancée suddenly had taken ill and died. Her loss hurt Solomon so deeply that he left his business in California and went to visit an aunt in Chicago. There he found many old Louisville friends, and in 1870 he decided to remain. Not long afterwards, Solomon's aunt introduced him to Dilah Horner, and a year later the dashing, adventuresome Westerner was joined by the Reform Jewish matrimonial ceremony to the eldest daughter of the socially prominent and well-to-do grocery family. The bridegroom was twelve years older than his bride and only nine years younger than his mother-in-law.[5] It is highly unlikely that any of today's marriage counselors would have predicted harmonious marriage for Solomon Levy. He and his mother-in-law seemed on a collision course from the start. The handsome Solomon had already condensed a lifetime of experiences in his thirty-two years. He had crossed the ocean many times, been shipwrecked, gone gold hunting. He knew his way around the capitals of Europe. And he had married on the rebound. Well-intentioned though she undoubtedly was, Hannah continued to be an unbending woman who meant to rule all who were within her realm; and sons-in-law were clearly not exempt.

Solomon worked for a time in the grocery but then quit and took a job in the more familiar export business. The newlyweds lived briefly with the Horners but then moved into a place of their own. Within ten months of their marriage, on March 14, 1872, a son, James, was born. The next year, on October 4, 1873, another son, Sidney, arrived.

The death of Henry Horner I in February of 1878 left Hannah, then forty-eight, with an expanding grocery business, ten children at home (Mattie was only seven), a married daughter with two babies and domestic problems, and an estate of $81,967. Ten months after the death of her father, on November 30, 1878, Dilah gave birth to a third son in their apartment on South Michigan Avenue. The birth certificate recorded his name merely as "Male Levy," indicating that Dilah's intention for the child to be named after her father, probably with some urging from her mother, had encountered resistance from her husband. But Henry it was, and young Henry Levy (Henry H. Levy, according to some family records) started life in a home that was filled with marital discord. Dilah said later in court that she could not remember "one week we lived happily."

Solomon forbade his wife to see her mother and struck her, in the presence of the children, when he suspected that she had disobeyed him. Once he grabbed her by the neck and threatened to kill her, until the boys pleaded with him to stop. Another time he caught her by the hair and beat her with his hand, leaving bruises that she later testified were visible for weeks. She said she hid in the kitchen until her husband had left the house.

Eventually in August of 1883 Dilah took her three sons and went home to Hannah's apartment above the West Randolph Street store. Solomon threatened to take the children from her and to remove the furniture, much of which had been given them by Dilah's father. Consequently, Dilah secured a writ of injunction to prevent Levy from carrying out his threats, and a short time later she filed suit for divorce in the Circuit Court of Cook County.

One relative, a Chicago businessman, offered his version many years later of why the marriage had failed: "He [Levy] was a student, an intellectual, always reading, extravagant. He just wasn't cut out for business." This remark is interesting when one recalls the earlier Dernburg family characterization of a non-conformist member, Anselm, who was a "student" and "not cut out for business."

Divorce was uncommon in the 1880's and exceedingly rare among Jews. Since family unity was the traditional foundation of Judaism, propagation of the race came first; personal marital happiness, when it existed, merely added frosting on the cake. But Dilah, nevertheless, filed her bill of complaint alleging cruelty. Following the procedure (which was normal at that time) for a so-called "consent" divorce, Solomon did not answer the complaint but filed a demurrer instead.

Just a few days after Henry's fifth birthday, Dilah appeared before Judge Thomas A. Moran. Her lawyer, Allan C. Storey, asked if she had been mistreated by her husband. "Yes sir," she responded, "I have been so mistreated by him I could not stand it any longer." Katie Zwach, twenty-four, who lived with and worked for the Levys, also testified. She said Levy "was always cursing her [Dilah]. He never came into the room but what he was swearing at her." Katie described Dilah's bruises and recalled a time when Solomon had thrown the dinner dishes at Dilah.

On December 11, Judge Moran entered a decree of divorce finding Solomon Levy "guilty of extreme and repeated cruelty toward the complainant for a period of upwards of two years." Care, custody, maintenance, and education of the two younger children were vested in Dilah. James was awarded to the father, in line with the court policy, prevalent at that time, of automatically giving custody of the oldest child to the father. Solomon received permission to visit his two sons in Dilah's house at least once every two weeks. No alimony was granted, but the decree stated that "the defendant shall contribute from time to time for the support of said children according to their necessities and his abilities." There is no evidence that he either took advantage of his visitation privileges or contributed to the children's support. Nor apparently did James visit his mother or grandmother. The household possessions went to Dilah.[6]

Solomon lived with his son in a downtown apartment hotel and went into the business of importing jewelry. Hannah offered her cramped quarters to Dilah and the other two boys with one significant condition: she demanded that the names of the two boys be changed from Levy (a name that she hated) to Horner. So not only did Dilah resume her maiden name, but Sidney Levy became

Sidney Horner and Henry Levy, five years old, became Henry Horner II. None of these name changes was made a part of the divorce proceedings, and no record can be found in the Cook County courts of authorization for the changes. Illinois law does not require such authorization, although it is usually requested in order to prevent future legal disputes. At the time of Dilah's death, the death certificate read "Dilah Levy."

If Henry's early memories of rancor and physical violence in his home had left an indelible mark, as indeed they must have, it must also be recognized that the years which followed in his grandmother's unusual household were of comparable significance in the shaping of his personality and character. As we have seen, Hannah ruled as Supreme Matriarch. She accepted the role of father-substitute with ease. Overseeing everything that everyone did, she devoted her attention first to operating the business, delegating the responsibility for household chores to Dilah.

Alongside Hannah's name in the old family Bible are inscribed the words: "We shall never see her like again." This is not mere exaggeration. As an illustration of her indomitable strength of purpose, when Hannah awoke in the morning, she wanted to look upon her favorite grandchildren, and without delay. Being a woman of direct action, she commissioned the painting of a picture on the ceiling of her bedroom. From a bank of pink clouds and flowers, three cherubic figures smiled down angelically from overhead. One was five-year-old Henry; the other two were his cousins. A half-century later when the building was being remodeled, the picture was discovered beneath several layers of wallpaper and varnish. The governor arranged for the picture—painting, plaster, concrete, and all, weighing some three hundred pounds—to be trucked to the Executive Mansion at Springfield.

A short time after the divorce, Hannah moved her brood to a new red brick building at 1705 South Michigan Avenue. It was a splendid dwelling with three bedrooms on the top floor, five bedrooms on the second floor, large separate parlor and living rooms, and a kitchen in the basement.

Already in this period the social distance between the Chicago Jewish aristocrats and the newer refugees, which was to become so pronounced later, had begun to widen. The wealthy German Jews, having learned the social graces, moved toward their Golden Ghetto on the South Side; and the newcomers from Eastern Europe poured into the West Side ghetto. The neighborhood in which the Horners then lived was considered to be an elite section of

Chicago. Along Michigan Avenue south to Twenty-second Street stood the lavish houses of rich families. The Armours, Fields, Pullmans, and Kimballs lived on nearby Prairie Avenue, the "street of the gifted few."

The importance of this pattern cannot be overstressed in the history of Chicago's Jewish community. As a gesture of their success, the German Jews moved to Hyde Park. In acquiring their wealth, many of the Jewish garment manufacturers, for instance, unmercifully exploited their sweatshop employees, Bohemian and Russian Jews who lived on the West Side. From the exclusive South Side, the managers then hastened to organize charities for the waves of Russian immigrants in the ghetto. Later in the depression a major social event would be the charity ball in the old Auditorium Theater with the Jewish "haves"—Leon Mandel, Milton Florsheim, Abel Davis, Philip Block, Melvin Rothschild, and others—dancing through the night for the benefit of the "have-nots" on the West Side.

In the Horner household, an enduring spirit of charity was drilled into young Henry by his grandmother. All the children were told, one of them said later, to "hold your head high, remember who you are, have pride in your ancestry, but be humble so you can help others." Henry learned reverence for race, family, mother. And he learned that a Horner must seek to excel in whatever the undertaking.

Grandmother Hannah's academy of learning convened on Friday night in her living room. Friday traditionally is Jewish family night, and in her house it was always a grand affair, especially during the religious holiday season. Dilah, who had become a skillful cook, prepared tubs of her special style of corned beef for Hannah's sons, daughters, sons-in-law, daughters-in-law, grandchildren, and other assorted guests who sat at a dining room table long enough for thirty. On Friday night the relatives *always* came to dinner. Hannah would have it no other way. After dinner, grandmother would preside from her large armchair. Son Joe would play the piano and sing "After the Ball Is Over" and the other popular hits of the day. The youngest grandchild, Henry's cousin Hazel Yondorf, would sit on the footstool beside Hannah's chair, and grandmother would stroke her hair to keep her from dozing. Hannah ruled her clan with a firm but gentle hand. She was loved and respected and feared by all the family. Henry basked in the affection of both Hannah and Dilah. Dilah adored her youngest son; he was the favorite, while his older brother Sidney enjoyed only secondary attention.[7]

Isaac, who was later elected alderman of his ward, helped his mother run the grocery business. Four of the other brothers followed, and the most astute businessman of the lot, Maurice, took over sole managerial responsibility in 1893. Among his other achievements, he invented a bicycle package-holder. In 1921 Henry Horner and Company merged with Durand and Kasper Company and McNeil and Higgins Company, becoming Durand-McNeil-Horner Company. The eldest son, Joseph, operated a small store of his own at Division and Clybourn Streets until 1877, when he married Minnie Kohn, daughter of the head of one of the largest men's clothing businesses in the country and one of Chicago's wealthiest citizens. He later helped found the successful insurance firm of Shoyer and Horner. Despite his unmasculine name, Angel was the handsomest of the men. He went to school in Heidelberg, Germany, and became a fish buyer. Several of Hannah's sons never married. Others did not do so until late in their lives—Harry, for instance, married when he was fifty.

Young Henry was a bright, imaginative, aggressive lad, fully endowed with a sense of humor and a sense of sympathy. Slightly smaller than most of his classmates, he engaged in at least the usual quota of scraps with other boys in the neighborhood. His school class pictures are of a youngster with a mischievous, inquisitive grin. His academic record was short of spectacular, but he liked to read, particularly about American history. During one phase of his boyhood he published a one-page weekly newspaper on a hand-press in the basement.

After attending Haven School, the neighborhood public grade school, he enrolled in Chicago Manual Training School, the South Side equivalent of a high school. This school, as its name indicates, taught the manual trades along with the scholastic subjects. He studied algebra, physics, chemistry, trigonometry, rhetoric, literature, physiology, French, Latin, German, history, drawing, woodwork, machine shop, and the use of tools. One of his scrapbooks contains a report card stamped "unsatisfactory" for one of the grading periods, presumably because of his 40 in deportment. He then ranked 47th in a class of 78 but rose to 18th in the next grading period. English was his best subject; drawing was his worst.

A year living with his aunt and uncle, the August Yondorfs, and the experience of working in his uncle's clothing store at Larrabee Street and North Avenue were more than enough to convince Henry that he was not destined to be a mercantile prince.

IV

These were years of a crackling social tension that a youngster growing up in Chicago could see, hear, and feel all around him. In May of 1886, eight-year-old Henry heard bursts of gunfire from nearby Haymarket Square before his mother whisked him indoors and away from the Haymarket riot. By 1890 there were almost as many foreign-born in Chicago as the entire population of the city had numbered ten years earlier. The year 1893 brought both the World's Columbian Exposition and horrendous economic depression to Chicago. Although the Horners were among the city's well-to-do, with a maid to assist Dilah in her mother's house, some families starved that winter in the city. The jobless slept in the corridors of City Hall.

By now Chicago's population exceeded one million. State Street remained unpaved south of Madison Street, and the floors of the mule streetcars were covered with straw in the winter. In the self-contained industrial community of Pullman City, some workers were earning 7¢ a week. When they struck for higher wages, federal troops were brought in to crush the strike. Hungry shop girls fled to the Levee, a notorious district of brothels and gambling houses hear the Horner residence, to become prostitutes.

In this same year Hannah visited her birthplace near the Rhine and saw her brother Aaron in Dieburg, about seven miles from Zeilhard. She donated funds for remodeling the rundown little Jewish temple at Dieburg.

Chicago was known as the "Gomorrah of the West." Englishman George W. Stevens called it "the most American of American cities and yet the most mongrel." According to Carter Harrison, Jr., who later became mayor, the city in the 1890's was ruled by "a low-browed, dull-witted, base-minded gang of plug-uglies with no outstanding characteristics beyond an unquenchable lust for money." [8]

One of Harrison's first backers was Billy Loeffler, a Bohemian Jew, a ward leader, and the most important Jewish politician in Chicago. Probably because of their memories of political suppression in their homelands, the Jewish immigrants had been slow to warm to the challenge of American politics. When Henry graduated at seventeen from Chicago Manual, having received at best a mediocre public school education, he was already bewitched by the law and politics. Hannah approved his decision to follow the normal course for that time and enroll as a night-school law student at Kent College of Law, later Chicago-Kent College of Law. At that time lawyers were able to pass directly from high school to night law school. Weymouth Kirkland, a law school classmate, remembers Henry as "well-liked by his classmates and considered one of the best scholars in the school." In the daytime he worked as a law clerk for Allan C. Storey, the attorney who had handled his mother's divorce, and after two years of study, Henry received the degree of bachelor of laws.

The years 1897 and 1898 were crossroads not only for Henry Horner but for the Democratic party of Chicago as well. John Peter Altgeld, who would be heralded in years to come as a great liberal governor, the "Eagle Forgotten," returned from defeat to fight with Harrison for control of the party in Chicago. Both were reformers, although their styles were individual—Harrison was a realist; Altgeld an idealist. Altgeld's backers were described by Clarence Darrow as "weird-looking idealists and worshippers . . . the poorly clad, the ill-fed, the unemployed, visionaries gazing off toward the rainbow espying something farther on than the very stars themselves." [9]

While still a student and not yet old enough to vote, Henry enlisted enthusiastically in Harrison's successful mayoral campaign. Through the combination of hard work, Uncle Isaac's long involvement in Democratic First Ward politics, and an assist from Billy Loeffler, he was elected one of the South Side vice presidents of a lusty, volunteer marching contingent called the Harrison Guards. Not far from luxurious Michigan Avenue in the downtown First Ward, where Harrison had been born and where the Horners now lived, existed a different seamy world of barrelhouse saloons and 10-cent flophouses. Marching in a plumed hat with the Harrison Guards down to Billy Boyle's Chophouse, downtown First Ward headquarters for Aldermen "Bathhouse John" Coughlin and Michael Kenna, Henry Horner the young law student had made his first important commitment to realism in politics and a life career in that unpredictable occupation.

CHAPTER THREE

Education... at the Knee of Hinky Dink ... and Lincoln

Fresh out of law school and anxious for postgraduate training in politics, young Henry Horner matriculated in a school that offered a diverse curriculum of hard knocks and lofty thoughts. On one level, his interest was absorbed increasingly by the life of Lincoln, who was undoubtedly the most perfect politician-ruler the nation has ever seen. Just as important, but in a different way, Horner learned about practical political tactics from the two imperfect Irishmen who ran the downtown First Ward, Hinky Dink Kenna and Bathhouse John Coughlin. The faculty of Kenna and Coughlin taught Urban Politics (Chicago Style) 101, a laboratory course in the precincts. However, his interest in Lincoln kept Horner in emotional and practical contact with the rural sections of Illinois which had produced Lincoln and which in due course would influence Horner's life too.

After being admitted to the bar in the summer of 1899, the twenty-one-year-old novice entered into partnership with another beginning lawyer in the Security Building at Madison Street and Fifth Avenue. His partner, Frank A. Whitney, was a son of Henry Clay Whitney, who had been Lincoln's friend in the 1850's when they rode the Eighth Judicial Circuit together as lawyers across east-central Illinois. This association with a man whose father had been so close to the living Lincoln stimulated Horner's curiosity. The younger Whitney gave him two books that his father had owned. One was an autographed copy of Whitney's own story, *Life on the Circuit with Lincoln.* The other was a treasured family possession, an old book worn by miles of travel in saddlebags, its pages singed by the Chicago Fire, that had been borrowed often by Lincoln during his journeys with Henry Clay Whitney from courtrooms between Springfield and Paris, Illinois.

Being introduced to Lincoln in this fashion touched Horner deeply. In the years that followed he regarded the lessons of Lincoln's life as complementing the teachings of his own grandmother. There was nothing contrived about Horner's interest in Lincoln. The more he learned about Lincoln's life, the more moved was this young American Jew by the story of the humble Kentuckian, his philosophy, his talent with words, his governing genius.

Some years later, Horner summarized his feeling of admiration in an address on "The Universality of Lincoln": "Notwithstanding his early ambition for political honors, Lincoln never was willing to sacrifice basic principles of justice for self-advancement. All through his gruelling experiences in private and public life, he never lost sight of the human equation. No man can know Lincoln too well and no man can know him at all without becoming better for that knowledge." [1] For a young man aspiring to success in the craft of politics, this seemed a worthy guidepost in the conduct of his own life.

In another speech about Lincoln, Horner remarked that "we honor him because of the man he was. He had both gentleness and strength. He was wise but in him there was no arrogance. His sympathy extended even unto those to whom a harsh fate made it his duty to oppose. . . . In his life he gave the world its best example of human nobility." [2]

Time and again during his life Horner sought the right combination of gentleness and strength and wisdom without arrogance; Lincoln's example of human nobility can be recognized as a cornerstone of Horner's thinking.

Starting with the two books that had belonged to Whitney, Horner accumulated a large and valuable Lincoln library. He found satisfaction not only in reading and rereading the books, but also in just owning and having them nearby. His collection grew to occupy 225 feet of bookshelves and 130 pamphlet boxes. It consisted of 1,996 books, 3,717 pamphlets, 185 programs of Lincoln meetings and dinners, 165 dealers' catalogues, and 410 miscellaneous items. Also included in his collection were 343 funeral addresses delivered after Lincoln's death. He owned biographies of the president written in 1860, Republican campaign manuals and song books of 1860 and 1864, and three original timetables of the Lincoln funeral train. To catalogue his collection, Horner organized a 13,000-card file of cross references.

In the company of serious Lincoln scholars, Horner was more an observer than a participant. Paul M. Angle, an authority on Lincolniana, former state historian and a friend of the governor's, explains it this way:

> He had an intense interest in Lincoln but could not be called an intellectual expert. He knew a great deal about the rarity and value of Lincoln books. His interest in New Salem [the restored Lincoln village] was primarily an emotional one. He had a depth of emotion commonly found among Jews. He certainly did not think of himself in any way as a successor to Lincoln, but he derived great emotional satisfaction from bringing himself as close as he could to a very great human being.[3]

If Lincoln can be considered one of Horner's instructors in these formative years, so too was Hinky Dink. And there is an absence of evidence that either Mr. Kenna or his partner Bathhouse John was ever inspired by the spirit of the Great Emancipator. Both hailed from Connelly's Path, an Irish district east of the Chicago River around Adams Street. From 1892 they were the aldermen in the ward that ranged from the river south to Thirty-first Street, taking in the Bad Lands, Little Cheyenne, and Bedbug Row. Operating out of the Silver Dollar saloon, in his pink gloves and billiard-green vest, the Bath resembled a Prussian general with his waxed mustache. Kenna, on the other hand, was a sad-eyed, quiet little man who peddled nickel beers and free lunches from the Workingman's Exchange saloon on the first floor of the Alaska Hotel.[4]

In order to get elected and re-elected, the strait-laced moralist Carter Harrison established a weird, not altogether holy, alliance with the overlords of the First Ward. Chicago was wicked and wide open, and the Hink and the Bath were two good reasons why. Kenna's most renowned pronouncement, that Chicago "ain't no sissy town," has never been disputed. At that time some two thousand professional gamblers plied their trade in the First Ward, and policy wheels and whores were in plentiful supply. The ward defense fund even financed trips to the West for consumptive prostitutes.

Because of the factionalism that prevailed within the Democratic party, Chicago's first native-born mayor felt obliged to solicit the support of the corrupt First Ward organization. Horner's family having been attached to the Harrison faction, he volunteered to serve as a precinct captain for Kenna. Like all the embryo neighborhood politicians, he spent his spare time at a pool hall and saloon at State and Eighteenth Streets, listening to lectures on a subject that has often been called the Cash Value School of Political Theory. An opposing Democratic faction emerged under the leadership of Roger Sullivan, an Irishman and clerk of the probate court.

When in later years Horner appeared as a candidate at a First Ward rally, Coughlin recalled that Horner's six uncles had "all played their parts consistently and well as true friends of the First Ward Democracy." The candidate proudly responded that every tidbit of knowledge about practical politics that he had picked up had been learned taking orders from Michael Kenna and John J. Coughlin. He sneered on cue at the names of several popular community reformers. "Has there ever been a cry of distress calling for aid that [they] have not been on the job?" Horner asked, referring to the aldermen. "The politics of the Democratic organization of the First Ward has been as fair, if not fairer, than those of any political institution." [5] The Kenna style was more colorfully described in a newspaper account by one of the alderman's unidentified precinct captains in this way:

> Kenna is a reformer. He is not the kind that hollers reform with his right hand uplifted and his left hand reaching out for the coin. He goes into the home of the poor man who has no bread on the table and whose children have no clothes and shoes. He goes into the home where the shadow of death has fallen and he calls the undertaker and says "Paddy Flaherty's mother is dead. Paddy is broke. I'll pay the funeral expenses." He takes the little kids and leads them up to the light of education.

Although Jewish workers were active in many Chicago ward organizations, they were slow to be represented on the state ticket. At the turn of the century, Samuel Alschuler of Aurora, who was Democratic leader in the Illinois House of Representatives and a Harrisonian, won his party's nomination for governor, the first Jew to achieve that distinction in Illinois. Since the 1896 election, Bryanism—which expressed so clearly the rural fears of the immigrant masses in the cities—had become the dominant theme in American politics. Although Alschuler lost to Richard Yates, the son of the Illinois Civil War governor, he ran ahead of Bryan (who lost Illinois to McKinley). Alschuler carried Chicago; Bryan did not. The Democrats would not carry Chicago again for a state-wide candidate until 1926.

II

Now there occurred two deaths in young Horner's family, one that touched him deeply and one that did not. On June 28, 1900, Solomon Levy died of a stroke at the age of sixty-five. Henry's father was buried on July 1 in a lot purchased by James Levy in B'rith Sholom cemetery in Louisville. A plain marble stone reads "S. A. Levy." Although he apparently did not attend the funeral of his father, Governor Horner visited the grave site many years later. No maintenance fees have been paid for the grave for a number of years, although cemetery officials politely tried to dun Horner after he became governor.[6]

Less than two years later, on February 15, 1902, while on a vacation trip to Pasadena, California, with her daughter Dilah, Hannah Horner fell ill and died. She was 72 years old, Dilah 51, and grandson Henry 24. Her amazing dynamo finally stilled, this grand old woman was carried by her seven sons to her grave in Mount Mayriv cemetery (Chicago's German Jewish cemetery), alongside the first Henry Horner.

It is much easier a century later to trace Hannah's influence on her grandson's development than it is to fairly evaluate Horner's father, Solomon Levy. He was an adventurer, an accomplished linguist, a dashing fellow. His marriage to Dilah Horner had followed quickly upon the tragic death of his first fiancée, whom he had known for many years. Levy did not fit into the niche in Hannah's matriarchy that had been provided for him and reacted in a rather extreme, ungraceful fashion. He was cruel and brutish. The unhappy memories of his father that Horner retained were reinforced by reminders from his mother and grandmother of his father's villainy. The masculine role in Dilah's life fell to her son Henry, and it was a role he would play for many years. As an adult, Henry Horner expressed regret occasionally that his parents had broken their family apart and, as he once put it, "parceled out the children like so many lumps of candy." But he also felt a lifelong sense of gratitude and perhaps even of some guilt that his mother had cared for and provided for him in spite of her own unhappy life. He believed that his success must have been due to the love and effort of his mother and grandmother. "I knew," he told one of his friends, "Mother must never regret what she had done. I must repay her for all her kindness and devotion. She has made so many sacrifices for me that I cannot bear the thought of leaving her alone."

Just as the fledgling attorney was commencing his political apprenticeship, he fell in love with a seventeen-year-old girl from a wealthy Jewish family in the east-central Illinois city of Paris. They were engaged to be married when Horner forced himself to analyze thoughtfully and traumatically his relationship with his mother. His first responsibility, he felt, must be his mother, who had only him to relieve her own life of tragedy. It would be unfair, Horner reluctantly realized, to expect a bride to share his devotion with his mother for possibly many years. Thus, in what he later described as the most painful decision of his life, his engagement was broken, and his fiancée eventually married into a socially and financially prominent Chicago family. Until the end of his life Horner often reminisced with close friends about his love for this girl and about what their life together might have been. "Don't make the mistake I did," he advised young bachelors. "You get married. A bachelor leads a lonely life. Nobody wants you when you're old."

After the death of his mother, the aging Horner developed an overcompensating affection for children. Over his bed in the Executive Mansion hung a picture of his mother—as a young woman. Earlier, when he lived in an apartment on the South Side of Chicago, a painting of his grandmother was placed over the dining room table. And here again it was not the woman he had known, but a young beautiful woman bearing little resemblance to any of the photographic recollections of his grandmother.

His interpretation of his relationship with these two women is both candid and revealing. In response to an inquiry from Lew Sarett, a speech professor at Northwestern University, about the influences in his life, Horner made this reply:

> The two greatest influences on my life were my devoted grandmother and my mother. It may seem strange to you that a bachelor of 55 should admit that the strongest influences in his life were wielded by two women. My grandmother was a typical pioneer woman who had 11 children, reared them all in an atmosphere of real respectability, and yet found time to inculcate in the character of her grandchildren those invincible and basic principles of honesty and earnestness and industry which she held. Mother and I lived with her for many years, until her

> death. I lived with my mother all my life and was never out of the joy and advantage of her good influence. While she was anxious that her sons succeed, she was unflagging in her efforts to instill in us the conviction that success won at the expense of integrity and good name was a very hollow and shallow achievement. These two great souls, although dead, still linger with me and I believe guide me.[7]

Another similar letter soliciting his views on Mother's Day found the governor "glad to reply to your letter regarding my very lovely mother." He went on to explain that she was the oldest of eleven children and helped her parents rear the other ten until she married and even after. He recalled that she had helped her parents and others at the time of the Chicago Fire when she was twenty.

> It was my happy experience to live with her from the date of my birth until her death in February, 1921. It was my good fortune to be her very close companion during all those years, and if there is any good in me at all, it came entirely from her. Mother was interested in all the finer things of life. She devoted herself entirely to her home and to her home duties. She was a lover of music and a devotee of the finer arts. She also did pottery work, painted on porcelain and tile, and I still have some of her precious and beautiful needlework. I am sure she enjoyed and got more satisfaction out of such success as life brought to me than I did. Perhaps this is natural in all true motherhood. She died in my arms with a smile on her face, bidding me to go on through life according to her own precepts. Her advice to me through life was far-visioned and unselfish. It is pretty hard to describe a perfect mother, but I have done the best I could . . .[8]

"I quite believe," he once said on another occasion, "that if it were not for women we should soon have not even a semblance of anything which we now call civilized living."

III

Unfortunately, the end of Hannah's life occurred just as her grandson's political career began to flower. A stocky, handsome young man with a steady smile and a virile black handlebar mustache, he already wore pince-nez. He specialized in real estate and probate law. In the early years of his practice, he did a good deal of collection business for Henry Horner and

Company and also for the Straus Brothers Company which was run by his uncle. His old collection books, which can be found among the Horner Papers, are full of notations like—"Get after him hard . . . see if debtors own their houses . . . stir up attorney . . . lives in good apartment—ought to pay . . . N. G. just now . . . wake up attorney"—the classic dialogue of the collection lawyer. Mayor Harrison in his autobiography recounted later that he was "fortunate in attracting to [his] retinue youthful sprigs of legal learning and more than ordinary character and ability," and he specifically mentioned Horner among them.[9]

As a practicing lawyer Horner was considered smooth and capable. In 1905 his partner Whitney moved to Florida, and a new partnership was formed at 30 N. La Salle Street with Lloyd Charles Whitman. This association continued until 1912. In 1902 when Horner advertised for a secretary, Ella Cornwall, a young lady just out of business college, applied for the job. After delivering some trial dictation, he remarked that her typing "wasn't so hot." "Oh no?" the applicant replied, "Well, that old second-hand typewriter of yours isn't so hot either!" A long association began, one that happily lasted for thirty-eight years thereafter.

It was a peculiar coincidence that provision was made by the state legislature for a referendum to be held in Chicago in 1902 on the question of abolishing the seven "towns" existing within Chicago—North Chicago, West Chicago, South Chicago, Jefferson, Lakeview, Hyde Park, and Lake—the same year in which the Harrison organization slated young Horner to be Democratic candidate for collector of South Chicago. He defeated John D. Shelhamer, a brick manufacturer, 15,161 to 13,770. But, alas, on the same ballot the elimination of the town governments likewise carried; the collector was legislated out of existence, and by an odd turn of fate Horner's first electoral triumph turned out to be a meaningless dry run. Some of his associates doubted the constitutionality of doing away with an elective office to which an individual had been simultaneously elected. "Speaking for myself," Horner told reporters, "I am not willing to make a fight. There is little use in combating public sentiment, especially when it has been expressed as emphatically as it was in this case." Within a few days a political item in a Chicago newspaper speculated that Horner "was being groomed for the judiciary."

After the death of his grandmother, Horner moved with his mother to an apartment on Forestville Avenue between Forty-eighth and Forty-ninth Streets on the South Side. His bachelor uncles took over a multi-flat building at 2945 South Michigan Avenue.

IV

The design of an apprentice politician's career must be plotted with meticulous care, especially if he is to utilize the ethnically-conscious big city machine. To this end, Horner cultivated influential leaders in both the Harrison organization and the Jewish community at large. His grandfather had been a member of the Standard Club, the exclusive German Jewish social club (Eastern European Jews not welcome), from the time of its organization shortly after the Civil War. By now its membership encompassed a sizable concentration of the economic power of Chicago. Balancing off his saloon politicking with Hinky Dink's crowd, Horner plunged vigorously into the activities of the Standard Club. Elevated to the board of directors in 1906, he patronized the club regularly, engaging in the casual pinochle game, the leisurely dinner, and the fat cigar with Abel Davis, president of the Chicago Title and Trust Company, and many other friends who were high in the city's economic elite. Later these Standard Club friendships would stand him in good stead.

Horner realized that another political requisite for a non-Catholic was a career in the Masonic order. Horner became a Mason shortly after leaving law school and seemed to enjoy his participation in the Chicago lodge. Unlike many politicians, Horner did not belong to organizations in name only. He willingly accepted the most thankless work assignments, all the while diffusing his friendly, cheerful personality throughout the group.

The decade beginning in 1910 dawned as a period of agitation in Chicago. Labor strife pitted Jew against Jew, forty-five thousand garment workers striking for better working conditions against Hart, Schaffner and Marx and other manufacturers. And although it was slow to come, reaction finally set in against the deplorable conditions that existed in Hinky Dink's so-called Levee—a district of gambling houses, barrelhouse saloons, dance halls, and more than two hundred brothels. The elegant Everleigh Club at 2131 S. Dearborn Street sparkled as the pride of the Levee. The gala of all galas was the annual First Ward ball sponsored at the Coliseum by Kenna and Coughlin for their subjects. The ladies from the Levee attended in the costumes of Egyptian dancers, Indian maidens, and geishas. Champagne and hundreds of kegs of beer lubricated the festivities, which usually degenerated with dispatch into an orgiastic riot. This was too much, even for Chicago, and Harrison finally felt compelled to clamp down on the annual ball. After an investigating commission identified 4,000 active prostitutes in 1,020 "resorts," most of them in the First Ward, Harrison took steps to suppress the Everleigh Club and other establishments on the Levee.

Thus the cement for the curious alliance was cracked; Kenna and Coughlin broke with Harrison, a move which marked the beginning of the end of the mayor's long reign. In 1912, as a result of the Republican Bull Moose split, a Harrison Democrat, Edward F. Dunne of Chicago, won the governorship, the first Democrat since Altgeld to hold that office. Although the Harrisonites occupied the mayor's office, the governorship, and a senatorship, the Sullivan faction controlled the large county patronage offices. The power shifted steadily from Harrison to Sullivan and then to another astounding figure who could have happened only to Chicago—William Hale Thompson.

In the meantime Horner was appointed attorney for the Cook County Board of Assessors, thereby acquiring another influential patron, the assessor David M. Phaelzer. In 1911 Harrison appointed Horner as a delegate to the City Charter Convention for Chicago, for which he became chairman of the committee on plan and procedure. Within the Harrison camp, meanwhile, new Jewish leaders were gaining prominence with ambitious plans for themselves and their associates. In terms of Horner's career it is sufficient to look for the moment at only three men.

Adolph J. Sabath came to America as a penniless Jewish Bohemian immigrant and advanced to Eighth Ward lieutenant under Billy Loeffler, the original Jewish political leader in Chicago. Sabath controlled several Southwest Side wards of Bohemian voters; in those days a Jew needed the sanction of both Loeffler and Sabath to go anywhere in Democratic affairs. Sabath first received a municipal court judgeship and then was elected to the United States House of Representatives. During the 1911 mayoral campaign Sabath organized the Progressive Democratic League of Cook County, a vehicle for Harrison's Jewish supporters, among them Horner.

One of Sabath's protégés was Harry M. Fisher, a Russian immigrant who worked days in a capmaking factory and studied law at night. Sabath helped Fisher reach the municipal court in 1912, and by then the young judge was a respected force in Jewish politics. Julius Rosenwald and other prominent Jews considered him to be a comer—bright, young, alert to social problems. A flowery orator, he assumed an active role in helping the new Eastern European immigrants acclimate themselves to their strange, often unfriendly metropolitan environment. While the German Jews could and did provide dollars, it was the Fishers who furnished emotional identification and understanding for their brethren from abroad. By organizing the Lawndale Club, Fisher laid the foundation for political strength in the burgeoning orthodox Jewish community moving into the west side.

A third individual whose importance cannot be exaggerated was Jacob Lindheimer. A German Jew from Stuttgart, he operated a saloon before starting in politics in the Bridgeport district, a predominantly Irish neighborhood near the stockyards. With their indefinable political *savoir faire*, the newly arrived Irish, then as always, managed somehow to run Democratic affairs most of the time. Lindheimer made the right friends and soon was managing the county treasurer's office for Patrick J. (Paddy) Carr, an influential Irish leader of that day. Previously Lindheimer had held the South Chicago collector's post, the one that was abolished just as Horner was to occupy it. Because of its tax collecting authority, the county treasurer's office could, with proper attention to proper details, closely audit the money arteries of the city. This Lindheimer did and in doing so he gained entree to the powerful banking circles of the city. And as it developed, he took a special liking to young Henry Horner. Ultimately the young lawyer would assume a relationship approaching ex-officio membership in the Lindheimer family. And in his fatherless life Horner's father-substitute would be old Jake Lindheimer.

CHAPTER FOUR

In the House of the Restless Ashes

In 1914 Jake Lindheimer put his finger to the winds and determined that Henry Horner, barely thirty-five years old, could be elected judge of the Probate Court of Cook County.

Through the mechanism of this court, the busiest single-judge court in the world, moved all the vast wealth of the county around and including the commercial center of Chicago once every generation. Its judge needed, therefore, to be an able administrator capable of handling a business with the equivalent of an annual inventory of $200,000,000, the value of estates placed before the court every year. Probate courts in America are an outgrowth of the English ecclesiastical courts presided over by the bishop of the Church of England, courts which were based on the premise that if the church knew best how to preserve a man's soul, it also knew best how to dispose of his worldly goods. Here existed the true court of last retort—death's retort. Among the racks of voluminous dusty probate dockets lurked romance, intrigue, mystery. In this court wills were examined, legacies parceled out, heirs ascertained, long-lost relatives scrutinized. Here the paths of wives and mistresses crossed in the gripping, often unemotional, struggle for the material possessions left behind by a dead man. A judge of this court would learn the hiding places for the skeletons of the most prominent families in town. He would be privy to the innermost secrets of the city's great financial institutions. As the presiding officer over what was essentially a massive service court, the judge could make important friends, do favors for influential people and institutions. By the same token he could ordinarily expect to avoid making enemies. A lawyer seldom argued with the probate judge because he knew he would be back tomorrow and the next day with routine business before the court. Under such circumstances it was natural for a judge sitting on this bench for many years to confuse his judgment with wisdom personified.

The incumbent state's attorney (elected county prosecutor) happened also to be a Harrison man, and he happened also to want his first assistant, Michael F. Sullivan, on the probate bench. Luckily for Horner, however, three others with good Gaelic names also filed. Sullivan polled 26,527 votes, John J. Coburn 25,961, and Thomas McEnerny 12,207. The Irish vote was effectively splintered, and Horner captured the nomination with 37,067. He campaigned hard throughout the county, hurrying from meeting to meeting in his impressive electric automobile. One day his fatigue got the better of him, and on the way to a rally he fell asleep at the wheel while driving through Lincoln Park. However, his long hours and the effective organization work by Sabath, Lindheimer, and other Jewish Harrisonites paid off. His old contacts in Hinky Dink's ward helped too.

He told the ward troops:

> Everybody knows the fighting Democrats of the First Ward, not only men who live in it, but men all over the state of Illinois. That's why every man who seeks to be a public official loses no time in turning handsprings to come down into the First Ward when he wants votes. I am aware that some candidates for purposes of newspaper publicity engage themselves with other interests outside the First Ward but . . . when they want to know the value of true democracy, they turn to the First Ward in election time, because as the First Ward goes, so goes the city of Chicago. What I learned of the practical politics of the city, I learned in the First Ward organization, and I am not afraid to say that I don't care what the men who criticize the democracy of the First Ward say about it. I was a Democratic captain of the First Ward here for years and I, like you, took my orders from Michael Kenna and John J. Coughlin. I have never stopped for an instant to regret accepting the advice given me as to what constitutes duty on the part of a Democrat in local, state, or national politics. One thing I learned here is that there is something bigger in politics than holding office. Something bigger than four-flushing about platforms and running after

> newspaper notoriety in the quest for public acclaim. That thing that is bigger is the true friendly interest of your fellow men. There is something higher and better than holding office, and that is standing for principle as exemplified in the battle cry of the First Ward and it is the battle cry upon which was founded the United States—personal liberty.[1]

He went on to say that if he were elected judge "everyone . . . whether coming with the staff of the beggar or the leper . . . shall get the same treatment as the most fortunate and pampered child of opulence." He said he valued the endorsement of the United Societies for Local Self-Government, which he had received, more than any other endorsement "because it carries the highest stamp of approval that any citizen of the United States can receive from his fellow citizens. . . . I am not a believer in personal liberty for today or tomorrow, but for all time. . . . I will try to be a square, decent, respectable, and humane probate judge. I will not forget that I have been elected by the people and solely by the people, and it is the people I will try to represent."

A speech befitting the First Ward, but hardly Lincolnian. Horner wanted desperately to win this election, and he reached out for any and all straws. But some semantic clarification is helpful here. In the First Ward context, translate "personal liberty" to mean the God-given right to get just as drunk as one desired, at any age, at any hour of the day or night, and to patronize prostitutes, gamblers, and/or other sundry merchants of vice on the way. A rough Bohemian former coal miner who appeared on the First Ward speaking program with Horner that night had organized the United Societies to mobilize the newly-arrived immigrant groups behind the liquor industry's campaign for a gloriously wide-open Chicago, all in the name of "personal liberty." That liquor lobbyist was Anton J. Cermak.

Of course, Horner's friends in the financial institutions and the other Standard Club members also had an interest in seeing him reach the probate bench. In the Chicago Bar Association poll of lawyers, he received the largest vote any Democratic judicial candidate had ever registered. Even at that, though, his Republican opponent surpassed him and obtained the bar endorsement. In the larger, more important balloting, the outcome was different:

Henry Horner, Democrat	154,752
Noble B. Judah, Republican	122,019

Albert Kales, Progressive	35,486
Edward Winston, Socialist	24,622
Orpheus Harding, Prohibition	1,268

For the next eighteen years Judge Horner devoted meticulous attention to his job.[2] He combined the incisive mind of the lawyer with the necessary feel for judicial administration on such a large scale. He found delight in pulling out the threads of human interest that were woven through the stacks of probate files confronting him daily. Maturing as a judge, Horner turned his sharp imaginative mind, the warmth of his personality, and a sensitivity for the overburdened to the business of his office.

The World War provided Judge Horner with a special opportunity to use his flair for innovation. To deal with the estates of dead soldiers and those combat casualties who had been declared mentally incompetent, he redesigned the entire procedural apparatus of his court. For widows and orphans, the judge brushed aside the legalistic red tape and assumed the role of protector against greedy undertakers, lawyers, bankers, and relatives.

By persuasive tactics that were not always gentle, Horner forced undertakers to scale down their funeral charges for veterans. The bar association was induced to furnish free legal aid for soldiers' heirs. Bankers cared for their money without charge. Court costs were trimmed. Under the judge's prodding the federal veterans' bureau expedited its financial settlements.

He made the rounds of the undertakers' conventions selling his educational program of more reasonable burial costs for the unknowledgeable, defenseless poor. In one typical case, a Lithuanian laborer died leaving an estate of $1,200. The first bill filed against the estate was for $950 in burial expenses.

"Who ordered such a fancy funeral?" the judge asked the undertaker. "Was it a relative?"

"No, your honor, but it was his best friend. He told me to lay out a funeral that the relatives back in the old country would be proud of if they could have been here. So I put him in a steel casket, hired a brass band of twenty pieces, furnished lots of flowers, and rented big cars to carry all the friends. You know, Judge, the Europeans go strong on funerals."

"So they do," Horner replied. "You are aware, I presume, that this man's surviving wife and child back in Lithuania would consider a legacy of $1,000 in American money to be a fortune. You will be allowed $200 for the funeral. You should not assume that you are called upon to bury the estate along with the deceased."[3]

He took similar steps against the vulturous lawyers of various ethnic groups who commonly solicited the permission of survivors in the old country to collect claims for them but then sent along only part of the money. Under Horner's policy these lawyers had to make full reports on disposition of the money within three months.

Every year about 9,500 estates were docketed in Judge Horner's court, and about 8,200 were settled. For an hour before court opened, the judge was available for informal conferences in his chambers. Here family hatchets were buried through friendly extrajudicial conciliation, and considerable incipient litigation was avoided. Lawyers came to complain about executors, executors about lawyers, wards about guardians, guardians about wards. Once a year all children under guardianship were called in for personal interviews with the judge. When the rights of children were involved, Horner took special care. In the courtroom, lawyers queued up in front of the bench, and the judge passed on fifty to a hundred motions daily at the rate of about one a minute. They involved applications of parties to estates of deceased persons, minors, or the mentally incompetent for permission to take action with money or property, in some cases with the objections of other parties. Horner's quick mind enabled him to grasp quickly the nub of the question before him.

Lawyers most appreciated his common-sense approach to the judicial process. One case involved the sinking of the "Lusitania" at the outset of the war.[4] The wills of an elderly couple who went down with the ship had been drawn by a Chicago attorney. It was, of course, hard to obtain accurate information about what happened in the lifeboats, and it became legally important to know which of the two had drowned first. The lawyer went to court armed with what cabled data he could acquire concerning the sequence of deaths. A timid judge, of whom there are many, would have demanded formal proof, resulting in interminable delay in the arrangement of his clients' affairs and the probate of their estate. But Horner realized that the best available evidence had been obtained, and he issued the necessary documents without delay. Before doing so, he asked for the lawyer's assurance that any later contradictory findings, if discovered, would be presented to him. Such experiences earned the confidence of the practicing attorneys and the admiration of their clients as well.

During his first campaign for judicial office, Horner promised his friends that "no act of mine ever will give you cause to regret what you did." However, he was often put to the test of judicial integrity. There were long, tedious trials over the admission of wills, involving complicated facts and law. Once when his mother asked what he thought of a certain pending case and volunteered her opinion, Horner immediately had the case transferred out of his court. His sixty-one-page opinion in the estate case of Emma Roche, concerning the struggle of two sisters for their mother's stock, followed fourteen months of evidence and arguments.

One notable case involved an estate of $400,000. The only heir was found to be a sister of the deceased who had been in an insane asylum for twenty years. Horner appointed an understanding conservator who bought a small cottage and a car and hired a nurse for her. Later a woman came to court with her lawyer claiming to be a daughter of the deceased. Using all the resources at his command, Horner traced life insurance policy records and determined her story to be fraudulent.

Probably the most sensational of all the judge's cases concerned the King will. James Clark King was a multimillionaire lumberman who willed most of his $3,000,000 estate to the Northern Trust Company as trustee for the creation of a home for old men on Chicago's South Side. Like many old men with money, he had taken a twenty-seven-year-old bride at the age of seventy-two. Twelve years after her husband's death, the widow was murdered at dusk on a lonely road near Concord, North Carolina. Her business manager and confidential adviser, the so-called Master Bad Man Gaston B. Means, cleared himself in court of murder charges. The murder victim, whose $100,000 share of the estate had been depleted by Means's cotton speculation, died while on an auto tour with Means and her sister, Mrs. Maisie Melvin. An authentically sinister figure, Means had been, admittedly, a German agent in the United States before the war. In 1915, after his acquittal Means announced that he had uncovered a second King will, which was said to have been executed less than a month before King's death in 1905. Mrs. Melvin and Mrs. King were supposed witnesses to the second will, which if accepted would have meant the loss of the old men's home. Roy Keehn, former publisher of the Chicago *Evening American* and then counsel for the Hearst newspapers in Chicago, represented Mrs. Melvin, who would have been chief beneficiary under the second will.

Thus the case had all the ingredients the sensational Chicago newspapers could hope for in a will case: the threat of old men being thrown out into the street if their homes were lost; a mean man named Means who had been a German spy; romance between Means and Maisie; then, murder on a country lane. And yet another juicy banner line for the newspapers came later. Means's lawyers released what purported to be a letter from an attorney for the Northern Trust Company to an assistant district attorney in New York. It read: "I also had a conference with Judge Horner. He is entirely in accord with the plan we have arranged and says he will carry out the matter on his part. He feels strongly that this plan ought to be carried out for the purpose of safeguarding the trust estate and bringing the guilty parties to justice in case they attempt to foist the forged instrument." Horner denounced the letter as fictitious and sued the *American* for $250,000 in libel damages after he was editorially criticized. The *American* subsequently retracted its criticism.

In December of 1919 Horner wrote a forty-thousand-word opinion dismissing the second will as fraudulent. The silence between Means's alleged discovery of the second will in 1915 and its disclosure in 1917 was, according to the judge, "a strange silence, a silence deep as death, a silence that almost speaks."

II

Horner, reacting to the everyday melodrama that filled his court, considered himself to be the "Keeper of the House of the Restless Ashes." The tone of his opinions revealed how his occupational adventures intrigued him. He once told an interviewer that the story of forged wills alone in his court would rival Poe's works for drama and mystery. As a member of the Chicago Literary Club, Horner discovered a whimsical literary outlet for the drama in his court files.[5] For his literary contributions to the club, he imagined a decedent reduced to a "restless ash" observing the devastating controversy in probate court that surrounded its own estate. Somehow the prospect of such figures "roving about in the celestial precincts," seeing their testamentary desires defeated and grumbling over how their control over their possessions after death had been frustrated, fascinated both the literary judge and his literary listeners.

"I am the Keeper of the House of the Restless Ashes," he recited. "The dwellers in my house are the ashes of men and women who, while they were on earth, made wills in which they attempted to direct the distribution of their accumulations and whose wills passed through the fierce fires of contests in the courts. Many of the wills could not be recognized by those who made them."

He quoted poetry:

> Let's choose executors and talk of wills;
> And yet not so—for what can we bequeath?
> Save our deposed bodies to the ground?

And:

> The boast of heraldry, the pomp of power,
> And all that beauty, all that wealth e'er gave,
> Await alike the inevitable hour;
> The paths of glory lead but to the grave.

In his first paper before the Literary Club, Judge Horner related how it had all started. One night while seated by the fire he said he heard a voice from the lapel of his coat.

> Upon looking there, I saw a small bit of ash which I supposed had fallen from my pipe. As I raised my hand to flick it, I heard the voice say, "Don't! Don't brush me off, for if you do you will not hear my story; and I am sure when you hear it you will be glad to let me rest in peace for a few moments upon your coat. I am not the ordinary tobacco or furnace ash—I am a bit of human ash—
>
> Remember ere you pass me by,
> As you are now so once was I;
> As I am now so you will be,
> So listen as I chat with thee.

The ash, as Horner described it, had once been a wealthy elderly gentleman who had yielded to the temptation of marrying a beautiful and young second wife, only to expire a short time after. As ash, he was blown about until

> I found myself on one of the boulevards of the city. Lying there helplessly, I noticed coming along at a fast rate of speed my own automobile, the very one in which I had so often ridden. Comfortably seated in it was my widow, very stunningly dressed in her becoming widow's weeds of latest Parisian fashion. I shall never forget my feeling of indignity as I was run over by my own car and my own widow. I attribute the fact that I was not crushed into a thousand pieces and not entirely destroyed to the tough texture of the ash atoms that constituted

me, evidently the result of the excellent firing I received at the crematory.

The ash continued to the courtroom riding on the widow's skirt, which, the ash observed, was somewhat shorter than a widow's skirt ought properly to have been. The judge looked solemn—"but I suppose a somber look is sometimes a sufficient substitute for wisdom."

"When I counted the number of lawyers present," the ash continued, "I began to tremble for my estate—and I wondered how much would be left after their appetite for fees had been satisfied."

Then the ash went on to tell of the many annoying developments occurring "at a time when I had a right to be at peace." One disquieting element was the rumor that a child would be born to the widow. "This was indeed news to me. I had been advised by my physician that I was destined to die childless. Nothing short of a miraculous conception could bring a child of mine into the world."

But if a child were born, he would qualify for two-thirds of the decedent's personal property, the widow receiving one-third; real estate would go to the infant subject only to the dower interest of the widow. Contrary to terms of the will, brothers and sisters of the deceased would be cut off entirely.

Being "only a lay ash," the ash had difficulty following the court discussion, which "reeked with big words and was clouded and shrouded in unnecessary legal terms. I wondered that some of the big words did not choke the lawyers and stagger the judge."

Six months after the husband's death, nevertheless, the woman went to Canada and arranged to take a child from a hospital for unwed mothers. She bribed a physician to perform the surgery necessary to give her the appearance of having recently given birth. Then the scene shifted to the courtroom, the baby forces on one side, the no-baby forces on the other, the ash in the middle watching.

"The lawyers," said the ash, "were apparently armed to the teeth with facts and arguments to hurl at the defenseless judge." The child was sickly, and if the infant died the widow—being sole heir—would get everything. "Horror filled me and a cold chill ran down my ashy spine. Could that be her game? Shades of Poe and Balzac, and the living Mr. Conan Doyle."

Observing the proceedings, the ash "almost envied the success of Shakespeare's revenge by which, under his will, he cut off his wife with nothing but his 'second-best bed' and some other old furniture. I was heartily sorry I was dead. How I then wished I could whisper the truth into the judge's ear. I knew it was contrary to good ethics to do that, but rules of ethics are made for the living, not for the dead."

Later the Canadian doctor confessed the scheme and six years of litigation ended. In a real-life case our fictional ash would have ended up in the probate court files where it would have met other ashes equally restless.

> We have delightfully gossipy times exchanging experiences and swapping reminiscences. Most of us had the great illusion that we could carry out after we were dead the plans for the future we built in our lifetimes, and of course we were disappointed. The disappointment in most cases is most pathetic. The tales of some of them are as romantic as the *Arabian Nights*. We are indeed a cosmopolitan and motley collection. . . . The dignified ash of Coke, who was in his lifetime England's famous judge and lawyer, complains every time he visits us because his will was stolen and never recovered.

Building on experiences in his own court, the judge improvised a series of imaginary meetings of his "whimsical and unnecessary club . . . a forum for restless souls." From time to time, James K. Polk, Benjamin Franklin, New York Governor Samuel J. Tilden, and Philadelphia mariner Stephen Girard were honored by appointment to the presidency of his club. Meetings of the club were enlivened by the singing of ditties ribbing lawyers, such as this:

> Ye lawyers who live upon litigants' fees,
> And who need a good many to live at your ease;
> Grave or gay, wise or witty, whate'er your degree,
> Plain stuff or state counsel, take counsel of me:
> When a festive occasion your spirit unbends
> You should never forget the profession's best friends
> So we'll send 'round the wine and a light bumper fill
> To the jolly testator who makes his own will.

This was all jolly good fun. But the founder of this amusing little club was much chagrined, some years after his departure from the probate bench, to find that he had a personal interest in an ironical gathering of some restless latter-day ashes. In 1927 his Uncle Albert died in California. Although there had long been an understanding that ownership of the grocery company would remain among the brothers, Albert's widow Georgia revealed that she had made a contrary discovery. She told of finding in Albert's private files a wax-sealed envelope with instructions "to be opened only by Judge Henry Horner." The envelope contained a new will dated December 28, 1924, which stated:

> Since my dear brother Joe's sad death last month without his wife near him has made me realize more fully what my dear wife has done for me. My health is failing fast. I want to protect Georgia's future years. She has not been too strong and will never be well again. I wrote M. L. Horner to send my will he has kept since 1922 when he made it for me to sign, and he wrote me he would destroy it. I worry about this, but have made my enclosed will that I am proud of. It is the only way my dear mother would have me do, and my heart will not be broken by the unfair and unjust will M. L. H. had. . . . This will explain everything I want done and I depend on you to see that my dear devoted wife gets a square deal. Love from, Albert.

Judge Horner sent the letter on to Georgia's lawyer in California. "She ought to have the best advice and help she can get because her devotion to her husband entitles her to that and all she can properly obtain from her deceased husband's estate," Horner's forwarding letter read. He volunteered to serve as executor of the estate, causing it to be probated in Cook County Court instead of his own court.

At a most inopportune time in his own career, however, in 1936, Horner discovered that Uncle Albert was a mighty restless ash indeed! A letter arrived one day from a man in Long Beach, California, who related that he had been one of two witnesses to the newly-found will of Albert Horner and that the affidavits swearing that the will had been drawn prior to Uncle Albert's death were fraudulent. The witness said that Albert had actually intended to leave most of his money and property to his only living brother, Maurice, who lived in Chicago, and not to Georgia. The witness' employer had been a friend of Georgia's who had forced two of his employees to sign the fake affidavits. The forged will had awarded $1,000 in cash, Albert's stock in the grocery, his share in some Chicago family property, and all his personal property to his wife.

Waiting until after his own personal political crisis had passed, Horner (who had himself been willed Albert's consistory ring with diamond setting in the fake will) wrote a joint letter to Georgia and to Maurice, Jr., in Chicago, informing them of the man's "strange, shocking, and astounding charges." Lawyers on all sides exchanged reams of correspondence. Two years later, according to documents preserved in the Horner Papers, without the dispute apparently ever being formally returned to the jurisdiction of the courts, the widow admitted a fraud and a settlement was made. The affair left the governor considerably shaken, but ash Albert presumably no longer had cause to be restless.[6]

III

One way in which a public official can effectively work to retain his office is to try to give such excellent service that the community thinks it cannot do without him. Following this principle, Judge Horner won re-election by progressively larger margins in 1918, 1922, 1926, and 1930. He polled 154,752 votes in 1914; 194,813 in 1918; 410,621 in 1922; 443,538 in 1926; and 691,854 in 1930. By 1918 the Chicago Bar Association committee on candidates recognized his "exceptional capacity and fitness for office." By 1926 he ran without Democratic party opposition in the primary election, and the Republicans had difficulty finding a strong candidate to oppose him. By 1930 he received more votes than anyone else on the county ticket, a distinction that carries a great deal of significance among politicians.

Attorneys who were contemporaries of Judge Horner's remember him as one of the outstanding Cook County judges. Although probably not as profound a student of the law as his predecessor on the probate bench, Charles S. Cutting, Horner was an efficient, personable judicial officer who made many friends in places of high financial and political power. His integrity was seldom questioned, except in the case of the King will letter, which if authentic would have constituted, of course, a serious breach of conduct.

In one other incident Horner's use of the probate bench as an opportunity for winning the favor of sources of political and financial power has been viewed with some suspicion. Stanley McCormick, son of the founder of International Harvester Company, suffered a mental illness and was declared incompetent. While he lived at Riven Rock, California, under the care of five physicians who were paid $90,000 a year, his wife and his sister and two brothers carried on a running legal battle for the control of Stanley and Stanley's fortune. His estate multiplied from $10,000,000 to more than $40,000,000 by 1930. Newton D. Baker, a Cleveland lawyer and an influential Democrat who had been secretary of war under President Wilson, represented the wife, Mrs. Katharine Dexter McCormick. In 1930 Baker suggested to

Horner, who had jurisdiction over conservation of the estate, that the services of his firm for a period of about two years were worth between $400,000 and $500,000. Opposing counsel maintained that a reasonable legal fee would be far less. Because of Baker's prominent position in Democratic affairs (he was being mentioned as a presidential candidate in 1932), Horner's decision granting most of Baker's fee request might be interpreted as having some connection with the judge's subsequent political good fortune in Illinois. It is significant to note, however, that Mrs. McCormick's petition to be appointed sole conservator of the estate was rejected by Horner.

On the bench Horner had an opportunity to see the muddles which little people could wander into and the way in which economic and social status provided a head start toward justice. By the end of his judicial tenure, however, Horner chafed at the drab, commonplace matters that made up most of the business of his court. His mind worked fast, and he became impatient and irritable. In the main, though, his judicial years were happy and stimulating. He enjoyed telling friends that his mother made him wear his muffler and rubbers to the County Building. "Downtown you're a big judge," she would say, "but here I'm still your boss, you're still my boy." In a more serious vein, the exasperated judge confided to an acquaintance, "You never grow up in your mother's eyes. My mother still considers me a little boy."

His defective eyesight ruled out any chance for military service in World War I. Prior to the war, during the Mexican border uprising, he had visited two of his National Guard friends, Abel Davis and Milton Foreman, at El Paso, Texas, where they were colonels in a field artillery outfit. Through the years his friend Davis, a prominent Republican, wrote letters of campaign endorsement for Horner.

Until January 8, 1921, the judge lived with his mother and brother Sidney in a West Side apartment at 4432 Grand Avenue. On that date, shortly after his forty-second birthday, his mother died of diabetes at the age of sixty-nine. She was interred in the family plot at Mount Mayriv cemetery alongside her father and mother.

After that, Judge Horner moved to a bachelor apartment in Madison Park between Fiftieth Street and Hyde Park Boulevard on the South Side, alone but for his Lincoln books and his parrot. The raucous bird's impertinent comments whenever a guest chattered too much earned him the name of "Shut Up." Horner and his bird swore at one another in Hebrew, and the judge once kept a sheet over the cage for two days, having found "Shut Up" in contempt for biting the judge of the probate court. Chinese lamps, model ships, a half-dozen different busts of Lincoln, a chair covered in needlepoint by his mother with the initials "D. H.," and other assorted mementos gave the apartment a cluttered appearance. Two doors away from Horner's home lived his Aunt Mattie and Uncle Eli Straus, a whiskey wholesaler.

Sidney Horner, Henry's older brother, was an impetuous individualist who decided after his mother's death that he no longer chose to live in a country where a man could not buy a glass of beer. So Sidney, who had earned a respectable amount of money in the picture frame business, exiled himself to Europe, a Prohibition expatrate. There he surely qualified as one of the Bohemians of the twenties. Sidney leased an apartment in Paris, wintered in Vienna, roamed over the Continent, and managed constantly to worry his judicial brother. The judge's brother loved nothing so much as stirring up petty trouble. In Paris, for instance, his favorite pastime was following American tourists until he witnessed one being shortchanged by a Frenchman, after which he happily informed his countryman of the fraud and gleefully watched the bilingual excitement. Sidney did not return to the United States until after his brother became governor. After having sown a variety of wild oats in many lands, Sidney married a woman twenty-one years his junior only a few years before his death at the age of seventy-five.

Nor could Henry's eldest brother, James Levy, be termed conventional. A champion bicycler as a youth, Jim started selling horseless carriages in 1897 and ultimately accumulated wealth as one of Chicago's leading Buick dealers. In Levy's agency the first order of business in the morning was the shining of a big brass sign on his office wall that contained a single word—"No." "That word alone has kept me in business," Jim explained. "It's the hardest word in the language for a man to use after he's forty-five, and yet it's the safest. When a salesman wants to knock down the price, he has to come to me for my okay. I always say 'no.' Sometimes on second judgment I can say 'yes.' You can go from 'no' to 'yes,' but you can't go from 'yes' to 'no.' " In many ways Jim was a nonconformist like his father and his brother Sidney. Once, late for a golf date at Idlewild Country Club on the far South Side, Jim chartered an airplane downtown and landed on the eighteenth fairway. After the board of directors of the club rebuked him severely for this, Jim resigned from the club and joined Bryn Mawr Club instead. He advised the directors that they were years behind the times, reminding them that a few short years before a man had been arrested for riding a bicycle in Lincoln Park.

Henry Horner was more conventional and less flamboyant than his brothers. He enjoyed attractive women, lively parties, and the convivial company of many friends. Among his fondest admirers, in an innocent kind of way, were the wives of his male acquaintances. They invited him often as the extra man at a dinner party. One of the hostesses, a strikingly beautiful woman, remembers Horner this way:

> He could never be considered handsome, but he liked the ladies. He had a disarming warmth—I suppose we'd call it a "line" today. He dressed sloppily, for lack of female counseling no doubt. Henry was an attentive, laughing man. His humor and personality made him fun to be with. When he arrived for dinner, he would always kiss me on the cheek and kid my husband that when I was ready for the discard pile to call him. Henry never seemed to be stuffy. He didn't go for small talk, but he could converse on any number of subjects.

Maude Lindheimer Lepman, Jake Lindheimer's married daughter, was an especially close friend of Horner's. Of all the magnetic Lindheimers, pretty Maude was probably the most vivacious and exciting. She liked Henry and called him "Hankie-Pankie." Belonging to the same German Jewish tradition in which Horner had been brought up by his grandmother, Jacob Lindheimer's wife Millie had also been a strong forceful woman. Maude duplicated many of her dynamic qualities.

By this stage in life Horner's scale of values had been established. Except for a good rich meal and a 50-cent cigar, he seemed to have little appetite for material riches. Money was to be spent quickly; much of it was given away or disposed of frivolously. Characteristically sweet and sentimental, he needed most of all to be liked, to bask in the fellowship of different types of men and women.

The judge seemed to use his generous outgoing nature as a shield for warding off the loneliness caused by the absence of a family. In turn his exposure to many different kinds of people contributed to his development as judge and politician. Having no one at home but "Shut-Up" the parrot, Horner enjoyed the social obligations of political life more than most family men would. He had the time to cultivate Moe Rosenberg, the ruthless, arrogant boss of the Twenty-fourth Ward. And after hobnobbing with the teacup set at the Lake Shore Country Club, the most exclusive Jewish country club in town, the judge could be found circulating easily around the pinochle table at the Democratic headquarters in the Sherman Hotel, where the crude and occasionally corrupt drones of the party machine sought recreation. Like any proper Democrat, the judge made the regular rounds of the Irish Catholic wakes.

Among his closest friends during this period were Jacob Loeb, an insurance executive and later president of the Chicago Board of Education; William Willhartz, a lawyer; and two bachelors like himself, Abel Davis and Ben Stein. On Sunday mornings without fail Horner breakfasted in his apartment with an eccentric and rare individualist, a former Chicago reporter who was giving birth to a book about Lincoln. Carl Sandburg loved to browse through the rare treasures on the bookshelves. Research for *The Prairie Years* led him first to the resources in Horner's collection. Sitting in front of the fireplace, the two men read the political oratory of Lincoln aloud and marveled together at its precise beauty. Sometimes Carl would stay overnight. Then Horner would unfold a hide-a-bed in his study and bring in sheets and pillowcases and act as maidservant for this guest whose enthusiasm for Lincoln was so infectious. Their only disagreement compelled Sandburg to periodically reprimand Horner for having delivered Democratic speeches in praise of Stephen A. Douglas. "You know of course that Douglas did not condemn slavery," Sandburg would lecture in his singsong chant. "He favored allowing any state to vote up or down on slavery. He favored human beings on the tax books, the assessor writing their valuation opposite their name like a piece of machinery. When the big pinch came, Douglas was for the Union, but the South had repudiated him. The facts that condemn your speech are right here in your own library." [7]

At intervals, too, Horner and another Lincoln enthusiast, Oliver Barrett, visited the Sandburgs at the poet's home on the shore of Lake Michigan in southern Michigan. Through these years Horner's study of Lincoln intensified, and he began writing newspaper articles and making speeches about his hero. His Lincoln's Birthday article in the Chicago *Journal* on February 12, 1926, pointed out that "one of the delightful things about Lincoln is that he never held himself out, or never set out, to 'set an example.' He lived his life simply and naturally, developed and spoke the thought that was in him, did the job that was laid out for him to do, and let his 'example' shift for itself." It was because of the annual meetings of the Abraham Lincoln Association that Horner's first trips to Springfield, the state capital, were made during this period.

On Wednesdays Judge Horner lunched with a club called the Bandarlogs. And on Saturdays, with the work week ended, the Skeeters convened in weekly luncheon sessions around a bottle of Scotch at the Midday Club in the First National Bank Building. Lunch, good conversation, and a bridge game or two continued until about four o'clock or until the Scotch ran out. Consisting of men who excelled in varying fields, the Skeeters comprised an extraordinary assortment. Horner was the only politician, and Democratic party sympathizers were few in number. Some of the other members were General Robert E. Wood, president of Sears, Roebuck & Company; Paul Steinbrecher, an insurance and real estate broker; Richard J. Finnegan, editor of the liberal tabloid *Chicago Times;* Burt A. Massee, vice president of the Palmolive Company; Herbert Bradley, attorney and big-game hunter; Dr. Horace Bridges, minister and director of the Chicago Ethical Society; Father Ed J. Mullaly, a Paulist priest; Dr. Solomon Freehof, rabbi at K. A. M.; Lee Metzenburg, jewelry buyer and collector of antique watches; Leonarde Keeler, pioneer of the lie detector machine; Fay-Cooper Cole, head of the anthropology department at the University of Chicago; and Col. Trygve Siqueland, vice president of the First National Bank of Chicago.[8]

Any prominent visitor who happened to be in Chicago would likely be invited to lunch with the Skeeters. At one meeting Count von Luckner, skipper of a German commerce raider in World War I, delivered a table-top lecture on the Battle of Jutland—and so intrigued Judge Horner that he sent someone to a nearby bookstore to buy fifteen copies of the count's book about the battle. This abrupt decision illustrated Horner's seeming disregard for money. Many of the other Skeeters were far wealthier than he. Burt Massee owned five lake yachts, one of them the 166-foot $500,000 vessel *The Margo* which tied up at Monroe Street harbor with a crew of 23. The Bandarlogs were a more fun-loving group without as much time for serious conversation. At one Bandarlog golf tournament, Horner, who was an occasional but abysmal golfer, brought along an Italian organ grinder and a monkey, who intercepted the balls before they could be holed out on the eighteenth green.

The Skeeters, Carl Sandburg, Abel Davis, Moe Rosenberg, the precinct captains at the Sherman, his dinner party friends on the Gold Coast and at the Lake Shore Country Club, the poor people whose heartaches were the raw materials in his courtroom—all these and many, many more contributed their part to the molding of Judge Henry Horner.

Religion also continued to be an influence in Horner's life. Drawn by the prestige of Emil G. Hirsch, who was succeeded in 1923 by Louis Mann, the judge belonged to Sinai Congregation on the South Side as well as to the older K. A. M. Other than by observing the High Holidays, Horner did not practice the rituals of the faith and cannot be considered to have been a devout Jew. However, he was conscious of the moral and ethical connotations of his religious upbringing; and he knew that as a politician he was judged closely as a representative of his fellow Jews. Horner, unlike other Reform Jews with indistinguishable surnames (like his), never attempted to assimilate into the non-Jewish world. He practiced his religion in many ways. He was president of Young Men's Jewish Charities, on the board of the Jewish Aid Society, chairman of the social service committee of Michael Reese Hospital, chairman of the governing board for the unemployment fund of the Garment Workers' Union, a member of the same union's arbitration board, labor arbitrator for the Federal Board of Mediation, on the executive committee of the Chicago Boy Scouts, chairman of the board of discipline of the federal Veterans' Bureau, legal adviser during World War I to the Illinois Draft Board, teacher of probate law at Chicago-Kent College of Law, director of the Central Council of Nursing Education, and a trustee of the Sarah Hackett Stevenson Memorial Lodging House. Through all of his service activities ran the central thread of his devotion to children. He was especially devoted to a camp for underprivileged Jewish boys which was located northwest of Chicago. Each year on the Fourth of July, he brought fireworks and other novelties for the campers. After his death, fittingly, the camp was named Camp Henry Horner.

IV

During the years when Horner perched serenely on the probate bench and enjoyed fellowship with the Skeeters and Carl Sandburg, Chicago's political machine came into being. Its evolution is part of the Horner story. In 1915 a forty-five-year-old political playboy who happened to be a Republican, Big Bill Thompson, replaced Carter Harrison in the mayor's chair. His partner was Fred Lundin, the "poor Swede," who a few short years before, in his black frock coat and flowing black string tie, had been selling juniperade to the Nordics on the Northwest Side.[9] Thompson and Lundin were the first to grasp an essential principle of urban politics in those days of heavy immigration—the importance of ethnic group identification and the way in which underlying nationalistic prejudices could be played off against one another. More than two-thirds of Chicago's 800,000 families were at least partly foreign born. Neighborhood contrasts stood out vividly—250,000 Negroes in the Black Belt, 285,000 Germans dominating the "Nord Seit," the Irish and their political know-how Back of the Yards, 130,000 Italians on the West Side, 200,000 Scandinavians, 315,000 Poles, 115,000 Czechs. When war confused the loyalties of these newcomers, Thompson skillfully inflamed the Germans and the Irish and capitalized on their mixed emotions.

In the natural course of events, Carter Harrison slid toward oblivion, and Roger C. Sullivan assumed control of the Democratic party. Jake Lindheimer switched his allegiance to Sullivan's "gas crowd," as it was called, because of the leader's affection for the People's Gas Company. From his insulated position on the bench, Horner maintained his good relations with the Lindheimers, including Jake's up-and-coming son Ben, but also stayed on good terms with the remnants of the Harrison faction.

In 1916 the Harrisonites sustained a death blow when Republican Frank O. Lowden, the master of the Sinissippi Acres of Ogle County, beat Governor Dunne by 139,000 votes. However, Lowden snubbed the patronage requests of Thompson and Lundin, and four years thereafter the Chicago group won a primary fight and elected Len Small of Kankakee governor. Small was re-elected in 1924 despite his indictment (and acquittal) for irregularities connected with his custody of state funds while state treasurer.

Appellate Court Judge William E. Dever, who had worked as a tanner on Goose Island at the north branch of the Chicago River, moved into the mayor's office in 1923. One of his decisions was to retain Thompson's city health commissioner, Dr. Herman N. Bundesen. As the Harrison administration drew to an end, Horner fastened an interested eye on the mayoralty of Chicago. By the early 1920's he considered this a possibility within reason if not reach. His judicial reputation had been nationally publicized, and his vote-getting ability demonstrated. He saw no reason why the same methodical, sensible approach he had used in probate court would not work equally well applied to the complex problems of metropolitan municipal government. Consequently, the judge was tempted in 1924 when Mayor Dever asked him to be corporation counsel—chief lawyer for the city—in his administration. It would, in one respect, have been a natural step toward the mayoralty. From another standpoint, though, Horner would no longer have been "his own man." His personal loyalty to the Mayor would be necessary even if differences of opinion occurred. He talked with his friends at the Standard Club before deciding not to give up his standing and prestige on the probate court. One of those consulted was his friend Max Epstein, head of the General American Transportation Company, which pioneered the rental of refrigerator railroad cars. Abel Davis' feeling that the Chicago Title and Trust Company would obviously be better served with Horner in the court carried considerable weight with the judge.

Democratic leadership had passed by now from Roger Sullivan to another Irishman, George E. Brennan. Until he lost a leg in an accident, Brennan had been a coal miner in the Braidwood region southwest of Chicago. Brennan turned thereafter to a school teacher's career. His chuckling good humor camouflaged an aptitude for cunning intrigue. If anyone can be called the father of the Democratic machine of Cook County, Brennan is the one. He assembled in a functioning unit the South Side Irish—Mike Igoe, Pat Nash, Tim Crowe, Denny Egan, and Kenna and Coughlin. A testament to Brennan's ability is that he was able to dominate the ward organizations with Irish, load the ballot with Murphys, O'Briens, and Farrells—and still expect the Jews, Bohemians, Swedes, Italians, Germans, and Poles to vote for them.

In 1927 the Brennan magic failed, and Thompson returned to power. Big Bill's organization, the Fish Fans Club, was jubilant. About fifteen hundred of his followers swarmed aboard the old lumber schooner which served as a clubhouse in Belmont Harbor—and the vessel sank in six feet of water. Swaggering back into power alongside Thompson came Al Capone, who was now free to move his gangland base of operations back into Chicago from suburban Cicero.

The legal repression of alcoholic beverages had drastic repercussions in a community which had lustily loved its booze for decades. Bootleggers, brewers, speakeasy proprietors, and gang leaders entered politics as the only means to obtain illicit distribution franchises. Police connived with businessmen, bootleggers, and gangsters. Much has been written about Prohibition as the Puritans' final heresy in America and about its influence even today on our politics and our attitudes about law enforcement. One short narrative will give some flavor of what those days were like in Chicago: Frank Loesch, counsel for the Pennsylvania Railroad and president of the Chicago Crime Commission, once called on the mighty Capone to plead that the people of Chicago be permitted just this once to elect their own prosecuting attorney. Above Scarface Al's desk hung portraits of Lincoln, Washington, and Big Bill Thompson. Capone, bless his heart, understood. Al said he would "have the cops send over the squad cars the night before the election and jug all the hoodlums in the Saltis gang of micks over on the West Side and keep 'em in the cooler until the polls close." Furthermore, he would direct the chief of detectives "to take care of the Dingbat O'Berta gang of Polacks" so as to prevent kidnapping and assaulting of Polish voters. Capone was a man of his word. Seventy squad cars were used to keep the Capone mob quiet on the North Side and the mobsters in the other districts under control as well.

Alfred E. Smith's try for the presidency in 1928 rocked Illinois along with the rest of the nation. Judge Horner's rise within the party earned him the honor of keynote speaker at the Democratic state convention on April 20 in Springfield. The only weapon that could be raised against Al Smith, Horner declared that day, "is the insidious weapon of religious animosity which has rusted in its scabbard since the birth of the nation. I warn you, beware of this issue."

The judge's name had spread far beyond the county boundaries. His activities for the Illinois County and Probate Judges' Association seeking legislation in Springfield introduced him to the state legislature. Other opportunities for meeting prominent downstate citizens opened up through his involvement in state-wide Masonic circles. He had progressed to senior steward of Chicago Lodge 437 in 1902, to junior deacon in 1903, to senior deacon in 1904, junior warden in 1905, senior warden in 1906, worshipful master in 1907, marshal in 1908, district deputy grand master of the Seventh Masonic district in 1921. And in 1924 Horner became grand orator of the Illinois Grand Lodge, a position that required him to deliver the order's annual "eloquent address." His speech to the grand lodge blended history with the sort of inspirational oratory that was expected at such an event. He listed previous Illinois grand orators, beginning with Stephen A. Douglas in 1840 ("had he lived in any other era of the United States he would have been its President"), and later including Adlai E. Stevenson I, former vice president of the United States, in 1896. "My brethren," the grand orator intoned, "each of us is a leader in our respective spheres of influence—be that circle small or large. We can be leaders for good or evil, as we choose. If we are true Masons, it will be for the good. By good leadership we can harness the best in our fellow men." After his subsequent elevation to the 33d degree of Masonry, Horner wore a plain band, the 33d degree Mason's ring, on the wedding-ring finger of his left hand.

Much more so than in heavily Catholic Cook County, advancement in the Masonic order has always been a requisite for political success in the Protestant downstate counties. (In Illinois, Chicago is in Cook County; the other 101 counties are considered "downstate," although some are in fact north of Chicago.) Judge Horner's talents were brought to the attention of influential downstate leaders at the annual state lodge conventions. One who met Horner and came away impressed at a Masonic convention in 1927 was Louie Lewis, a weekly newspaper publisher in Christopher, Franklin County, and a dabbler in Democratic politics. "Horner made a speech that year for a resolution that we downstaters were against," Lewis later recalled, "but he made such a striking impression that we remembered him." [10] Another whose Masonic friendship Horner nurtured was the Republican secretary of state for Illinois, Louis L. Emmerson of Mount Vernon in southern Illinois. Emmerson mirrored the very qualities that were most revered downstate: he was charming, conservative, prohibitionist. In 1928 Emmerson defeated Len Small in the Republican gubernatorial primary and ran against a Chicago justice of the state supreme court, Democrat Floyd Thompson.

At the peak of that 1928 campaign Horner received a letter from a fellow Mason asking, "As a Mason can I vote for a Catholic for president without violating my Masonic obligations?" In a seven-page typewritten reply, Horner answered that the society never tried to influence the political views of its members. "Occasionally," he said, "persons seeking political preferment have sought to aid their cause by an appeal based solely upon their Masonic affiliation. . . . There have been instances in the past when Masons have rejected such a class appeal. . . . The large vote among Masons which Mayor Dever, a Catholic, received at the last election is but one instance of the fair and open-mindedness of the fraternity in our city." [11]

He pointed out that Masonry is a progressive moral science which does not attempt to influence attitudes on church questions, other than to require belief in God. "But the fraternity has never undertaken to influence its members as to the manner or form in which its members shall worship God; and to that policy, Masonry —properly practiced—has ever adhered, and I hope will ever adhere."

If the writer believed Smith would make the better president, Judge Horner said he would be violating his Masonic principles by not voting for him. The judge reminded him of that portion of one Masonic lecture which says: "By the exercise of brotherly love we are taught to regard the whole human species as one family—the high and low, rich and poor; who are created by one Almighty parent, and inhabitants of the same planet are to aid, support and protect each other."

Horner's letter reached this conclusion:

> The founders of our Republic were the descendants of those who came to this country to escape religious intolerance abroad, and in framing the Constitution they wanted to be sure that this question—religious intolerance—could never be raised in this country. The birth of Masonry in this country is almost coincident with the formation of our government. Our fraternity was rocked in the cradle of liberty by the men who won our freedom. These noble patriots would rise in protest from their graves if they thought that Masons would vote on any presidential candidate because of the manner in which he worshipped his God.

In spite of such noble sentiments, Judge Thompson fell alongside Al Smith under the force of anti-Catholic votes in many downstate areas. Emmerson succeeded to the governorship.

The reorientation that had occurred in American politics was, to be sure, far greater than a flash of religious prejudice. The 1924 Democratic convention fight, Smith versus McAdoo, the urban Catholic versus the rural Klansman, had changed the direction of the party for at least a generation to come. Four years later, Al Smith broke the Republican hold on the cities for reasons more basic than religious identification. In Illinois the rural-urban cleavage was even deeper than elsewhere. Bryanism, repellent to the big city, was strongest in the southeastern part of the state where Southern Baptists prevailed. The total vote for governor in Chicago increased between 1920 and 1928 from 797,000 to 1,248,000.

Midway in the 1928 campaign, George Brennan, the former country school teacher, died unexpectedly, leaving the Democrats without a leader. In preparation for such an emergency Brennan had designated, as his heir apparent, Mike Igoe, party leader in the state House of Representatives. Igoe, a chubby-faced Irishman, had served his party well since coming to the legislature with Governor Dunne in the Bull Moose upheaval. Brennan, however, had underestimated one of his former pupils at Braidwood and made the grievous error of continuing to treat him as a schoolboy.

V

Anton Joseph Cermak was born in the coal mining region of Kladno near Prague in Czechoslovakia.[12] His immigrant family settled in the mining town of Braidwood, a community of fifteen thousand Bohemians and Irishmen and ninety-nine saloons. The Chicago and Wilmington Coal Company owned most of the town. Tony became a mule driver in the coal pits in his early teens and attended school about three months out of the year after that. Czech social life revolved about the saloon, and it was not out of the ordinary that this pugnacious youth with powerful shoulders, bull neck, and thick chest should have learned to drink at sixteen. He moved to the Pilsen section of Chicago, got a job driving a kindling-wood wagon, and inquired around about how to score in politics. Legend has it that George Brennan, his old mentor, advised him to "go live among the Bohunks" in the Twenty-second Ward. By the time he was thirty Cermak had been elected to the state legislature, where in 1909 he was accused of selling his vote for United States Senator. From there, Cermak progressed to Chicago alderman, bailiff for the municipal court, and in 1922 to president of the Cook County Board. A member of Loeffler's organization, Cermak remained one of Carter Harrison's lieutenants until 1914, when he defected to the Sullivan-Brennan faction of the party. In the Bohemian neighborhood around Twenty-sixth Street and Kedzie Avenue, one of Tony's precinct captains and a personal friend was Otto Kerner, Sr., son of a Bohemian cabinetmaker. Under Cermak's guidance, Kerner ran for alderman and later was elected judge of the circuit court.

Cermak pursued parallel careers in public office and as a lobbyist for the liquor industry, a conflict of interests that was not frowned upon in that period. United Societies, which he served as secretary and leader, was a federation of saloon, brewery, and distillery interests working, in the name of the thirsty and the foreign-born, for a wide-open Chicago. In 1912, before a city council hearing, he described the organization's goal as the passage of "liberal" laws. "You know," Cermak pointed out, "that we have state laws providing that liquor shall not be sold after midnight. But we get permits for our dances allowing sales up to three o'clock in the morning. The one o'clock closing ordinance is also a violation of state law. We don't want these laws enforced." His group exploited the foreign-born and opposed the efforts of the Juvenile Protective Association to force compliance with closing laws. Minors were served drinks in these dance halls, and investigators once estimated that two hundred thousand boys and girls frequented the halls in the days before Prohibition.

His gruff, two-fisted manner did not retard Cermak's rise. Playing both wings of the party, he took advantage both of Harrison's personal popularity and the organizational durability of the Sullivan-Brennan forces. While building up the Slavs and Italians, Brennan had kept Cermak and the other ethnic leaders in comparative subjection, continuing to concentrate leadership in the Irish. Cermak made a try for the gubernatorial nomination in 1928 but was refused by Brennan. But after the death of his teacher, Cermak employed the logical tactic of coalescing the Jews, the Bohemians, the Poles, and the other non-Irish on the West Side, so as to snatch party control from Igoe and the Irish. He drove his machine ruthlessly but with dexterity, conciliating business, labor, reform, nationalistic, and neighborhood groups in the process. For the most part, Igoe and the other Irish leaders were left holding the bag, unaccustomed as they were to such a load. Two who committed their loyalties to Cermak were Joe McDonough and the party leader in the state senate, Thomas J. Courtney. Another Irish leader who exercised considerable influence on A. J., as he was called, was Edward J. Kelly. Ed Kelly's acquaintances included Frank Hague, the Democratic boss of New Jersey, and Colonel McCormick, the flamboyant Republican editor of the *Chicago Tribune*. For county Democratic chairman, Cermak installed the only Irish name he thought he could trust, Pat Nash, a ward committeeman and sewer contractor.

One of the strongest links in the chain used to pull the Irish off the throne was the Jews. Along Twenty-sixth Street in South Lawndale, Cermak commanded the Czechs of the Twelfth Ward. But the North Lawndale and Douglas Park area from Tripp Street west to California Avenue had now expanded into the largest concentration of orthodox Jews in the nation. There were fifty synagogues in Lawndale alone, and on Thursday nights Jews from all over the city flocked to the kosher markets in the Roosevelt Road and Sixteenth Street shopping district. From this mass of humanity living in dreary buildings, two men assembled a mighty political organization in the Twenty-fourth Ward. Moe Rosenberg, arrogant and unrefined, supplied the brawn. His protégé, Jacob Arvey, whose parents came from a town near Mir in Lithuania, added the brains. At Passover time Rosenberg and Arvey personally handled out matzoth, baskets of noodles, chickens, and sometimes shoes from fleets of trucks. In return, Boss Rosenberg demanded votes and respect.

Rosenberg and Horner had little but their political interests in common. But this was more than enough. It had by now become apparent to any Jewish leader in Chicago that the most popular Jewish candidate in their midst would be Henry Horner. Although technically detached from the anti-Irish coup in 1928 because of his judicial position, Horner nevertheless gave whatever comfort he could to Cermak and Rosenberg, mindful of what it might mean to his own future.

Rosenberg's relationship with Samuel Insull influenced Democratic politics during these years. Born in England, Insull came to Chicago as president of the Chicago Edison Company. He cultivated the friendship of Roger Sullivan and proceeded to acquire a power monopoly over electricity, gas, and rapid transit. To this end, Insull bought politicians. Rosenberg said later, when he became involved in income tax trouble, that in 1929–30 he had distributed $500,000 to fellow Democrats representing profits of the Rosenberg Iron and Metal Company that had accrued through bargain purchases of scrap metal from Insull utilities, and that he had given Cermak $50,000 to pay off party debts.[13] The crumbling of Insull's utilities empire precipitated the closing of Chicago banks and triggered the depression that followed.

In the meantime Horner went on participating liberally in campaigns for good causes. He took part in efforts to obtain greater home rule for Chicago, prompting the Illinois Municipal League to advertise him as a possible candidate for governor. He led a campaign by the Illinois Society for Mental Hygiene for better conditions and larger budgets in mental institutions. When the legislature voted a $3,000-a-year salary increase for judges in 1926, Horner directed that his raise be turned over to the newly formed Institute for Juvenile Research.

Since the beginning of the century it had been stylish for Chicago leaders to complain about the lack of equal representation in the legislature. Reapportionment was badly needed if the legislature was to reflect changes in population, particularly the growth of Chicago at a faster rate than the rural regions. Dominated by rural Illinois, the legislature shackled the city government, and there was little that Chicago representatives could do about it. In the mid-1920's Horner enthusiastically volunteered to serve as chairman of the subcommittee on legal procedure of the Illinois Apportionment Committee. Inasmuch as the state constitution explicitly required that the legislature be redistricted every ten years, it was obvious that the basic law was being ignored. But because of the separation of powers between the judicial and legislative branches, no one had been able to figure out how the courts or anyone else could force the legislature to do something it did not want to do. With this objective in mind, Judge Horner's committee of fifty-five of the state's most astute legal minds set about to find the legal means with which to accomplish reapportionment, an achievement not actually completed until 1954.

Horner made other contributions to state government as well. He was appointed by Governor Emmerson to a commission that marked the Lincoln Memorial Highway along the route taken by the Lincoln family from Indiana through Vincennes in 1830. He also served on a commission appointed by the governor to dedicate a statue of Lincoln at Dixon, where Lincoln had been mustered into the army fighting Blackhawk in 1832.

The momentous events ahead could hardly have been imagined as 1930 ushered in a new decade in Illinois. On New Year's Day Governor Emmerson radiated optimism. Industries, he said, were on a sound basis, bank reserves sufficient for orderly development, and the state's people thrifty and capable. The reduction of employment that followed the stock market crash of 1929 had given way in many instances to what the governor termed a more normal production and resumption of manufacturing.

But despite the governor's wishes, normalcy was a thing of the past in Illinois. In Chicago, police broke up a fight near a bank, and a crowd gathered. Somebody yelled "run," $1,600,000 was quickly withdrawn, and the bank closed. Paul Douglas, a professor of economics at the University of Chicago, warned that economic competition between socialistic Russia and the Western nations could lead to the destruction of mankind. Already $290,000,000 in debt, the city of Chicago fired 473 policemen and 240 firemen. For years, dishonest real estate tax assessments and delayed collections had prevailed in downtown Chicago. Governor Emmerson complained that Chicago had not paid its share of state property taxes for the previous two years, jeopardizing the solvency of the state government. Former Governor Lowden proposed, instead, a tax system based on income rather than property. On Washington's Birthday, Communists marched on City Hall demanding "wages and work" before they were dispersed by mounted police and riot squads. A few weeks later, Governor Emmerson declared hopefully: "At no time during my public career have I sensed a more friendly spirit among our people. I believe we have come to a day when each man is willing to assume his fair share of the cost of advantage which community cooperation, expressed in the form of government, has afforded him." [14]

This friendly spirit was not evident in November when the Democrats elected J. Hamilton Lewis to the United States Senate by a landslide vote of 770,000. Horner wrote a friend that "we unwashed idealists have elected a senator and many congressmen on the Prohibition issue." [15] In the interim Emmerson had vetoed a bill repealing the Illinois prohibition laws, and Cermak strained anxiously to have the spigots turned back on.

J. Ham Lewis was plenty colorful, but no unwashed idealist. He had salmon pink whiskers and sported a high silk hat, beige waistcoat, pearl spats, mauve gloves, and gold-headed walking stick. The son of a Confederate officer from Georgia, J. Ham opposed involvement in the World War, the World Court, and the League of Nations. As a boy he suffered from asthma and could not sleep well, so he memorized selections from the Bible and the classics. According to legend, whenever he quoted facts or figures, he carried a couple of rolled-up sheets from a Sears catalogue to make himself appear authoritative.

The same election produced a thirty-year-old state treasurer: Edward J. Barrett. American political historians of the postwar years have devoted scant attention to the influence on both parties of the American Legion and other veterans' organizations. In Illinois this influence was substantial. Veterans who obtained control of their local and state organizations were able to use this broad bipartisan base to build general political support. Two politicians who employed this technique in Illinois were Eddie Barrett and his Legion friend from southern Illinois, John H. Stelle.

Barrett, who had been wounded and gassed in the war, was one of the organizers of the Disabled American Veterans. His jobs as secretary to the leader of the Chicago Streetsweepers' Union and precinct captain in an Irish ward gave him further confidence, and in spite of his youth, Barrett decided to run against Cermak's candidate for treasurer, Mike Zacharias. Barrett hired thirty chorus girls to collect the necessary ten thousand names on his petitions of candidacy. He invested $100 in his campaign, most of it for postage on letters to leaders of veterans' organizations throughout the state.

Barrett turned out to be a better ballot name than Zacharias, and the brash young man won. However, he was startled to discover that he had three thousand fewer votes tabulated at 7 A.M. the morning after the election than he had when he went to bed at 3 A.M. "Take it easy, kid," Cermak assured him. "You're going to win. We just don't want such a big margin that we'll have a million independents running next time." A short time later, Cermak called Barrett over to his Sherman Hotel headquarters, plopped $10,000 on the table, and told him: "Here, grab on to this, kid, and give us your withdrawal." Barrett refused, and the wiry chap who wore striped suits with wide lapels, a mammoth pearl gray hat, spats, and an overcoat with velvet lapels was on his way to Springfield. He appointed John Stelle from McLeansboro in southern Illinois, one of the organizers of the American Legion in the state, as his first assistant.

Emmerson's crystal ball, meanwhile, fogged up all the more. Unemployment rose in Chicago by 168 per cent from mid-1930 to the beginning of 1931. The governor appointed an Illinois Emergency Relief Commission and asked a special session of the legislature to authorize new state taxes for relief, supplementing local programs and private charities. Out of this special session emerged only one relief bill—a measure to protect pheasants from hungry hunters.

Assisted by big business and Moe Rosenberg, Tony Cermak ran for mayor in 1931 and defeated Big Bill Thompson, 671,000 to 477,000. Judge Horner acted as treasurer for the Cermak campaign fund and in keeping with his own practice returned unexpended contributions after the election. One of Julius Rosenwald's secretaries forwarded the check to her hospitalized employer with a notation that "I think this is the only letter of its kind in captivity. Do you want to send Henry any special message?" "Write him," the millionaire marked on the memo, "that this almost gives me a relapse."

Cermak's own operating methods were more direct. A reporter

who was close to him at the time says that Cermak selected certain Republican ward committeemen and paid them $5,000 each to "lay off" the mayoral election. The same system was used in the 1932 gubernatorial campaign. One of Cermak's potential opponents, business leader A. A. Sprague, who was a friend of Horner's, was dissuaded from running by the promise of a job as public works director. He headed the businessmen's committee for Cermak. Ben Lindheimer, with whom Horner had invested $25,000 in a real estate venture four years earlier, was committee secretary and fund raiser.

Sensing the desperation of his cause, Thompson conducted a campaign of mud-slinging ridicule. He spoke derisively of Cermak's national background. "Hey, Tony, where's your pushcart at? Can you imagine a World's Fair mayor with a name like that? [The World's Fair would shortly be starting in Chicago.] You want a Bohunk for mayor? I won't take a back seat to that Bohunk—Chairmock, Chermark, or whatever his name is." Thompson promised the Poles, on the other hand, "Elect me mayor and you can call City Hall the capital of Poland." [16]

Some Chicagoans felt that the choice between Cermak and Thompson left much to be desired. Rabbi Louis Mann suggested publicly that by his standards neither candidate was qualified and that a third candidate, Dr. Herman Bundesen, should file. Bundesen had compiled an impressive vote for county coroner in 1928 and wanted to be health commissioner in Cermak's cabinet. The promise of that appointment, which dissuaded him from running as Mann had suggested, was delivered to Bundesen on Cermak's behalf by Burt Massee, Horner's fellow Skeeter. Nevertheless, because Moe Rosenberg, Ben Lindheimer, Harry Fisher, Jake Arvey, and many of the city's leading businessmen both in and out of the Standard Club already were planning their move to secure the gubernatorial nomination for Horner a year later, the rabbi's public pronouncement understandably embarrassed the judge.

Considered in this perspective, as a message from a man who sensed that the state's highest office might be within his grasp, Horner's letter of January 29, 1931, to his rabbi is revealing:

> The chief objection urged against Mr. Cermak's candidacy is that he is a politician. True, he has taken an active leadership in politics for many years, but that could also be truthfully said of every President since Washington up to Hoover. When I speak of politics or politicians I mean it in the better sense of

the word, not in the evil sense that excludes ethical principles. I do include in the term those who properly promote the interest of a political party as such. Lincoln, all through his adult life, was one of the active politicians and party leaders of his day. So were Jefferson, Cleveland, McKinley, Roosevelt, Wilson, and Coolidge. Grant and Hoover are the two outstanding Presidents who were not considered politicians. Grant's administration was a failure. Hoover . . . is futile as a president, and seems to be more so every day. The reason is that neither knew government or politics or the people. Government is not so much a matter of mechanics as it is understanding one's fellow citizens and that government is instituted to bring them the greatest happiness, security, and progress.

I do not mean to say, or even imply, that a man who knows politics alone and offers nothing else would make a good mayor for Chicago. I do say a man who is equipped thoroughly with everything else but lacks an understanding of politics and the political methods of government cannot accomplish the hoped-for result as mayor.

The only other criticism I have heard of Mr. Cermak is that his name does not rhyme with the names of the descendants of the Mayflower passengers and that he has no Pilgrim fathers in his heredity. While I know that such criticism makes no impression upon men like you, yet . . . there are many ready to believe, without proof, any unpleasant rumor against one whose parents were foreign born and who bear a foreign sounding name. The fact that Mr. Cermak started as a coal mine boy and worked his way up through life, step by step, fighting every inch of the way to his present position surely does not disqualify him.

Chicago's mayor ought to be qualified to be a city manager so far as its business and financial affairs are concerned, and he also must be able to combine with high motives and ideals sufficient understanding and experience to enable him to effectuate them in the operation of the city government. Mr. Cermak, in my judgment, fits into that picture. His administration of the county's affairs spells, insofar as he has been responsible for them, a high degree of efficiency. I do not mean that he is perfect—perfection in government has seldom been reached. Perfection in government is usually reached in campaign speeches and Utopian hopes . . .

It looks to me that the suggestion of an independent candidate . . . is for the purpose of attaching devoted men like you to Dr. Bundesen. Dr. Bundesen and I have been good friends for a long time and I am fond of him. He was an excellent health commissioner, is a good coroner, is very popular and altogether a fine fellow. But what experience has he to fit him to act as chief executive of our government?

. . . Fortunately, I have no illusions about politics in a large city like Chicago—for my opportunity has been great to observe it on all sides. You may think that I am a partisan politically, but everyone who really understands me knows that my big hope in this mayoralty campaign is that Chicago obtains the very best mayor it can get—for the Lord knows Chicago needs it . . .

The difficulty in getting men of great prominence to enter politics is that the campaigns alone, with their unsustained rumors, false charges and petty buncombe, discourage them. Furthermore, public life is becoming very unattractive to those who conduct themselves properly in it.[17]

One can only conjecture the extent to which this letter represents Horner's actual views rather than a rationalized belief that he championed partly for reasons of personal aspiration. Prior to his campaign for mayor, Tony Cermak became a millionaire on a modest salary. There is some reason, therefore, to suspect that all the accusations against him were not, as Horner contended, "mere unpleasant rumors."

The political philosophy of Carter Harrison, who had been mayor for five terms, had an influence on Horner. To do good things, Harrison believed that a leader had to be politically strong and had to use the full powers of his office; this he demonstrated by his working arrangement with Kenna and Coughlin. Impressed by Horner's judicial record, the *Tribune* said in 1926: "The Democrats are proud of Judge Horner, although he has no record as a ward leader. He is said to be helpful but not a leader in those highly practical matters that determine ward control." But what about Horner and these "highly practical matters"? One of his friends offered this analysis when questioned many years later:

He did not have very strong insight into some of the things that were going on around him. In some cases he chose to close his eyes to these facts. Horner fully recognized the ladder that he had to climb if he expected to reach high public office, and he understood the type of appeal that the party used on the immigrant voting blocs. He considered himself independent of party leadership that might condone corruption, but at the same time he knew he had to be quietly tolerant. For one reason or another he was naïve about how some people in the party interpreted political power to mean financial gain for themselves. This naïvete changed as he grew older.[18]

Another friend was astounded to hear Horner say one day, "I'm a Democrat. It's my party, right or wrong." At a testimonial dinner for Jake Lindheimer in 1918, he spoke glowingly of loyalty to party organization, principles, and candidates. To another associate in 1931, he wrote, "There is more to running the government than knowing the mere mechanics of its various departments. The government operates on human beings."

The development of Horner's reform instincts can be traced with comparative precision. He associated with and talked the language of reformers. It is important to stress, though, that he had no political involvement with those who wanted to operate outside the framework of the two parties. Possibly because his uncles had been active party workers, Horner would forever be a Democrat. The beginning of his political career coincided with the upsurge of the Progressive movement in the Midwest, and many of his reform notions were undoubtedly nurtured during this period. But he could not embrace one primary tenet of Progressivism, that an alliance between "big business" and government had corrupted the American democratic tradition and must be broken. Horner devoted himself to causes that many bread-and-butter politicians sneered at: settlement houses, the clothing workers' union, cleaner elections, constitutional reform, and better mental institutions. Nevertheless, his entire social milieu, his devotion to the Standard Club crowd, did not exactly foster radicalism. The judge, furthermore, was an intelligent and practical man who knew better than to tinker with independent movements.

Fletcher Dobyns, in his bitter book *The Underworld of American Politics,* expressed the attitude of the typical reformer of that period:

> [Horner] had not been aggressively good or bad as probate judge. . . . He simply went along and repeatedly received nomination and election from the Democratic machine. He had not been notorious for any political "rough stuff," but in the berth he occupied he was the beneficiary of work of this kind on a grand scale. He never lifted his voice against the system of public betrayal and exploitation exemplified by Tammany; he did not join the fighting patriots of the city, but he lunched and drank tea with the type of reformers who exhaust their patriotic fervor in solemn conversation and who are as dangerous to

> Tammany as a puff of wind is to Gibraltar. He was ideally equipped to act as a rubber stamp and to adorn a Tammany show window.[19]

Dobyns' words bear the frustration of "fighting patriots" who were incensed about conditions in the city and considered total war the only means of combat. The events that followed will show that Dobyns was much too uncharitable.

CHAPTER FIVE

South into Egypt

". . . Like his ancestors of old, he went down into Egypt; but unlike them he captured the affections of the Egyptians so that they became his staunch adherents ever after."

—Ulysses S. Schwartz, at the dedication of the Horner portrait in the Standard Club, Chicago.

In the middle of 1931 Big Bill Thompson, the repudiated former mayor, hosted a Republican picnic to boom Len Small for governor again. A banner unfurled over the picnic grounds—"Back to Prosperity with Coolidge and Small," a slogan verging on the ludicrous. The depression gripping the nation was tightening its painful hold on Chicago and the rest of Illinois. Unemployment and hunger spread out beyond the metropolis into the hamlets and countryside. National sentiment seemed to presage a massive shift of power to the Democrats. Surely the Republicans would offer something other than the tired old duet of Thompson and Small, whose electoral welcome had seemingly been worn out.

The anti-Republican tide rising across the country had not escaped the notice of Anton J. Cermak, newly ensconced as mayor. In fact, His Honor had convinced himself that as much as Chicago needed his administrative talents, the state of Illinois cried out for them even more. Especially if the Republicans trotted out seventy-year-old Len Small again, the election of a Democrat might be assured regardless of who ran; and victory would make the coal miner's son the invincible political boss of the whole state, with control over all the accompanying patronage. "I'm going to be the candidate," Cermak confided to his close associates. "Why should I be mayor when I can run the city from Springfield?" [1]

However, Moe Rosenberg and Ben Lindheimer refreshed A. J.'s memory. Old Jake Lindheimer, nearly blind in the final years of his life, had died, imploring his family to remain united and dine together at least once a month. Ben quickly moved into his father's shoes as a political operator. Cermak was reminded that before the mayoral election he had recognized that only a clean, dignified figure from Chicago would stand a chance to be elected governor, someone who looked like a governor and could remove some of the Cook County odium, someone who would be a respectable front for the organization. Even if Cermak had not intended fully to commit himself, Rosenberg and Lindheimer understood that Horner would be the candidate. He could attract contributions from the bankers and the Standard Club crowd. State Street liked him. He had been a phenomenal vote-getter in Cook County through the years; and his Masonic connections provided an entree downstate.

Mike Igoe made his own availability for the governorship quite plain. There is some evidence that Cermak held out the promise of the 1932 gubernatorial nomination to Horner only in order to get the Jews behind him in 1928, hoping that by 1932 the Irish would return to the club and prefer Cermak instead of a Jew for the highest office in the state. It is also clear, though, that Cermak feared a race against Igoe because it might disintegrate the party again and inspire the Jews to flock to Igoe. In the third floor corner suite at the Congress Hotel where he lived after the death of his wife, Cermak told visitors that "Horner's not the candidate; I'm the candidate."

In any case, if the Horner logic did not penetrate to A. J., Lindheimer mustered a display of the sort of pressure that Cermak had to respect. Not only were all the important Jewish Democratic leaders pushing for Horner, but Horner had arranged for the help, when needed, of some potent Irishmen like Pat Nash, Joe McDonough, and Al Horan; Mel Traylor, president of the First National Bank of Chicago, and an aspirant himself for the Democratic presidential nomination; Abel Davis; and D. F. Kelly, president of The Fair store. These men tightened the screws on Cermak.

Inasmuch as Igoe had already declared his intention of running for the nomination with or without organization endorsement, Cermak could not risk losing the Jewish segment of his coalition and still hope to again subdue Igoe's Irish insurrectionists within the party. The mayor's final hope lay in arranging a deadlock between the Horner and Igoe supporters when the slate-making committee representing the county and state organizations met on February 13, 1932, at the Sherman Hotel. Then Cermak would step forward and volunteer to break the deadlock by being the compromise candidate. The plan fell through when one of Igoe's supporters failed to appear. So it was, to the cheers of two thousand precinct captains responding to their leader's command, that the Democratic party endorsed Judge Horner for governor. Cermak thought even then that he could talk Horner into withdrawing, a prospect which the judge and his backers would not consider. Henry Horner, then fifty-three years old, had come a long distance from his marching days in the Harrison Guards and his apprentice duty on a bar stool at Hinky Dink's saloon. Any objective forecast of the state's political climate would have to acknowledge that he stood an excellent chance of occupying the governorship at a crucial point in the history of Illinois.

"Everything that I possess and all that I am," the candidate told the slate-making committee,

> I owe to the state of Illinois; and all through my life I have hoped to repay that debt. I have one ambition now, and that is to be the best governor Illinois has ever had. I am for the return of the simple system of government which interfered least with the rights of individuals and placed no great burden of taxation upon them. The principles of Jefferson and Jackson will help our people most. It is because we have departed from these principles that most of the evils which afflict the state today have occurred. With federal interference with the rights of states, with state interference with the rights of municipalities and individuals has come the establishment of a bureaucracy as wasteful as it has been harmful. Offices have been multiplied, enterprise hampered, and individual liberty destroyed. Today, with local governments facing bankruptcy, the men who are responsible for these conditions have to offer as their only solution more taxes, more burdens, more controls.

After this unstudied and extremely shallow, not to say irresponsible, analysis of the state's ills, Horner added an after-comment for Cermak's benefit: "I have no ambition to become a political leader. Therefore, such time as governors usually devote to party politics, I shall be able to save and devote exclusively to public service."

Having hesitantly repressed his personal ambition, Cermak put together an organization slate he could depend on: an Irish Catholic from downstate for lieutenant governor; his old friend Otto Kerner, Sr., for attorney general; Congressman-at-large William H. Dieterich, the son of German-born parents who were downstate farmers but who had been solidly connected to the Cook County organization through an earlier patronage appointment with the Chicago Sanitary District, for United States senator; that demonstrably successful ballot name of Barrett again for state auditor; and a Methodist Mason from downstate to take Barrett's place as state treasurer. A well-balanced Cermak ticket. Harry Fisher, who had been in line for the Cook County state's attorney endorsement, had to be sidetracked on the theory that one Jew on the ticket was the limit. Instead, State Senator Tom Courtney, a handsome Southwest Side Irishman, was chosen. Igoe and the Democratic state chairman, downstater Bruce Campbell of Belleville, who was also a nationally prominent officer in the Elks, filed against Horner in the primary. All three ran as "dripping wets," for the prompt repeal of Prohibition.

Some of Horner's Chicago friends frankly feared that his candidacy was miscast. They believed that he was not enough of the "politician type" to run for governor and suggested that he might become enmeshed in a web of sordid commitments that would compromise his integrity. Horner assured his friends that such fears were groundless. He told Edward Low, a Masonic acquaintance who often joined the Sandburg Sunday breakfasts: "I'm my own boss, and I'll run my own show. Don't worry about that. Once I get in, they can't control me." Low and others who had watched Horner's career progress over the years maintained their private doubts. By temperament and personality, the judge hardly seemed the type to stand up against the aggressive Tony Cermak. At a rally in Moe Rosenberg's ward, the candidate acknowledged that his debt of gratitude to Rosenberg was second only to the one he owed Cermak for having delivered organization endorsement.

Dick Finnegan, the fellow Skeeter who had known Horner for twenty years, expressed no doubts whatever in this editorial in the Chicago *Times:* [2]

> A governor needs executive and administrative ability. There is no greater test of this ability anywhere in the United States than Judge Horner has undergone [as probate judge]. His duties have been less judicial than administrative. . . . The governor should know about politics and the ways of politicians. In political vernacular, Judge Horner is able to get around, but he is not a professional politician. Nor is he the kind of man who can be "owned" or "run." . . . In Henry Horner the people know they have a man with motive power, and not merely a man anxious to squat down on any available public job.

Campbell, the popular downstate leader, thundered the warning that Cermak yearned to extend his dangerous influence to Springfield. Igoe used a similar approach. In response, Horner stressed party loyalty, as well he might. "Never in the history of the party," he asserted, "is there such need for every loyal Democrat to subordinate his own ambitions to the interest of the party." [3]

Igoe and Campbell ran well downstate, but in the process canceled out one another's effectiveness. Hence, the power of the organization in Cook County carried Horner to his resounding primary election victory. He polled 397,499 votes to 255,527 for Igoe and 134,972 for Campbell. In Moe Rosenberg's Twenty-fourth Ward, where it was rumored that votes were sometimes weighed instead of counted, the tally read:

Horner	15,614
Igoe	241
Campbell	17

All of Horner's companions on the organization slate won nomination. Scott W. Lucas, another American Legion politician, lost the senatorial nomination to Dieterich. Born on a farm near Chandlerville in the duck hunting paradise along the Illinois River in Cass County, Lucas now lived in nearby Havana and had been national judge advocate of the Legion and its state commander in 1925–26. He sent his congratulations to Horner and offered to help in the fall campaign. "Thanks for your cordial congratulatory letter," Horner replied, "and also your fine friendship. I am mighty glad to have your offer to help and you can consider yourself enlisted during the period of the war. . . . You made a fine run." Lucas, John Stelle, and Campbell later were named coordinators of Horner's downstate campaign. To the delight of most Democrats, meanwhile, Len Small won the Republican primary, beating state treasurer Omer Custer and other minor contenders.

With his control over the state party decisively established, Cermak now turned to the big stakes of presidential politics. In July the Democrats were to nominate a president in Chicago—and Cermak's concern reached even beyond that. Waging his unrelenting war on "the old women of both sexes" who brought on Prohibition, he wanted a dripping wet plank in the party platform for unconditional repeal of the 18th Amendment and immediate modification of the Volstead Act.

One of the active aspirants for the nomination, Governor Franklin D. Roosevelt of New York, was looked upon with some suspicion by Cermak. Roosevelt had been busy for months lining up delegates in Illinois. Carter Harrison and former Governor Dunne supported his cause in Chicago; and downstate a Springfield newspaper editor, V. Y. Dallman, worked in his behalf. They succeeded early in corraling 15¼ of the 58 Illinois votes for FDR.

Horner's friend Mel Traylor, the conservative bank president, admitted that his chances as a dark horse were dark indeed. Banking institutions enjoyed something less than full public esteem; bankers were sometimes called "banksters" by disrespectful Americans whose savings had vanished behind closed doors. Cermak preferred Al Smith, of whose drinking philosophy he was more certain, or Governor Albert Ritchey of Maryland, or Traylor, to the New York governor. As his own belated contribution to the stop-Roosevelt movement shortly before the convention, Cermak put up Senator J. Ham Lewis as the Illinois favorite son candidate.

Cermak's convention views were adopted by Horner as his own, although the judge's pretensions at cracking the whip for his chief were out of character. In his autobiography, Carter Harrison mentioned Horner's "bluffs and scowls" and referred to the judge's leadership gestures as "crude, if not a bit brutal." [4] Most of the Illinois delegates were fully prepared to follow Cermak's lead without Horner's help. However, one delegate, a young insurance claims lawyer from Peoria named John Cassidy, would stay with Al Smith through the first three ballots.

Eventually, though, the individual who outfoxed Cermak was none other than his nominal favorite son, J. Ham Lewis. Dallman prompted Lewis to announce his support of FDR (without consulting Cermak) in return for an advantage in the matter of Illinois federal patronage. Cermak retaliated by bringing a second favorite son, Mel Traylor, off the bench, but the game was all over. Nevertheless, Cermak still managed to obtain Roosevelt's support for the ultra-moist "Illinois plank" on Prohibition repeal, against the wishes of many Eastern delegates. This accomplished, the mayor then deserted his New Jersey and New York allies and delivered Illinois and Indiana to the Roosevelt camp, but not until after the nomination had been cinched. Rushing to the airport to greet the nominee, Cermak bore him in triumph to the convention hall and heard FDR's assurance that "from this hour the 18th Amendment is doomed."

Far less accustomed than his leader to the sudden, unpredictable changes of sentiment that a successful politician must manage, Horner did not adjust so easily as Cermak to the nomination of Roosevelt. He brooded and sulked in his conviction that the party had been rendered a disservice by chicanery of the worst sort. Cermak understood how political friends change into enemies overnight, but his candidate for governor did not. On the day after the convention, Horner's speech writer, Harry Barnard, inserted a line in a Rockford speech to the effect that Roosevelt would carry the party standard forward with dignity, possessed many sterling attributes, and would of course be the salvation of the nation. Horner balked. He did not regard Roosevelt as the best candidate, and he felt that to utter these oaths would be hypocritical. Barnard phoned Harry Fisher who phoned Tony Cermak who phoned Henry Horner who praised Roosevelt the next day in Rockford.

As it was, the Illinois candidate had more than enough problems of his own. Delegates from one hundred Illinois Ku Klux Klan chapters convened in Chicago and officially endorsed Small for governor. The Fulton County *Democrat* provided a preview of what the campaign would be like with its report of "rumors" that Judge Horner not only came from Chicago, which was bad enough, but had changed his name some years ago and was, in fact, a Jew.

The object of this curiosity wheeled south out of Chicago down the eastern border of the state in his big Packard automobile to begin his downstate campaign. "This ain't goin' to be no bed of roses, Judge," offered one of his campaign troupe. "When folks down here think of a Jew, they see a fellow behind a wagon peddlin' pots and pans."

II

The state of Illinois is formed like a carrot, the thick end nestled against Lake Michigan, the tip pointed at Dixie. That thin part of the carrot, down to the southern extremity at the charming old river town of Cairo, has long been known as "Egypt." Socially, culturally, economically, and politically, Egypt and Chicago are more different than many states or nations. Successive waves of European immigrants made Chicago into a robust urban center that Hinky Dink could boast "ain't no sissy town." The remainder of the state was heavily rural, conservative, and Protestant.

Egypt has been appropriately called "the Other Illinois, south of prosperity." The scenic Shawnee Hills rise from the claypan soil in the Ohio River bottoms. From the Carolinas, Virginia, Kentucky, and Tennessee, rural mountain folk—too poor to own slaves—arrived before the Civil War to populate this wedge between the Mississippi, Ohio, and Wabash rivers. The Southern Baptist church made its influence felt in the morals and the politics of the region. As early as 1839, Prohibitionist sentiment began emerging in the interior sections where the anti-saloon league was active.[5] Because of its southern heritage Egypt was torn apart ideologically and emotionally by the Civil War. As late as 1868 a Republican parade in Franklin County for presidential candidate Ulysses S. Grant was interrupted by two men in a horse-drawn buggy whipping into the line of marchers from the side, shouting "Hurrah for Jeff Davis." Jefferson and Williamson counties both mustered Confederate army volunteers. The southern half of one county, Union, had been inhabited between 1813 and 1840 by German Lutheran farmers from three counties in North Carolina. Union army deserters hid out and were given protected refuge in the peach orchards of Union County during the war.[6]

Force-fed Baptist morality mixed with other elements to produce a volatile compound. From its earliest days Egypt acquired a reputation for bloody violence and disregard for law and order. Many of its people were prejudiced, stubborn, and hot-blooded. Social control was deemed a family function. Law enjoyed no particular prestige value. In Horner's time this tradition erupted on the surface in two ways—brutal inter-union warfare in the coal fields and flourishing activity throughout the Prohibition era by the Ku Klux Klan, an anti-Negro, anti-Catholic, and anti-Jewish movement. The Kluxers and their leader, Glenn Young, took over law enforcement responsibilities in southern Illinois in 1923 and 1924, ostensibly to do battle with the Italian-American bootleggers. Bands of armed Klansmen roaming the streets were accepted as a law enforcement expedient by Protestant ministers. When Young died, his funeral attracted fifteen thousand mourners and was conducted by a platoon of five ministers. One plausible theory for the regional history of violence is the fact that the region was peopled before it was governed. There were no courts, sheriffs, or constables, so the people learned to solve their problems themselves by direct action rather than through the recognized channels of organized society. The nature of southern Illinois and of southern Illinoisans slips more clearly into focus when one examines an individual who would play an important role throughout the remainder of Horner's life: John Stelle of McLeansboro.

John Stelle was a rugged son of Egypt who had been a machine gun captain in the AEF and a member of the original executive committee of the American Legion in 1919. His great-grandfather, Thompson Stelle I, of French Huguenot stock, came to the Illinois Territory from New Jersey in 1816. He settled on a farm near McLeansboro and fathered fifteen children. One of these, Jacob, served in Company A of the 87th Illinois Volunteer Infantry in the Civil War. His son, Thompson II, married Judith Farmer, who hailed from the hill country in Tennessee. Thompson taught school when he was only sixteen and was elected Hamilton County judge in 1869. Another Stelle, Samuel, walked alone after the War of 1812 from New Jersey across the Alleghenies to Calhoun County, Illinois, where he married a woman whose parents had migrated from Tennessee and North Carolina. One of their sons, John Patterson Stelle, was a leading agrarian agitator in southern Illinois.

In a history of Hamilton County, Judge Thompson Stelle II (who was John's father) lamented the decline of the manly art of self-defense and the substitution of other more civilized methods for settling disputes. His pioneer forefathers in Hamilton County

> had a "stray pen" in which they placed the runaway stock; and it was also used for fighting exercises in which our ancestors occasionally tried their power of endurance and the strength of their muscles in a cool and friendly knockdown. It was a forum where all controversies were settled in a manly way by wager of battle and without the aid of lawyers, judges or juries. It was cheaper fighting in those good old days and not half so dangerous as it afterward got to be when the cowardly practice of using clubs, rocks, knives and pistols came into vogue. After the knockdown was over, no difference which whipped, all hands would make friends and go in to have a drink all around. It had a tendency to develop the muscle and strengthen the nerve and occasionally resulted in a black eye. It is certain that no improvement has been made in the manly science of pioneer fighting. Fighting should always be avoided when possible but when human nature is overcome by a rude insult from a cowardly braggart, there is nothing more effective in settling the "bile" on the stomach than a good old pioneer twenty-pounder knockdown.[7]

Here can be traced a parallel with the rough, tough Clary Grove boys of Lincoln's New Salem. Writing of New Salem, Benjamin Thomas has pointed out: "On the frontier, men settled their disputes with fists, feet and teeth as often as they resorted to the courts; or fought first and sued each other afterward. Sometimes they fought for the sheer love of fighting." [8]

Despite having been wounded and seriously gassed during seventeen months of combat service, young John Stelle plunged into the American Legion's peculiarly bipartisan brand of politics when he returned to Illinois. Interestingly enough, bipartisan politics has always been fairly routine in southern Illinois. The first great southern Illinois politician, Congressman, and later General, John A. Logan of Jackson County was a rabid Democrat who took a leave of absence from his army command to come back to Illinois in 1864 and campaign for the Republican president, Mr. Lincoln. Logan's family loved racehorses and the general loved to bet on them, a passion shared by Stelle. Many of the same adjectives used to describe Logan—straight-built, Indian-like, energetic, restless, impulsive, and daring—fit John Stelle perfectly, and in fact come close to a timeless composite formula for gaining political fame in that part of the state. And whereas Logan helped to organize the Grand Army of the Republic in order to protect the interests of Union war veterans, Stelle helped found the American Legion to promote the interests of World War veterans.

Stelle, however, encountered a good deal more difficulty in both his political and business ventures than Logan had. He ran unsuccessfully for the state senate and for local state's attorney. His brickyard and dairy businesses had just failed in 1913 when this "plain hillbilly," as he referred to himself, made the long trek to Chicago in a Model-T Ford coupé to ask Eddie Barrett for the assistant treasurer's job.

Further north, the more prosperous downstate counties were Protestant and Republican—settled by New Englanders or Scandinavians—and as far removed emotionally and culturally from Chicago as the southernmost tip of the state. In 1927 a resolution was introduced by a Chicago legislator for a division of Illinois into two states, Northern Illinois (the eight metropolitan Chicago counties) and Southern Illinois (the rest). Downstate legislators believed that Chicago representatives had no regard for any public problems south of the Cook County border and that the city was bursting with crime and "undesirable elements," which usually meant swarthy foreigners and Negroes.

At about this time, though, hard roads and bridges were built connecting the city and the country, Chicago and downstate. Symbolic of the change, a bridge across the Illinois River at Hardin linked Calhoun and Jersey counties for the first time. Calhoun is a peninsular county that juts down between the Illinois and the Mississippi rivers, little more than an hour's ride from Springfield. Old German, Irish, and French farmers lived on its isolated apple orchards. Families intermarried within their clans—the separate Lutheran and Catholic clans among the Germans, for example. Steamboats brought provisions into the southern end of the county. After the last steamboat landed with the winter's supplies before the rivers froze over, much of the county was cut off for the rest of the season. Now the bridge at Hardin changed that and symbolized the opening up of rural Illinois. The development of the "hard road" system elsewhere served the same purpose of exposing the provincial isolated areas of Illinois.

It was at this moment in Illinois history, with the afterglow of the flaming Klan torches not yet fully faded away, but with rural residents now able to travel more easily and to learn to know people in neighboring counties, that Henry Horner, the Chicago Jew, moved south into Egypt.

As he did so, the most urgent and immediate necessity was to deal with what his campaign staff referred to as the Jewish Question. Typically, the campaign scene would be a Democratic barbecue in a city park in July, perhaps the candidate's first visit to a coal mining county like Christian, south of Springfield. In middle Illinois, the Lithuanians, Poles, Irish, and Welsh had moved along the Illinois Central railroad tracks to work in the mines alongside the earlier settlers from the south. Before the speechmaking started, Horner summoned all the precinct committeemen around a big shade tree. He reached over and confiscated a cigar from the county chairman's shirt pocket, lit up, and invited the men to fire away with whatever they had on their minds.[9]

"If there is anything bothering you, anything at all, I want to hear about it and this is the time to come out with it," he said. "I don't care if it's political or personal or a little of each."

Some rambling, half-hearted questions about issues were proffered while the men squirmed uneasily. A committeeman named Sheehan cleared his throat and then stopped without saying anything.

"I think I know what some of you are thinking and don't want to talk about," Horner piped up, rolling the cigar in his lips and blowing out a geyser of smoke. "You're thinking I can't win this election because I'm a Jew from Chicago and a Jew from any place, even from Springfield, couldn't possibly get votes in this part of the country. Isn't that so?"

Some of the men hung their heads or looked aside as Sheehan nodded uncomfortably.

"Well," replied the judge with a smile. "I can see the map of Ireland all over your face. And you didn't have anything to say about who your parents were, did you? Or what religion you were born into? I learned my religion at my mother's knee, and I wouldn't trade it for all the gifts or all the patronage in the world. I believe in the same God you do. I wouldn't forsake either my mother or my religion. You're going to hear that my name isn't really Horner. And it isn't. Originally it was Levy. But it was changed to my grandmother's name of Horner."

And then he would proceed to explain why the name had been changed, telling of the divorce of his parents and citing docket and page number where the divorce was recorded.

Horner's forthrightness impressed the downstate Democrats. They took it all in and then (many of them) went into the river valley Bible Belt counties and solemnly passed the word that Horner had been born a Jew but had had his name changed and had been raised as a Gentile.

Otherwise his campaign rested on a few fairly simple appeals. Reduce taxes. Reduce government expenses. Relieve unemployment. Protect bank deposits. To relieve the disproportionate real estate tax burden on farmers, small homeowners, and industry, Horner proposed constitutional reform. In Illinois the tax system was based almost exclusively on assessment of property. As a result, the farmer paid heavily, and the big income-earner with little tangible wealth got by lightly. Raymond Warren, a Lincoln biographer, prepared an imaginative campaign pamphlet entitled "Henry Horner, a Governor for the Whole State." A sketch of a widow and her children gazing at the kindly, benevolent, smiling judge featured the slogan: "They know Horner! The Devoted Humanitarian." He declared that "the prosperity of Illinois depends on the farmer's security" and pledged, accordingly, to "lighten the tax burden on all the earth's surface lying within the boundaries of the state, whether it be city real estate or farm land." And, of course, he promised to be a vigorous fighter for repeal of the 18th Amendment.

By the standards of that day, his was a slickly handled, smooth, and expensive campaign. Ben Lindheimer managed it and introduced imaginative billboard advertising techniques. Albert D. Lasker, a nationally recognized advertising executive, made his agency available. Julius Rosenwald and others at the Standard Club contributed money freely. Harry Fisher helped with the speechwriting. Mort Kallis, a printing company owner, who was Moe Rosenberg's brother-in-law, made his services available. Fred Sargent, president of the Chicago and Northwestern Railway, and other Republicans in the business community also worked for Horner, partly because of their displeasure with Small.

Campaigning down the eastern edge of the state, Horner discovered that Paris was full of Lincoln recollections. In a daily campaign journal which he kept for a while, the candidate noted that Paris had been Lincoln's headquarters when he practiced law in Edgar County in the 1840's. Judge Horner also observed in his journal that "the tide seems to be turning against the inequities of bogus Prohibition even in the driest parts of the state." [10] His speeches on Prohibition were carefully reasoned expositions intending to prove that the noble experiment had failed.

In straw hat and white carnation, Horner enjoyed the rustic charm of downstate Illinois, delighting especially in the other towns on Lincoln's old eighth judicial circuit—Metamora, Bloomington, Mount Pulaski, Clinton, Monticello, Urbana, Danville, Shelbyville, Sullivan, Decatur. At Eldorado in the revolt-ridden mining country, Judge Horner talked to miners in their lighted hats. Speaking to farmers, he usually worked in the line, "Some folks say there ain't no hell, but they ain't farmed so they can't tell." He seemed to sense where and when the quaint, folksy touch could safely be exploited, though it was unnatural for a big-city judge. (He refused, incidentally, to resign his judgeship during the campaign in spite of continuing heckling from the opposition.) His farm speech went something like this:

> I want to admit frankly that I have never turned a shovelful of earth. I am not a farmer. I am the only candidate who admits he is not a farm expert. But I believe I understand your problems, and if elected, I pledge to do something about them. All the farmer asks of his state government is a square deal, a deal based on the principles of equal opportunity with other industries. He doesn't want the government to sow and reap for him. The state can and should take off your backs some of the heavy load of taxation which is bending you over.

In Franklin County, Horner sought out Louie Lewis, whom he had met at the 1927 Masonic convention in Chicago. Even though many of these downstaters were committed to Campbell in the primary, the judge's memory for Masonic names and faces made friends that would be helpful in the fall. The small towns of southern Illinois were exceptionally receptive to candidates who promised something different, because of the severity of the depression and the mine wars. In the little town of Christopher, the school teachers had been paid $9 a month for three years. Many mines were shut down, and at those that were operating, rival unions battled for domination.

In July, when Judge Horner came to town to open his southern Illinois campaign at a barbecue in the park, fifteen thousand people turned out for one or both of two reasons: they were curious to see what the "Jew from Chicago" really looked like; and they were hungry and the food was free. Farmers donated four tons of calves, pigs, and chickens, which were butchered without charge by a local packing company. But the audience perked up and listened; this man had a knack for speaking their language. He promised that there would be no sectionalism if he were elected governor, that he would recognize the needs of people "whether in Chicago or Podunk." He said that as governor he would be like the cow who was a good old critter and would give all the milk she had to give. His concept of the governorship, he said, would be to keep busy—"to do something except wear a silk hat on inauguration day." He said his decisions might not always be the wisest, but he would do his utmost. The lean-faced hungry miners from southern Illinois liked what they saw and heard, and enjoyed the taste of a free barbecue. Here was a candidate who seemed to be something other than the ordinary Chicago politicians who had been dropping by for their votes for decades.

From this point onward Horner's downstate campaign went well. In Ziegler, the central part of the coal battleground, the local Democrats tried to steer him away from a confrontation with the leader of the Progressive union. Pat Ansboury, the Progressive leader, was there. As the miners of both factions crowded around the truck where he spoke, Horner again vowed to do his best to bring an armistice to the coal fields. "And I'll tell you something else," he shouted. "If I'm governor there's going to be law and order. The violence will stop." Horner varied the level of sophistication in his speeches to fit his audience and the locale. In one speech, he said, "Every public officer ought to be ready to account for his stewardship every day, and not just at election time. It seems to me that the greatest contribution anybody can make to government is to simplify it so that everybody can understand it. Government is the concern of everybody." [11] He wrote the president of the University of Illinois in July that "you may be assured that if I am elected governor, you and your great university will have no more earnest ally than myself." Governor Emmerson, a Republican, but a factional enemy of Small's, covertly gave comfort and advice to the Democratic candidate.

In the meantime the opposition carried on one of the most unorthodox campaigns to which Illinois had ever been exposed. Small and Thompson campaigned on a river steamer, the "Cape Girardeau," which floated down the Illinois and Mississippi rivers and up the Ohio to Shawneetown, trailed by a barge with an orchestra for free dancing after the talkin'. Thompson assailed "Tony Baloney the Dictator" and warned the corn-hog farmers that the price of pork would surely drop if a Jewish governor were elected. Within a year of Small's inauguration, steamboat whistles would be blowing on the inland rivers from Cairo to Chicago, Thompson predicted. He doubted that Horner could stand up against the Loop bankers in Chicago and characterized him simply as "a rotten judge." In Chicago, Thompson said the slogan of "Tony the Tyrant" was "No Irish need apply." He claimed to have searched the entire city payroll and discovered only one O'Brien! "Come on, you Irish, vote for Len Small and me," he implored. "Punish the Democrats that put us in the war, punish the Democrats that made this nation and are keeping this nation *dry*."

At a rally in the gymnasium of Loyola University, one Thomas V. Sullivan, by his own genealogical description an Irish-Scandinavian, stirred his audience with this report: [12] "Why, down in Eldorado, Horner was introduced as the Second Messiah, comparing him with the Savior of Mankind. That fellow sat on the platform and made no objection to it. Why, that was an insult hurled at every Christian in this state. He accepted it without raising his voice in protest of having himself compared with the Gentle Nazarene who drove the moneychangers out of the temple!" And in Quincy a local Republican leader asserted, ominously, that "here we have a man who calls himself Horner. But his name isn't Horner. His Christian name is Levy!"

At another campaign stop in Harrisburg the candidate was running behind schedule. Art O'Brien, his campaign assistant, asked a nearby state policeman to help clear the crowds so Horner could get through. "For that Jew son-of-a-bitch, no!" the policeman replied. O'Brien duly noted his badge number for future reference.

Not only the Democratic Chicago *Times*, which had been helpful to Horner when Cermak was wavering at slating time, but also the normally Republican Chicago *Tribune* and Chicago *Daily News* hammered away at their long-term Republican enemies, Small and Thompson. Small, in turn, attacked Chicago's "Trust Press."

When some of Thompson's friends pleaded with him to discontinue the religious smear, Big Bill explained, "You know I've been a friend to Jews and still am. I'm saying what I've got to say to make Len Small win. He has got to win." Horner in a letter to his editor friend Dick Finnegan related that

> I do not meet [the religious question] at all now. However, the other side—Thompson and Small—is pressing very hard and making every prejudicial suggestion it can. They seem to be champions in spreading poison. That seems to be the only campaign they are making, other than their reckless and abundant employment of promises of jobs, roads and other things which I am sure they have no intention of making good. . . . I get little opportunity to do anything else but meet people throughout the state. This seems to take up most of the day, except the six or seven hours I try to reserve for sleeping. However, I do not want you to think "out of sight, out of mind." For I think of you frequently and take unto myself the conceit that you think of me occasionally.[13]

In another letter Horner asked Finnegan if he had heard the ferocious things" Thompson had been saying about religion on his river cruise campaign. "They are the filthiest I have ever heard coming from human lips. Small and Thompson are using the same methods used in the Al Smith campaign, but much more viciously." He expressed encouragement that his views on legislative reapportionment seemed "to be getting over to the folks in this area." He thought he had "knocked most of the pins from under" Small's anti-Chicago approach.

During a late September pause in Chicago, Horner dined with the Finnegans at their home on Sheridan Road. The Irish editor and the Jewish judge had been friends for many years. More than Horner, Finnegan had been swept up by the midwestern Progressive movement and had run for Congress in 1910. Lacking the judge's unquestioning attachment to the Democratic party, Finnegan could be more of a liberal idealist. Horner spoke that night of the oceans of human faces he had seen—forlorn miners in southern Illinois, farmers at Bloomington, city-dwellers by the thousands at a Riverview Park rally for Chicago German-Americans, and, everywhere, dispirited elderly couples. "The people I have seen," he said, "do not deserve bad government. They deserve the best kind of government." After dinner he lay on a couch for a brief rest and slept until 8 A.M. instead of working on the speech he had planned. Finnegan wrote the speech for him.

Cermak vacationed in Europe in September and came home boasting that he had convinced the Europeans that Chicago was no longer a hotbed of violence. He pointed with pride to the fact that there had been only eighty gangland bombings so far that year, compared to one hundred the previous year. After his return Cermak took a personal hand in the campaign strategy. The candidate made frequent trips to Antioch for late-night conferences at the mayor's summer home in a Bohemian settlement on Channel Lake. Relations between the boss and the candidate were generally smooth. At one major party rally in the Congress Hotel, however, Cermak talked so long that there was no time for Horner to deliver his prepared speech. Afterwards, in the hotel suite, Horner wanted to summarize his speech for Cermak privately. "Now A. J., I want you to hear what I was going to say tonight." "Oh forget it," jibed Cermak, "that's your lost speech," a poke at the judge's Lincoln interest, which A. J. did not appreciate. Cermak ventured downstate for one speech during the campaign, a talk by an ex-miner to a group of coal miners in Carlinville. Despite predictions of disaster by the campaign staff, most of whom wanted Cermak quarantined to the Chicago reservation, his speech created no problems.

Horner's carefully plotted campaign covered all the bases. Leaflets proclaimed his endorsement by two hundred professors at the University of Chicago and carried an explanation of why the chancellor, Robert M. Hutchins, supported him. Edward J. Kelly, chief engineer of the Chicago Sanitary District, a Cermak intimate and a hard worker for Horner, delivered radio speeches. The party leaders, he said, had not chosen Judge Horner because of his political power. "As a matter of fact," continued Kelly, "he is not a politician in the strict sense of the word, except that he was elected the last time by about four hundred thousand votes. He has no political ambitions except serving his fellow man." How those words would echo in Kelly's memory in the years to come.

In the midst of the campaign the last blocks of Samuel Insull's power empire—which he had acquired by buying politicians from Roger Sullivan to Moe Rosenberg—tumbled down. Dick Finnegan wrote Horner on September 22:

> Do you realize that the [Insull incident] is probably the most colossal failure and the most enormous financial gambling fraud ever perpetrated on the public in the history of the world? The whole circumstance is a challenge to every citizen, but particularly is it a challenge that can take you to a leadership of public opinion which has been available to few men in the thirty years that I have known anything about Illinois politics. No one else can see this the way you can see it. It is beyond the grasp of most men because it needs a spiritual depth which few men in politics have and which, unless I have seriously misread you, you possess.[14]

To a degree, the silver-haired liberal editor *had* misread his old friend. For although Horner did denounce Insull in moderate tones, now, with the governorship almost within grasp, he could not risk touching the sensitive nerves of a Cermak or a Rosenberg. Insull's lines of influence were almost beyond comprehension, touching even such important men as the cardinal of the Catholic archdiocese.

III

Election day finally dawned, and the Skeeters wired their luncheon companion:

> Little Henry Horner
> Steps out of the corner
> Challenged by Thompson and Small
> From November and after
> He will drive out each grafter
> And be the best governor of all.
> Some Skeeters buzz
> Some Skeeters bite.
> Henry the Skeeter
> Is our state's delight.

On election night at an appropriate location, the Standard Club, Henry the Skeeter awaited the returns in the company of a most unpolitical conglomeration: some of the Skeeters, members of the Rehearsal Club of the bar association, and a few of his club friends. The national tide turned out early in the evening to be overwhelming. Horner polled 58.6 per cent of the vote and was elected by 566,287 votes, at that time the largest majority in the state's history. It is entirely possible that Tony Cermak, Moe Rosenberg, or the lowliest saloonkeeper might well have won on the Democratic ticket in 1932, but hardly by that much. Roosevelt carried Illinois with 56.8 per cent, a margin of 449,548. Dieterich beat Otis F. Glenn for senator by only 198,652. Horner outdrew Roosevelt in Cook County, 1,033,789 to 919,231. That the "religious question" did in fact carry some weight downstate is indicated by Roosevelt's 963,078 to Horner's 896,541. Later in the night the governor-elect phoned the president-elect, and congratulations were exchanged.

In an editorial following the election, Colonel McCormick's *Tribune* rejoiced at the Small-Thompson defeat:

> Illinois was particularly fortunate in the sisterhood of states in this election because surely none other escaped from such a nightmare as the people of Illinois voted themselves out of Tuesday. [No other state] was threatened with such wholly unbelievable political conditions as those from which this state escaped by electing Judge Horner and defeating the attempt of a certain seemingly imperishable outfit of politicians to reproduce an administration which already had given eight indescribable years to Illinois government. . . . A fantastically scandalous organization of Republican politicians has been thrown in the garbage can. The lid is on. There is the prospect of a new era.

There was, indeed, to be a new era. But not much of it would please the colonel for very long.

Congratulatory letters poured in, including many from Jews in New York City and elsewhere expressing their happiness that Illinois had risen above bigotry and prejudice. One of his new neighbors-to-be, James A. Griffin, the Catholic bishop of Springfield, wrote: "Frankly, I am personally and officially delighted with your election. It is time that the great commonwealth of Illinois would have a scholar, a courageous man, a gentleman and a representative of the entire commonwealth. . . . We welcome you as a neighbor and we pray that your administration will be fruitful in good achievement for the state as a whole and a source of much happiness to yourself and your friends." Peter F. Rossiter, Sangamon County Democratic chairman and an Igoe man, wired that he was sorry that "we could not add Sangamon to the roll of honor. Done the best we could." Sam L. Nudelman, a haberdasher from

Bruce Campbell's town of Belleville, sent a letter saying "I am at your service and if there is anything I can do to help you and the administration I hope you will feel at liberty to write." In response to a letter from Roosevelt's campaign manager, James Farley, Horner said: ". . . while you rode an unbeatable winner to victory, let's not forget to recognize the fact that the exceptional jockey knew how to ride the thoroughbred." Carl Sandburg's message was seconded by the rest of the Skeeters: "I don't want no jobs from nobody, but I just want to feel close enough to the new governor that I could be sure he would call on me at anytime whenever it might happen that I could help out with voice or pen." [15]

After the election Horner recuperated briefly in French Lick, Indiana, with Cermak and Campbell. There he informed reporters that there would be no mansion hostess. "I am going there to work. I am a bachelor and I am accustomed to its hardships. There should be no social functions at this time. It will be time enough when the people are happy and contented again."

Both he and Governor Emmerson attended a cornerstone laying for a restored cabin at New Salem Park later in November. Shortly after, Emmerson summoned the legislature into special session and a $17,000,000 non-referendum bond issue was approved for Cook County relief. The governor-elect tried, meanwhile, to crawl out from under the more than one hundred thousand Democratic job seekers, many of them desperate for a paycheck. He named seventeen businessmen and economists to a committee on unemployment. The committee listed a thousand public works projects in five hundred communities and recommended a quick program to stimulate such activities as a spur to employment.

Horner spent Christmas with Cermak at the home of the mayor's son-in-law, Dr. Frank Jirka, in Miami. Back home, as the inauguration drew near, the problems multiplied. Governor Emmerson withdrew the National Guard from Taylorville on Christmas Eve. On the evening of January 3, a body of striking miners attacked a group of working miners, using machine guns and rifles. Two men and one woman died. Fourteen were wounded. Fourteen strikers were arrested. The troops returned January 4.

CHAPTER SIX

Inauguration... Liberation... Frustration

Winter sunlight sifted through the narrow windows of the old State Arsenal, a huge feudal fortress of stone in Springfield. For only the third time since the Civil War, the Democrats of Illinois were installing a governor, and enjoying the rare occasion thoroughly. The patronage-hungry party dignitaries welcomed the sunshine as a happy omen of good fortune. On a morning back in 1893 the temperature in Springfield had plunged to 15 degrees below zero and the musicians' instruments had frozen for the inauguration of another Democrat, the German-born John Peter Altgeld, in another era of economic uncertainty. But this time, on the special train down from Chicago, Paddy Bauler's Forty-third Ward German band made merry. Proud of this high moment in the twilight of his own career, Bathhouse John Coughlin came resplendently attired in tan suit with cream-colored vest and red, white, and blue cravat. Tony Cermak squirmed inconspicuously at the rear of the platform.

His prominent ears standing out from under his silk top hat, the outgoing Governor Emmerson smiled warmly and took pride in presenting "my personal friend, Judge Henry Horner." Before doing so, in his parting address, Emmerson conceded that "probably in no similar period since the Civil War has there been so much financial distress." However, he criticized the government for its "unwarranted encroachments on private business" and reiterated his opposition to "the dole system."

The chief justice of the Illinois Supreme Court, Oscar E. Heard, administered the oath of office to the first Jewish governor of Illinois. A soldier in the Revolutionary War, David Emanuel of Georgia, had been the first Jewish governor in any state. And before the expiration of Horner's term there would be three others: Herbert H. Lehman of New York, Julius Meier of Oregon, and Arthur Seligman of New Mexico.

At the instant the new governor lowered his right arm, his executive assistant Art O'Brien slipped out a side door of the arsenal and hurried to the governor's office in the Statehouse. He telephoned the state police and, reciting the badge number of the trooper who had called the judge a "Jew son-of-a-bitch" in Harrisburg, carried out the administration's first executive decision: That man is to be fired immediately.

Governor Horner droned through a forty-page inaugural address, enumerating many problems and as many hoped-for solutions.[1] He said, "We are face to face with a crisis which demands militant leadership and broad human sympathy and understanding." The election was not so much a disapproval of one party, he added, as "a very definite demand for a complete change in certain of our governmental affairs—a new era in government functioning."

The first responsibility, as Horner saw it, was to prove that our form of government was still adaptable to the requirements and service of the citizenry. To fight the "war against economic unhappiness and suffering," he proposed a tax on retail sales. "It should be remembered," he emphasized, "that this tax is received at this time solely with a view to the tremendous emergency."

> We have failed to heed the warnings of history. We refused to believe that the germs of decay are sometimes incubated in the warmth of prosperity. While we basked in the sunlight of it, we discarded all caution and abandoned ourselves to a standard of expenditures much beyond our present ability to meet. It will therefore be our compelling task to find salves with which to heal our self-inflicted wounds. . . . As governor of this state, I shall dedicate myself to the great cause of restoring the harmony, the prosperity and the happiness of all the people of Illinois.

His speech ranged the plentiful supply of problems: legislative reapportionment; constitutional tax revision to loosen the rigid requirements that prevented taxation of different forms of property at different rates; consolidation of local governments, including the separate Chicago park systems; repeal of Prohibition, but with the restoration of strong state regulatory laws and a tax on alcoholic beverages; improvements in the public welfare institutions; humane and scientific treatment for the "accidental and occasional delinquent"; home rule for Chicago transportation; greater controls over life insurance companies and public utilities.

He mentioned the possibility of eliminating the primary election because he said it had not been the remedy for corrupt or inadequate nominations. "It has frequently given nominations to men of large wealth or to men able to collect large campaign contributions, some of dubious propriety," he declared. Repeatedly, he said that Illinois deserved to be first among the states in many different fields of achievement.

In place of the traditional inaugural ball, which would have cost $25,000, Horner escorted Mrs. Clara Tanner, the widow of former Governor John H. Tanner, to a reception in his new home, the Executive Mansion. Lincoln had walked over with his sons to watch construction of the big white house in 1856. Horner, finding the beds too soft, moved in his own bed as well as a pair of worn-out bedroom slippers and a moving van full of his six thousand books and documents about Lincoln. At the reception, a throng of well-stuffed politicians and lean and hungry aspiring politico-civil servants filled the mansion to the danger point, and the National Guard finally had to shut off the inflow. A stubby little man with Eastern European features tried to get in but was rebuffed by a state policeman. "But I am Cermak," insisted Tony Cermak. The policeman refused to budge, and the state leader of the Democratic party finally ducked through a back laundry-room window, dodged under a maze of pipes, and emerged at the reception in an irritable mood.

Mr. and Mrs. Emmerson left the arsenal by a side door and were driven by the governor's chauffeur, Patrolman Everett Van Diver, back to Mount Vernon in the new 1933 Packard which his department directors had presented Emmerson as a parting gift. Although Van Diver, a tall, strapping, extremely handsome man of thirty-three, had been appointed to the force as a Republican, Emmerson informed him that the new governor would be asking him to stay on as his driver. Horner did just that, saying, "They [meaning Democrats] will be after you and they'll be after me, but just don't say anything to anybody and we'll wait 'em out."

Among the jubilant celebrants, the Rehearsal Club of the Chicago Bar Association was moved to song, praising the "morn of gladness" that would follow the state's "long dark night":

> Listen boys
> What is that noise
> From Cairo to the lake?
> Everyone is asking
> What'll you take?
> That's the sign to sit in line
> Beside the tavern bar—
> Though we don't say bar
> We know where we are!
> Liquor control? What is it for?
> It's for our state and gov-er-nor.

The next day, before going back to Chicago, Dick Finnegan penned a note to his friend: "I have just one worry," it said, "about which I constantly remind you—your propensity to overdo and overtax your personal strength. Above all things, please take care of your health. When you are tempted to pile the last straw on the camel's back, remember old Dr. Finnegan's advice." [2]

Advice of another sort, on how to be a good governor, came from Harry Fisher:

> With few exceptions, a governor cannot hope to accomplish major results without dealing with the fact of politics. I mean politics in its narrow and disagreeable sense. One who believes that the force of his character and personality and the justice of the cause will suffice to produce results in a democratic government is doomed to failure. This is not altogether a nice situation. It is a valuable incident to representative government, where results *should* be dependent upon the concurrence of many. While your labors might be lessened and more pleasant if all the men upon whom you have to rely for cooperation or assistance were morally and socially minded, as you are, the fact that some of them are not so must not be permitted to interfere with the production of intended results. The greatness of a democratic ruler lies largely in the art of dealing with men. . . . Therefore, my dear Henry, let your work be within the real world, and not within an imaginary one.[3]

This is a lesson, of course, that Horner had learned from Carter Harrison and Hinky Dink; he had enunciated it himself less than two years before in his letter to Rabbi Mann. But would it be as easy to follow as it sounded?

II

With a handkerchief carefully folded in the pocket of his double-breasted overcoat, the man with the broad nose and pince-nez walked the two blocks to the Statehouse and set about his work. The big "captive balloon," as Vachel Lindsay had described it, had taken more than twenty-one years to build and had been completed in 1868 at a cost of more than three million dollars. The circumstances surrounding its design seemed to prescribe the moral tone for many of the events that would transpire inside. A legislative commission had offered a $3,000 prize for the best architectural plans. The winning architect revealed later that he had spent $2,700 of the $3,000 bribing the legislative commission.

Although he had suffered persistent flare-ups of high blood pressure during the campaign, Governor Horner was anxious to pitch into his duties. His desk was heaped high with chronic difficulties. Unemployment continued to rise. Private charities and local sources for relief had run dry. Banks were closing. Property taxes were going unpaid, as were salaries to school teachers and other public employees. The state government tipped on the brink of bankruptcy. Debt-ridden farmers could not meet their mortgage payments.

If the new governor arrived with any doubts about the gravity of the situation, they were dispelled by one of the first documents placed on his desk. It bore the title "Military Intelligence Report to the Commanding Officer, 33d Infantry, Illinois National Guard—Confidential." As the public mood grew more tense, leaders of the civil government in Illinois had begun to expect the worst. Every month officers of the National Guard prepared a summary of state-wide conditions that might spell trouble, a report that dealt with such danger signals as the activities of local Communist and other radical parties, an estimate of unemployment in various communities, the extent to which local leaders were not meeting relief needs, threats of union violence, areas where the police might not be able to cope with crises. The report for December told of two additional factories closing down in Quincy; of twelve hundred totally dependent residents in the livestock center of Monmouth and the failure of a campaign to raise relief funds locally; of the more than twelve hundred men in the 132d National Guard infantry unit who had no civilian employment. In

Bloomington the American Legion was sponsoring a work project using jobless veterans to cut firewood, and Norman Thomas and Clarence Darrow had been booked as speakers for the Unitarian Church's Sunday evening forum, a choice of program which was evidently reason for concern. In Danville a township had taken over the operation of a strip mine with jobs for one hundred. In Mount Vernon the Third National Bank had shut its doors, leaving the whole county without banking facilities. The guard had something to say, too, about Champaign-Urbana: "There is considerable radical activity in this vicinity, but it is practically confined to the 'intelligentsia' group. There has always been a radical element around the University. These activities have been quite well confined to the 'debate' stage and no direct action on the part of this element is anticipated." A final cryptic comment caught Horner's eye. In the section on Joliet, site of the largest state penitentiary, the report stated: "The prisoners of the penitentiary appear more resigned to their situation because of outside conditions." [4]

The new administration went right to work. Artie O'Brien, the chubby Irishman from Chicago's West Side who had been Mayor Dever's secretary and had worked with Horner during the campaign, functioned now as his chief of staff with control over who could or could not see the governor. His exercise of this power made friends and enemies alike. One day an irascible visitor from Chicago flew off in a huff after he had been denied an opportunity to call on the governor. Harold Ickes wanted only to inform Horner as a courtesy that he soon would be named secretary of the interior. Johnny Casey, who had been campaign chauffeur, was made superintendent of transportation. Gray-haired and heavy-set Ella Cornwall functioned as the governor's personal secretary, performing such diverse duties as writing his personal checks and seeing that he wore his rubbers in bad weather. Alex Wilson, a former legislator from Cairo, was named legislative liaison assistant.

To another West Sider, William J. Walsh, went the hapless task of dealing out patronage equitably. Hundreds of hungry Democrats lined the halls of the Statehouse and milled around outside Walsh's patronage headquarters in the St. Nicholas Hotel. The governor was inundated by job seekers and pleading letters: "Have five votes in my family of eight . . . nobody working. I shure [*sic*] need a job that is worthwhile as I am back six months on my insurance and owe coal bills and am in debt up to my ears. I made the nineteenth precinct of the Thirty-seventh Ward go Democratic first time in history." Men offered bribes and scuffled in the lobby of the St. Nick for $45-a-month attendants' jobs in state institutions.

One of Horner's old classmates at Haven School enclosed a school class photograph along with this letter:

> I am just another one of those victims of circumstances, having been fairly successful in the commercial world up to three years ago. The depression has hit me like so many others a very hard blow, and I lost all I had. I am taking this opportunity to impose on your good nature and am wondering whether or not it is fitting to ask your assistance in placing me in *any kind* of a position anywhere. I trust that for our old school days' sake that I shall hear from you a favorable response. I am a man of family and I need work and I want work.

Beneath his signature, this correspondent scribbled in his Masonic affiliation, "member of A.A.O.N.M.S., Medinah, Chicago."

Ben Lindheimer, beginning by now to reap the benefits of profitable real estate developments and becoming intrigued by race track enterprises, was appointed to one of the most powerful jobs in the administration, the chairmanship of the rate-setting commerce commission. The medical profession reacted with astonished disappointment when Cermak's son-in-law, Dr. Frank Jirka, was named director of public health. A second son-in-law, Richey V. Graham, had been elected president pro tem of the state senate. Joseph Triner, a close friend of Cermak's, and president of the Illinois Wholesale Liquor Dealers' Association, was appointed chairman of the state athletic commission.

Not all of Horner's appointments were similarly pleasing to Cermak, however. The mayor had his eye on the sensitive post of director of insurance. When the governor selected a Republican from suburban Evanston, Ernest Palmer, Cermak is said to have exclaimed, "Who the hell is he?" Palmer had been an insurance lawyer for many years, a member of the board of governors of the Law Club, manager and general counsel of the Chicago Board of Underwriters, and one of Horner's golfing companions at the Lake Shore Club. He accepted the job with an understanding that he could hire and fire as he pleased, unconfined by the regular party patronage channels.

Into the job of chief highway engineer, with jurisdiction over the awarding of road construction contracts, went one of Lindheimer's protégés, Ernst Lieberman. Cermak was enraged by that appointment. "Where did you get that fellow?" he exploded. "They tried to hand him to me." There were a number of these patronage disputes, and someone overheard Cermak telling Horner, during one, "Well, goddamn you, you're governor in name only. Who the hell do you think you are?"

A labor leader to whom Cermak was indebted, Martin P. Durkin, received appointment as labor director. Ernest Hoover, Christian County Democratic chairman and Horner's downstate primary campaign manager, wanted to be conservation director. Informed that he lacked the necessary qualifications, Hoover protested, "But I'm a hunter." "What do you know about forestry and fish hatcheries?" the governor insisted. "No, I'm going to get people for these top jobs who can do them well. You'll get another good job." Another leader of Hoover's Christian County organization, Harry Hershey, who was counsel for Peabody Coal Company, was placed under Palmer in charge of insurance company liquidations.

Barnet Hodes, another Lindheimer protégé, who had been in charge of campaign literature, wanted to run the state tax commission. Despite limited assessment powers, it was the function of this commission to devise a more uniform system of taxation in the various counties. Originally from downstate Havana, Hodes had become a successful Chicago real estate lawyer and had exhibited a flair for promotional publicity in his service to the Democratic party. Horner appointed him one of the tax commissioners, made Scott Lucas chairman, and enlisted a non-politician, University of Chicago economics professor Simeon Leland, to actually operate the commission. At first Leland had said no—he had earned a year's sabbatical that he hoped to use for a trip to Italy. "That's just the trouble with you fellows who are always telling us how things ought to be done," Horner lectured. "Then we give you a chance to do it and you're always too busy, you've always got something else. All you want to do is talk about these problems. I try to go out and get my friends, people who are qualified, and they won't do it. Where can I turn but to the political organization?" Leland had no choice but to accept the challenge. He recruited a staff of able young men, former students and others, operating—like Insurance Director Palmer—with a dispensation from accepting the patronage referrals of county chairmen and other party officials. If a candidate endorsed by a Democratic organization for a staff job was rejected, Horner always backed up Leland with a simple explanation to the complaining sponsor:

"Now, you know you don't send stuff like that to the professor." The blunt-spoken professor managed in a brief span of time to insult most of the influential politicians across the state. At commission meetings politician Lucas sometimes prefaced the session with an advance statement that fellow-member Leland might find himself treading on some political toes; and indeed he invariably managed to do so by such comments as: "A good assessor will last only one term because if he does his job the way it should be done he will be run out of office by the people with power and influence."

Horner brought in yet another academician to confound the politicians further. Some years earlier at a South Side garden party given by Albert Loeb, he had met a University of Chicago professor who not only looked like him, being bald and mustached, but who also lived a bachelor's life with his devoted mother. To John Weigel, who was later administrator of the Institute for Juvenile Research in Chicago, the governor handed the purse-strings of the most colossal of the state agencies, the department of public welfare. This department exercised administrative responsibility over the state institutions with their nearly forty thousand hospital patients (most of them mentally ill) and twelve thousand penal inmates. Horner promoted another Republican, Arch Bowen, a former newspaper editor and for twenty years state superintendent of charities, to be department director. But Weigel, reporting directly to the governor, was given the special assignment of cutting costs in the institutions. In 1933 the state government could not tolerate a single wasted tax dollar, and Weigel was instructed to proceed without regard for political ramifications. Budgets were reviewed, and although there were 8 per cent more patients and inmates in 1933 than there had been in 1931, the operating budget was reduced by 28 per cent. Bowen and Weigel clashed frequently with two of the most aggressive patronage promoters, Ben Lindheimer and John Stelle, but always with Horner's complete support. Weigel was especially infuriating to politicians. A typical letter to Horner from State Senator Lynn C. Sieberns of Gridley contained these words in capital letters at the top: "YOUR FRIEND JOHN WEIGEL IS A FATHEAD." Sieberns complained that Republicans were being given jobs by Weigel. "If they think they can place people in the contact services who are primarily Republicans and expect Democrat success," asserted the senator, "then they should go into the legerdemain business rather than handling public office."

Endorsement of the county organization was required of applicants for the routine, non-technician jobs filled under Bill Walsh's supervision. A youth of twenty-one, Joe Knight, had impressed Horner during the campaign by dashing about Jersey County in order always to be in the front row of every Horner rally. His mobility paid off with an appointment as an assistant commerce commissioner. Al Horan and Artie O'Brien's brother, Marty, a Chicago ward committeeman who had been one of Cermak's original Irish foes but who was helpful to Horner in the campaign, landed the lucrative state insurance and bonding business.

Taken as a whole, however, Horner's disbursement of patronage managed to dissatisfy Cermak, Lindheimer, Stelle, and many others. Palmer and Bowen were Republicans. Emmerson's appointee as Cook County public administrator (an office highly lucrative in fees) stayed on, in spite of the fact that many Democrats longed for the post. Horner refused time and again to fire Republicans just to make room for Democrats. His insistence on capability and honesty was a brand of logic that did not sell very well at the height of the Depression to a party that had not occupied the Statehouse since the World War.

Serious troubles also developed at another level. In the early days of the new administration the leaders of the party gathered at the Sherman Hotel with Senator J. Hamilton Lewis to reason with him about the federal patronage situation. During the conversation the sometimes uncouth Moe Rosenberg had occasion to call the senator a short, explicitly descriptive, but quite obscene name. J. Ham's expression turned several shades more crimson than his whiskers, and he announced to one and all that Mr. Rosenberg would regret his remark. He did. A few weeks later the Bureau of Internal Revenue commenced an investigation of the Twenty-fourth Ward leader's income taxes. Neither a visit to Washington by Governor Horner nor all of Moe's raving and ranting could forestall his doom.

It was not long before the new governor discovered that the highest officer of the state did not enjoy judicial powers. No longer could Horner render decisions from on high and hold in contempt all who differed. It was a critical time. The state appeared to be on the verge of fiscal disaster. In February the University of Illinois could not meet its faculty payrolls, for the first time in its history. After the elected state officers volunteered to take a 10 per cent personal salary cut, the governor called them together and proposed a similar across-the-board reduction for all state employees.

Eddie Barrett, the youthful state auditor, took the position that he could not impose a cut without legislative authorization unless the employees signed waivers. Furthermore, he said he had had difficulty attracting qualified bank examiners even at the salaries now being paid. Horner snorted and suggested that bank regulation belonged in the insurance department under his jurisdiction anyhow. "Don't ever try that," Barrett shot back, "or I will get the legislature to put the finance department under the auditor where it belongs." And so it went. Horner leaped to his feet, and the meeting adjourned. Barrett sent word the next morning that they would get along better if they had conferences instead of merely listening to judicial decisions.

Trouble in another sector added to the governor's painful period of adjustment from the princely probate bench to the realities of governing a state in which many of the noises sounded ominously like the death rattle for peaceful government. Early in his administration Horner set about trying to resolve the differences between the warring coal mine unions. On the first Sunday after taking office, he summoned fifty men—officials of both unions, representatives of the Peabody Coal Company, and mayors of all the towns involved—to a meeting in the Governor's Mansion. Two large urns of coffee were wheeled in. But when the mansion butlers laid out trays of dainty finger sandwiches, Horner realized that they were more appropriate for a League of Women Voters tea than for a congregation of ill-tempered coal miners; thick roast beef sandwiches were substituted. Asserted the chief executive:

> We're not going to bed tonight until this thing is ironed out and there's some area for peaceful agreement. If the troubles continue in the mines, people are going to be locked up, and I don't care what their names are. If Illinois keeps going down as a coal-producing state, it will be the fault of all of you. The best thing that can happen for the country is for all laboring men and women to present a united front. The worst that can happen to the necessities of the laboring man is divided strength and internal dissension.

III

The genesis of the coal mine wars is found in the march of a band of Scotsmen and Welshmen up the Wabash tracks from Gillespie and Staunton. These hardy men who spent their working days underground were determined to drive the dictatorial leader of the UMW, John L. Lewis, out of the Illinois midlands. But their mission failed and Christian County remained a Peabody Coal Company barony, operating in harmony with Lewis for the mutual benefit of both. At first, miners chased each other with chunks of coal, then with pick handles, and finally with guns. Mining coal was a dirty, dusty, noisy, backbreaking way to make a living, and the men who did it were a tough breed. Bloody warfare soon spread to Kincaid, Bulpitt, Springfield, Virden, Mount Olive, Tovey, and then over much of southern Illinois. Soldiers with bayonets patrolled the mineheads and prodded townspeople to step lively on the sidewalks. The rival Progressives mounted a machine gun on a tripod atop a grocery store roof in Bulpitt, near where one of their men had been ambushed from the roadside. Coal trains were dynamited. Citizens of Springfield came out in their automobiles on Sunday afternoons and parked near the mine entrances in hopes of seeing some gladiatorial excitement. Even without the terror of the mine wars, the coal industry had started to decline in Illinois, a state with one of the richest deposits of bituminous coal in the world. One hundred mines had shut down in Franklin, Saline, and Williamson counties since 1923, a loss of twenty thousand jobs. The countryside was dotted with weed-covered railroad sidings, rotting tipples, and burnt-out slag piles.

From the beginning, Governor Horner had seriously underestimated the depth of the emotions and the antagonisms. Consequently, his ultimatum to the all-night meeting at the mansion failed to accomplish its purpose. He then tried sterner measures by issuing a general disarmament order in the Christian County battlefields. Union members, the one thousand special deputies, and all citizens with unauthorized firearms—whether for shooting squirrels or people—were required to turn them in to the National Guard. Mass picketing was prohibited. Horner had worked marvels as labor arbitrator for the Chicago clothing workers, and his efforts here were equally well intentioned. But he failed to reckon with the background and the stubbornness of the principal figures involved—especially one of his fellow-members of the Abraham Lincoln Association of Springfield.

John Llewellyn Lewis thought of himself as an emancipator of slave wages in the coal mines.[5] Of Welsh extraction, John Lewis started digging coal at Panama, Illinois, when he was fourteen years old. He grew into a formidable man, with a huge head, a mud-colored mop of hair, red bushy eyebrows, a face dull with miner's pallor, heavy jowls. Outfitted with the short, powerful arms and gnarled fingers of a miner, his deep, booming voice prepared him for the sort of leadership that earned respect and authority in the coal fields. Courageous confidence carried him through the early leadership disputes within the Illinois District of the United Mine Workers of America. At one district meeting he told one of his rivals to "take that gun out of your pocket or I'll shove it down your throat."

At another convention he had words for his antagonist Pat Ansboury. "All I can say," growled Lewis, "is that I mined coal in Illinois when delegate Ansboury was herding sheep in Bulgaria." Much later in the day the furious Ansboury finally gained the floor to demand an apology for this insult. Everybody knew he was an Irishman, not a Bulgarian. "Delegate Ansboury asks for an apology from the president of the United Mine Workers," exclaimed Lewis. "The president of the United Mine Workers does owe an apology, but the apology is not to Pat Ansboury but to the committee of twelve Bulgarians who came to see me at noon and protested this insinuation against their group. I hereby apologize to the twelve Bulgarians for having even suggested that such a person as Pat Ansboury could be associated with them."

Peabody dominated the industry in Illinois and to a considerable extent controlled the United Mine Workers Union too. The Peabody family had been closely associated with important Chicago Democrats since the days of Roger Sullivan. They received a substantial portion of the city coal business and contributed greatly to Democratic campaigns.

There is much in the early pre-Lewis history of the UMW to commend it. Abuses in the company camp were ended, wages and other benefits were improved, and the truly democratic union took care of its own disabled members. After a general soft coal strike in 1928, a basic daily wage of $6.10 was agreed upon. In 1932, presumably because of his close relationship with the company, Lewis proposed a $5 daily rate, which the membership rejected by a vote of 25,239 to 10,084. "Big Boy," as the miners called him, liked to use big words which "Adam Coal Digger," as he called them, could not understand. But the issue of a drop in pay of more than a dollar a day they understood only too well. Lewis resubmitted the issue to referendum. Enroute from the State Arsenal to the UMW headquarters in Springfield, the tally sheets disappeared, reputedly stolen by a UMW vice president. Lewis proclaimed a union emergency and signed the contract with the coal operators before sunset on the day of the election. Many of the miners rebelled at such autocratic tactics and founded the Progressive Miners of America. Thereafter, any pretense at democratic methods such as elections was dispensed with by the UMW. The president appointed his own officers to "provisional organizations" anywhere his leadership appeared threatened.

In a Peabody county like Christian, where the company controlled the local newspaper, the Taylorville *Breeze*, as well as most of the public officials, the Lewis forces held an upper hand. Only UMW members got jobs. Faced with starvation, the Progressives decided that their only course of action was to close the mines through picketing and violence. In other counties, of course, where the companies were more friendly to the PMA, the situation was reversed. On balance, however, the Progressives had become far more desperate, subsisting from the produce in their backyard gardens. Although they had right on their side, or so they contended, they were also going hungry.

On January 25, 1933, two hundred Progressives stormed the Statehouse. After being expelled from the gallery of the House of Representatives, they marched on the governor's office. The demonstrators jerked a doorknob off the reception room door and stomped on the polished table. Horner walked out of his office and offered to meet with five of their representatives. "Nothing doing," they shouted. "We voted for you, we'll tell you what to do, right now, all of us." The governor ordered the state police to evict them. Police clubs were used, a few heads bruised, and the casing ripped from the doorway as the mob was pushed out into the hall. Nine ringleaders were detained in the county jail.

Horner said it was deplorable that mob rule should have been substituted for the orderly processes of popular government at a time when all resources were strained for the relief effort. He regretted that "would-be terrorists" had confounded recognition of the right of petition with invasion of legislative halls. "The governor is determined," his statement made clear, "that there shall be no effort to use the right of petition to attempt to terrorize either the legislature or the executive. The worst excesses of the First French Revolution were directly traceable to the influence exerted by tumultuous mobs which filled the galleries of the national convention. . . . There must be no confusion between the people and a mob." [6]

Extra units of the National Guard were mobilized the next day when ten thousand women members of the PMA auxiliary marched through the streets of Springfield. Horner met with their leaders, who demanded cash relief, unemployment insurance, restoration of civil rights in the coal fields, and no sales tax. Horner told them that a sales tax was the only conceivable means of raising money for relief.

As the mood of the miners became more unruly, Horner realized that conferences were meaningless and that only one man held the power to bring peace to the mines. But that supreme individualist, bushy-browed John L. Lewis, wasted no time in informing the governor that he held all the good cards and would therefore make no concessions. Nor would he ever back away from a fight. He would not agree to a miner referendum on union recognition, or to divided work in the Christian County mines, or to submitting the conflict to a board of arbitration, or to leaving the Progressives alone. Horner seems now to have been both sympathetic to the plight of the Progressives and fearful of their ripeness for Communist takeover. In the weeks to come, however, Lewis' power in the national administration would enhance his strength even more and nullify whatever Horner might have considered doing to challenge his dictatorial stand in Illinois.[7]

Consequently, on February 4, the peace talks broke off, and the truce ended. Horner said neither side had been willing to give ground. "I feel that the termination of negotiations for settlement and the apparent lack of hope for an agreement is a severe blow to the welfare of our people as a whole. I shall expect all groups involved in this controversy to cooperate with me in my determined effort to prevent further bloodshed and suffering in the coal fields." Muttering under their breath as they left the Governor's Mansion, men on both sides vowed to settle this matter in their own way—just as the Herrin Massacre had settled something in its own way eleven years before.

Horner took steps in the meantime to cope with the many other recurrent problems of the gathering depression. He issued a formal appeal to holders of farm mortgages to "use the utmost forebearance in foreclosing on mortgages . . . when the owner is in such desperate financial circumstances that he is actually unable to pay." The governor did not go so far, though, as to urge a moratorium on mortgage foreclosures. His cousin, Milton Yondorf, who was in the investment business and dealt in mortgages, wrote him several letters during this period warning that the lack of a moratorium would "either put out of business or make go into bankruptcy the few remaining mortgage houses."

IV

It was at this discouraging moment, buffeted by patronage pressures, disappointed by his failure to unknot the troublesome coal mine crisis, that Henry Horner experienced an unexpected political liberation. Endeavoring to work himself out of the patronage predicament involving Senator Lewis, Mayor Cermak made a pilgrimage in mid-February to visit President-elect Roosevelt in Miami. There, at a reception in Bay Front Park, a bullet from the gun of a demented assassin, Giuseppe Zangara, presumably meant for Roosevelt, struck Tony Cermak instead. "I'm glad it was me instead of you," Cermak whispered to Roosevelt. Whether the shot was fired by a would-be Roosevelt assassin or by a sharpshooter of the Chicago crime syndicate intending to nail Cermak is still debated. Horner and Mrs. Helena Cermak Kenlay, the mayor's daughter, rushed to his bedside in Miami. On March 6 the immigrant coal miner who had learned his big city politics living among the Bohunks died.

Cermak's funeral must be remembered as one of the most spectacular in Chicago history. Thirty thousand marched in the funeral procession and twenty-three thousand attended services in the Chicago Stadium. Another fifty thousand gathered for the burial in Bohemian National Cemetery. Horner's eulogy was a florid one: "No assassin's dart shall stay the course of progress which Cermak's genius has stamped out for Chicago . . . Safe in the repository of our hearts, beyond the reach of vandal hands, lies the precious gold of our memories of Anton Cermak." Horner lauded Cermak's "tireless industry and sound judgment of men. Men could not frighten or cajole him. Cermak took command of his own political party and vitalized it into an instrument for unselfish public service."

The death of Tony Cermak represents a crucial juncture in the life of Henry Horner. For reasons that are undoubtedly connected with the governor's family background, he needed to lean upon strong, forceful men. There can be no question but that Horner derived some measure of emotional fulfillment from his relationship with the aggressive, domineering Cermak. But the shot that killed Cermak gave Horner both his political freedom and his political opportunity. Horner could, quite plainly, have become the party leader if he had chosen. Cermak's term still had more than two years to run. Rather than hold a special election, the legislature passed and Horner signed a bill authorizing the Chicago City Council to select a new mayor. On April 10, ten men met secretly in Chicago to talk about their choice. One of the ten was seventy-year-old Patrick A. Nash, a wealthy sewer contractor, breeder of thoroughbred race horses, and Cermak's Democratic county chairman. P. A., "the old man" to Democrats, had known and liked Horner for many years. Also present at the meeting was Jake Arvey, alderman from the Twenty-fourth Ward and heir to the influence of the fallen Rosenberg. Others were Al Horan, bailiff of the municipal court and beneficiary of Horner's state bonding patronage; Nash's nephew Ed Hughes, the Illinois secretary of state, who was dependent on the governor for legislation and appropriations; Tom Courtney, the state's attorney and also close to Horner politically; and Ed Kelly, chief engineer of the Sanitary District, president of the South Park Board, and a resident of Horner's ward.

With such a variety of power sources, Horner could have stepped in and assumed control of the Democratic party in Illinois. Nevertheless, he permitted the chance to slip by, for several reasons: the chores that fell to a political boss, to a Cermak, Sullivan, or Brennan, were basically distasteful to him, no matter how much he claimed to understand their justification. As a judge, furthermore, his broad vision had not been as fully developed as his eye for detail. Certainly, the responsibilities of his own job seemed overwhelming right now, and he thought the inherent powers of his office were obvious for all to see. In this sense the governor was excessively naïve—because of the national emergency he thought the party would unite easily behind its new national leader to pursue a progressive program as one big happy family.

The most likely successor to Cermak seemed to the governor, and to many other observers, to be William Sexton, a lawyer who had worked with Horner for Carter Harrison at the start of the century. It was with some astonishment, therefore, that the governor had listened to Nash's telephoned inquiry before the meeting —did he have any objection to Ed Kelly for mayor? Did Tom Courtney agree to that? Horner asked. When he was informed that Courtney had agreed, the governor said Kelly was acceptable.

Later, it would seem incredible that the governor, a Chicagoan, would not have played a more prominent role as the virtually leaderless party chose a new mayor for Chicago. Be that as it may, the next morning thirty-six of the fifty aldermen voted to make Edward Joseph Kelly the mayor. Since Nash was in the sewer contracting business and Kelly was chief engineer of the agency in charge of sewage disposal, it is not surprising that they were already well acquainted. Kelly's father had migrated from Ireland during the Civil War and operated a saloon on the Southwest Side. Kelly had started his working life as an undertaker before going to work for the Sanitary District, where he rose rapidly from rodman to chief engineer without the benefit of any engineering education beyond high school. Along with five trustees of the district, he had been indicted, but acquitted, in the late twenties for alleged misuse of public funds. At the time of his selection for mayor, the federal government had been pursuing him for $450,000 in unreported income during 1926, 1927, and 1928. It was in this connection, on March 24, that Horner made a trip to Washington on Kelly's behalf as he had done for Rosenberg. But the mayor was required, nevertheless, to make a sizable settlement of his tax debt. Although one of Kelly's closest friends was Colonel McCormick of the *Tribune*, an acquaintanceship that dated back to the days when McCormick had been president of the Sanitary District, the story of Kelly's income tax troubles leaked to the newspapers by way of the United States attorney in Chicago, Dwight H. Green, a Republican.

Nor was the governor beyond polishing a few newspaper apples himself in those days. Colonel Frank Knox of the Chicago *Daily News* had absorbed another afternoon daily and had employed the ex-publisher of that paper, K. L. Ames, Jr., as a carryover assistant at $25,000 a year. Knox made Ames available after Cermak's death to help promote "the things we are interested in in common, including securing a competent mayor for Chicago." The selection of a "*Tribune* man"—Kelly—naturally did not meet Knox's specifications for competency. Ames, nonetheless, continued with Horner and later became director of finance. Knox, for his part, offered a barrage of advice to the governor, including a suggestion on March 21 that officials of the various executive departments make no publicity statements until they were cleared by the governor's office. "I suppose I ought to be encouraging these birds to talk as much as I can get them to talk," confided Knox, "but I am trying to subordinate my instincts as a reporter in the higher interest of the Horner administration." A curious statement from the head of a Republican newspaper, but a suggestion readily accepted.

V

In the last two weeks of February the Chicago banks paid out $350,000,000 and drew nearer the brink of disaster. Governor Horner went to Chicago on March 2 with train reservations for Washington and the presidential inauguration. As he was about to leave for the station in late afternoon, he was intercepted by a committee of bankers requesting that he meet with them at the Chicago Club. Mel Traylor, his old friend from the First National Bank, believed the time had come for a moratorium on withdrawals to prevent runs on the banks. But other leaders of the Illinois Bankers' Association hoped that if they could pull through the half-day on Saturday, March 4, Inauguration Day, they could weather the storm. The banking crisis had struck Michigan on February 14 and had spread quickly to the financial centers of New York and Chicago. Other states were declaring bank holidays, and now Governors Lehman in New York and Horner in Illinois were in touch by telephone. At almost 4 A.M. Horner returned to his room at the Congress Hotel and abandoned any chance of attending the inauguration. He went to the Federal Reserve Bank of Chicago on Friday afternoon for further conferences. By now there had been large withdrawals during the day, and most of the bankers agreed with Traylor and Horner that something had to be done. That night, Franklin Roosevelt, Ray Moley, Cordell Hull, and Jesse Jones were meeting in Washington and debating the wisdom of a national moratorium. At midnight there came word from the New York banks that they were shipping gold to Europe. Horner expressed concern over this. At 1:45 A.M., the groggy Illinois bankers phoned Horner at his hotel and unanimously requested a state moratorium. Following phone calls to Lehman and to the Washington group, Governor Horner issued an order at 3:15 A.M. closing all Illinois banks for ten days. At 4:20 A.M. Lehman did the same in New York. Horner based the legality of his executive action on his constitutional power to "preserve the public peace, safety, health and welfare of the people of the State of Illinois." [8]

On Saturday the Chicago Board of Trade—which the governor's grandfather had helped found—closed for the first time in its eighty-five years. In Elgin, storekeepers learned that a sixteen-year-old boy had saved 11,357 pennies toward his college education and surrounded his house in siege. Joseph Rizzi, a banker in Benld, had been on his way to the inauguration, as had the governor. But he turned back when he heard of the moratorium.

The sky was the color of slate that afternoon in Washington as Franklin Roosevelt, coatless and uncovered, braced himself in the chill wind and officially assumed the presidency. Banker Rizzi in Benld sat by the radio in his closed bank listening to FDR assert that "the practices of the unscrupulous money-changers stand indicted in the court of public opinion, rejected by the hearts and minds of our men. The money-changers have fled from their high seats in the temple of our civilization." Thirty-seven hours after his inauguration, the president closed all the banks in the nation. On March 13, after scrutiny by state or federal examiners, banks began reopening in Illinois.

President Roosevelt's first hundred days constituted America's "orderly revolution." To head the Public Works Administration, Roosevelt named Harold Ickes, a veteran of Chicago reform politics, battler against Thompson and Insull, a pugnacious individual who trusted no one and considered everyone but himself potentially dishonest. His law partner, Donald Richberg, went along to Washington as another cog in the New Deal. In his capacity as a lawyer for the agency which administered the Industrial Recovery Act, Richberg agreed with John L. Lewis, among others, that a policy of carrying out existing contracts should be followed in the coal industry, even though the act also specified "a union of their own choosing." The Roosevelt administration had faith in Lewis, and "Big Boy" from Springfield manipulated the coal code hearings behind the scenes.

In early October Richberg arrived in Springfield to inquire first-hand into the mine union problem—on the very day, as it happened, that hundreds of armed pickets poured a steady stream of bullets for twelve hours into the buildings of Peabody Mine No. 43 near Harrisburg, where fifty miners were under siege. Four companies of National Guard infantry and one howitzer company hurried to the mine, and the Progressive pickets retreated into the hills. Fourteen UMW members and two Progressives were wounded. The next day the governor ordered the mine closed.

Richberg reported:

> It is evident that no agreement for a peaceful solution of the Illinois situation can be obtained so long as a substantial number of miners involved are encouraged to believe that they can gain their ends by rioting, intimidation, and wholesale violence.

> . . . Nor is it tolerable that any group of men with guns in their hands should be permitted to threaten that government must either support their demands or that they will resort to murder to gain their ends.[9]

With that, Richberg returned to Washington, and the machine-gun fire resumed. A state legislative commission looked into the problem and, under pressure from all sides, came forth with an innocuous recommendation that the only solution would be "one union under wise leadership and a fair distribution of the work among the men." At the Peerless mine, near the state fairgrounds in Springfield, seven hundred miners were routed by troops with tear gas and bayonets after ten United Mine Workers had been wounded. In Christian County the soldiers clubbed miners with gun butts and prodded them with bayonets. People were forbidden to sit on their porches and on more than one occasion a tear gas shell was lobbed onto a porch. Those who caused trouble were herded into trucks and expeditiously driven out of town.

By December, the National Guard intelligence report described the situation in Saline County as very tense. In Springfield, the situation was said to be "quiet except for a few scattered bombings. One bombing resulted in considerable damage to Peabody No. 59 when a dynamite bomb was thrown into the air shaft of a mine."

Farther south in DuQuoin, meanwhile, five young miners drove past a deputy sheriff's house, one firing a random rifle shot which deflected from the eaves and killed the officer's daughter, fourteen-year-old Laverne Miller, inside the house. Their trial was transferred to Union County, where four received life sentences and the fifth was sentenced to forty years in prison.

CHAPTER SEVEN

The Battle for the Dole

In the context of today's social dialogue, Henry Horner's Standard Club orientation would probably warrant the label of social "moderate" or "conservative with a heart" or something of that sort—his political posture fell short of social liberalism as we know it in the modern welfare state. He combined an intense feeling for people with an emotional reverence, typical of his well-to-do cronies, for the platitudes that are said to have made the nation great—private initiative, business enterprise, etc.

Oftentimes Horner spoke of the "constant danger of the establishment of a permanent dole and a pauper class" in America. To one friend he wrote that "a dole . . . is bound to be enervating to what we have been proud to call American vitality and courage." Another time he wrote, "I realize how difficult it is to get out of the dole once we are in it. However, all of us must realize that the dole is one of the dangers of American life, and the sooner we get out of it, the better it will be for the normal process of both government and community life."[1] Horner coupled fundamental economic conservatism with a feeling for people in trouble. In 1933, though, theoretical pronouncements about the danger of the dole were to be proven academic.

Three hundred policemen donned steel helmets and took up axe handles to deal with hungry demonstrators at city relief stations in Chicago. "It has been brought to our attention," reported the National Guard military intelligence officer, "that the possibility or desirability of revolution is being openly discussed . . . in Chicago, the Tri-Cities area, Springfield, and Granite City. . . . Certain leaders of farm organizations prophesied that unless the economic condition of the farmer improved in the near future there would be revolution within twelve months. . . . Talk of revolution is common through Illinois among the small businessmen's group." [2]

Looking back, it now seems incredible that Horner's hardest legislative struggle involved a proposed tax for the feeding of starving families. The tax structure bore heavily upon land, buildings, and farm equipment. An income tax already had been held unconstitutional. And Horner had promised to relieve the disproportionate load on property owners. But in 1933 no tax—including his only practical alternative, the sales tax—would have been greeted with anything like pleasure in Illinois. Although Democrats had majorities in both houses of the legislature, a rare privilege, the minority Republicans made political capital by being against taxes—period. The sales tax did not set well with either the ideological liberals, who were disturbed by its regressive impact upon the poor, or with the retail merchants. Horner's old friendships in the commercial community proved helpful though. D. F. Kelly of The Fair store wrote the governor in February that although he could not publicly advocate the tax, "my private opinion is that there is no other way to take care of the poor during these trying times." Kelly became Horner's ambassador on State Street, trying to persuade other leading merchants to see his point of view.

For more than a year now local governments and private charities had been unable to hold back the waves of destitution and suffering. The Illinois Emergency Relief Commission administered bond issues and other appropriations, with county relief commissions being formed to set local standards for assistance. Later this aid was supplemented by the first of the special federal programs, the Civil Works Administration. Governor Horner and Pat Nash traveled to Washington pleading for still greater federal assistance. As it turned out, in the year ending August 1, 1933, the federal government contributed 99 per cent of the $68,000,000 spent for relief in Illinois.

By the middle of the regular six-month legislative session in 1933, Horner had learned to adjust his judicial temperament to the conciliatory attitude necessary in dealing with the makers of law. He also confided to a friend that already "this job of governor is no bed of roses."[3] The administration's bill for a 3 per cent tax on retail sales, excluding farm products and motor fuel, passed both houses with the bare two-thirds majorities necessary to levy the tax immediately instead of waiting until the new fiscal period started in July. But a test case was brought quickly to the Illinois Supreme Court, and on May 11 the tax was struck down as unconstitutional. The "uniformity" clause in the taxation section of the constitution requires that taxes be imposed uniformly; a tax on automobile fuel cannot exempt farm tractors. So a new bill covering all retail sales, without exemptions for farm products, was introduced at a lower rate of 2 per cent. Chagrined by these developments, the Illinois Agricultural Association, followed by many rural legislators, changed sides and opposed the measure. Six roll calls were needed before the new bill passed the House, but pass it finally did.

"High Tax Henry" thereupon took the brunt of the indignant protests. Typical of his mail were comments like, "Reach for your hat, governor, and don't slam the door on the way out." A sales tax on food is tyranny, declared a Chicago neighborhood newspaper, adding that "the people of Illinois have just been treated to one of the grandest gyps in its history. . . . The bill to tax the bread in the mouths of the poor was jammed through the legislature, signed by the governor, and inflicted without delay on the helpless people of Illinois."

Merchants often overcollected the tax, by taking a penny for the nickel sale of a package of gum, for instance. Not only were the citizens in no mood for taxes, but in many small towns and rural areas there was a notable absence of concern by the haves for the have-nots. It was widely suspected that loafers were on relief rolls, that many of those drawing relief were not entitled to it, and that the administration of public aid was riddled with graft. Robert E. Wood, Horner's former Skeeter companion, enunciated a not uncommon point of view when he said: "While it is probably true that we cannot allow everyone to starve (although I personally disagree with this philosophy and the philosophy of the city social worker), we should tighten up relief all along the line, and if relief is to be given it must be on a bare subsistence allowance."[4]

Those who expected the benevolent New Deal to continue its prolonged bankrolling of virtually all the relief burden in the industrial states failed to reckon with Harry L. Hopkins. The son of a harness shop proprietor in Sioux City, Iowa, this former social worker on the lower East Side of New York City was brusque, cocky, and ambitious. As much as Governor Horner admired Harold Ickes, he despised Harry Hopkins. And Hopkins functioned not only as federal relief administrator but also as administrator of the New Deal's work-relief program, the Civil Works Administration. In both capacities he cultivated Mayor Kelly and the other big-city leaders with an eye on the presidency in 1940. This farsightedness was shared, though, by two of his enemies within the administration, Postmaster General Farley and Ickes.

In the fall of 1933 Hopkins advanced federal funds to Illinois on condition that the state take immediate steps to raise money on its own for the winter needs. Governor Horner recalled the legislature in special session and proposed a $30,000,000 bond issue for the November referendum ballot:

> You are asked to consider means to provide food and other necessities for those of our State who by reason of the industrial depression have been prevented from earning their livelihood and supporting their dependent families. They have been caught and crushed in the economic disaster that has engulfed nearly the whole of the civilized world. While nearly all our citizens have suffered some degree of financial loss, the majority of our people are fortunate in comparison with the legion of workers who are unable to find employment. You well know that all of these unfortunates, with few exceptions, are willing to work if employment can be provided for them. . . . The Federal Administrator [has] indicated emphatically that Illinois could expect no more than is provided under the matching provisions of [the act]. The federal agencies for unemployment relief have been generous to the extent of carrying practically the entire burden of our State for about 15 months. There are open to us only two courses. Either we must provide additional funds without delay or shut down our relief stations and abandon over 223,000 families aggregating nearly a million people to privation, suffering, and even death. Either the State of Illinois must help them now or there is no help for them. There is no choice between these two courses. I doubt that there will be a single voice raised . . . to urge that relief work stop and these helpless persons be abandoned. The results would be too frightful, too disastrous, too inhumane to contemplate.[5]

Although the bond issue did succeed, the petty, politically inspired bickering in the Statehouse chambers over this relief project and others that followed is one of the sorry chapters in the history of Lincoln's state. The Decatur *Herald* commented, sympathetically, that "politics [in the relief situation] will not be adjourned until the specter of anarchy is in sight."[6] Bishop Griffin, whose casual friendship with his neighbor in the Executive Mansion had now been bound firmly through personal fellowship, told the governor in a letter:

"I fear that the United States is becoming one big insane asylum. . . . Our elected representatives are watching the passing show and leaving you to take full responsibility before the public. When there is any honor and credit, they like to take it. When there is any grief, the Governor is expected to go it alone."[7]

Whenever the sniping opposition lacked for ammunition, they were helped by the barely disguised animosity between Horner and Harry Hopkins. The federal official recognized no Illinois authority other than Mayor Kelly, and the governor finally had to complain to the president that he could not even get through to Hopkins by telephone. Hopkins dispatched two investigators to check into alleged irregularities in the Illinois CWA program and later made an army district engineer the state administrator of CWA instead of placing this responsibility with the relief commission. A tapering off of the CWA in Illinois at the end of the year also proved damaging. In November, two hundred thousand heads of families were working on CWA projects. But the National Guard reports informed the governor that in Rock Island "much of the money paid CWA workers has gone to pay old bills in neighborhood stores." In the same community "some mass meetings have been held by the so-called CWA Protective Association and another to raise funds for the Daily Worker. Efforts are being made [by the Communists] to organize the steelworkers' union. Curtailment of only 11 per cent in CWA work brought people back to the relief agency." "Pessimistic utterances" were also reported in Kankakee and Bloomington "about what will happen when CWA funds are depleted." In Springfield "the mental attitude of the public has taken a distinct turn to the pessimistic, caused mostly by the cut in CWA workers. . . . The Communist Party has been holding a series of meetings. Mining conditions are very unsettled. Loaning agencies, both farm and city, report their borrowers depressed and pessimistic."

Nature did little to soften the hardship on the farms. In 1933, hail, wind, and rain devastated fifteen hundred farms in the northeastern part of the state. Half the farmers were without resources to buy seeds for replanting, until the relief commission and the state agriculture department came to their rescue. Then in the following summer, severe drought, cinch bugs, and ear worms cut the corn crop to about twenty bushels per acre, the lowest yield in sixty-eight years.

Another part of the National Guard report stated that "stevedores on the barge lines at Cairo are being organized by the Marine Workers Industrial Union, a purely Communistic organization of the most direct actionist type." In Rockford, said the guard, "the Unemployed Councils (slightly red) holds regular meetings and makes demands upon relief agencies—nothing serious."

Nothing serious.

II

In Illinois the legislature meets in regular session every other year from January to the end of June. Because of the recurring problems Governor Horner kept the legislators in special session much of the rest of the time too. After the regular session of 1933, there were four special sessions. Except for a two-week break, the two houses were in session from October of that year until May of 1934. The second special session was convened to consider liquor control, a subject that will be treated in detail in a later chapter.

The third, called for February 13, 1934, took up three topics: legislation to enable state cooperation in the federal recovery programs that were rolling out of Washington on a mass production assembly line; legislation empowering the state courts to delay mortgage foreclosures; and the problem of dwindling public school funds. A bill was passed to temporarily divert one-third of the state motor fuel tax to the school fund, with half of it going to Chicago. Horner also sought, unsuccessfully, to force the consolidation of many of the ten thousand one-room schools in the state. In downstate areas there were more school board members than there were teachers, and some school districts covered only three families. But the Illinois Education Association, an organization representing teachers, resisted consolidation and also fought other measures to withhold state aid from schools not meeting certain sanitary standards. Eighty per cent of the one-room schools had been judged to have unfit drinking water.

After approval of the sales tax, the governor suspended the state property tax, resulting in reduction of local property tax bills by between 7 and 19 per cent. Operating budgets of state agencies were trimmed by about one-fifth over the previous biennium. At one important institution, though, Horner's zeal for economizing got him in trouble and resulted in political damage. The University of Illinois submitted its lowest budget request since 1919, but the governor dispatched a team of management consultants to search for additional economies. The firm of J. L. Jacobs and Company proposed the saving of $1,500,000 more by abolishing certain scholarships, raising tuition, and cutting back the work of research agencies. "This would save money at a terrific social cost," protested President Harry Woodburn Chase, who pointed out that his was not a rich man's college. Horner finally retreated under alumni pressure and approved the requested appropriation of $7,810,000. Later, as he departed for a new position as president of New York University, Chase sympathized with Horner. "Perhaps no governor in Illinois," he said, "in recent years at least, has been confronted with so difficult a task as you have on your hands. It is comparatively easy to expand governmental functions and services, and so difficult to shrink them." [8]

The members of the Illinois Legislature, like those of other states in which the business of legislating is an underpaid, part-time job, have generally not been of superior quality. Independent of mind, hungry for patronage and other favors, they are usually convinced that they could govern the state better than the man elected to try to do it. An impetuous, quick-tempered orator from Chicago, twenty-eight-year-old Benjamin Adamowski, became Democratic House leader in 1935 after Horner had rejected him as being too young in 1933. The governor had barnstormed the state in 1934 asking for the election of legislators who sympathized with FDR's recovery program. His campaigning evidently helped, for twenty-two additional Democrats won.

Another event of political significance in 1934 was the death of Moe Rosenberg just as the income tax scandal caved in on him and just after he had started blowing the whistle on some of the fellow-Democrats who had shared in his Insull fortune. "To those who really knew and understood him," Horner wired the widow, "he will live in our memories for his loyalties, his charities, and the beautiful sentiment of his family life."

Upon the death of the congressman from the Havana district, Henry T. Rainey, the speaker of the United States House of Representatives, Scott Lucas was elected to his seat. And a choice federal patronage job, that of United States attorney in Chicago, went to Mike Igoe with Senator J. Ham's backing. A young Chicago lawyer, Adlai E. Stevenson II, also was recommended for the post by Walter J. Cummings, treasurer of the Democratic National

Committee and chairman of the board of the Continental Illinois National Bank and Trust Company.

In April of 1934 the White House forwarded to Horner a bill making the state the policing agent for the NRA (National Recovery Act). The state courts were to enforce the various industrial codes which businesses had agreed to conform to. The Illinois Manufacturers' Association and the Chicago Association of Commerce organized squads of businessmen who assembled in Springfield protesting that Horner would be elevated to "business dictator" of Illinois. "Worse than Prohibition," complained Representative Clinton Searle of Rock Island. "All state police would become snoopers under this bill." Another Republican representative, Richard J. Lyons of Mundelein, called it an attempt at super-government that would put every line of business in the state under political dictatorship. Nevertheless, Dick Finnegan's Chicago *Times* asked: "Today the citizen closest to President Roosevelt's heart is the man without a job. . . . Does Illinois propose to secede from the New Deal?" Horner told businessmen that the NRA in the last eight months had increased stability and brought about greater returns for industry and more employment and higher wages for workers. "I have full confidence in the leadership of President Roosevelt," he said, "and so have a vast majority of the people of this state and nation. It is my sincere desire to follow his masterful guidance, his integrity and his genius of statecraft." The governor's pleading for "concerted and unselfish and united action in the nationwide effort to overcome the worst economic disarrangement in the history of the world" finally yielded—many thousands of disputatious words later—legislative ratification of NRA in Illinois.[9]

Bishop Griffin thought he could discern a lessening of domestic tensions. "A year or two ago," he told Horner, "nearly everyone was in the firing line heaving bricks at every head that happened to be a little higher in the social scale than others." By now, with 675,000 Illinoisans still on relief, the federal WPA (Works Progress Administration) had supplanted the CWA, and the governor fretted at reports coming from Chicago and Washington. The Chicago Democratic machine adopted WPA as just another form of patronage, dispensing jobs upon the endorsement of precinct captains. The Cook County Council of the American Legion complained to Horner that "the one prime assurance for WPA employment is a letter from some elected member of the Administration political organization." Harold Ickes recorded in his diary that he once told

Roosevelt that any WPA funds distributed through Mayor Kelly were "subject to 20 per cent for graft." According to Ickes, the president said he was afraid that was true.[10]

Despite his yeoman's service implementing the New Deal in Illinois, the governor's federal patronage rewards proved disappointing. Hopkins, furthermore, made it plain that federal relief money would be cut off if the state did not raise its ante and implied that there had been wasteful political administration of the Illinois program. Auditor Barrett, a member of the state relief commission, clashed repeatedly with the professional social workers, alleging "looseness" in the issuance of relief checks. A legislative investigating committee was formed to look into these charges. Howard O. Hunter, Chicago field representative for the Federal Emergency Relief Administration, wrote Horner that he considered the investigation "an obscene farce." He said the committee members had no idea what they were supposed to be investigating and studiously avoided the assistance of anybody who knew anything about the subject.

Even before the new legislature could organize in January of 1935, the governor was compelled to bring back the old legislature for a fourth special session. If the property tax were to be suspended again, forfeiting $30,000,000 a year in potential revenue, Horner had to be certain that the sales tax, due to expire in mid-1935, would be continued. "After fifteen months of experience," he informed the legislators, "the sales tax has been found practical and efficient. . . . No tax is of itself popular. It can only be said to be popular in the sense that it is preferred over other taxes. To my mind it is unthinkable that we shall take the backward step of discarding our present constructive and beneficial method of obtaining state revenues."

The Monmouth *Daily Review Atlas*, a downstate newspaper, disagreed. "Who is best able to pay for expenses of state government?" asked the paper. "The rich, the big corporations, or the poor to whom Jewish Horner's 2 per cent toll is a real hardship? The sales tax is a blessing to the rich. It is a damn outrage on the poor and those unable to pay it." [11]

Such talk pained Horner because he knew it to be essentially true. But there seemed to be no alternative to a sales tax when economic conditions made property no longer a practical base for taxation, an equitable income tax appeared to have been ruled out by the Constitution, and Mr. Hopkins was warning from Washington that unless the state discovered a means to raise $3,000,000 a

Governor Horner's grandmother,
Mrs. Hannah Horner.

Governor Horner's mother,
Mrs. Dilah Levy.

Rudolph M. Schaeffer, an artist, pictured while retouching a portrait painted on the ceiling of Governor Horner's boyhood home. Left to right are: Irene Horner, 4, and Milton Yondorf, 6 months, both cousins of Horner's, and young Horner himself. Herald and Examiner photo.

Judge Horner and his Lincoln library. By permission of Field Enterprises, Inc., Newspaper Division.

Judge Horner, nominee for governor, with Mayor A. J. Cermak, at the Democratic county convention. Photo by The Chicago American.

Judge Horner, seeking the
Democratic nomination for governor,
is introduced at a workers meeting
by Clayton F. Smith, chairman
of the managing committee.
Photo by The Chicago American.

Judge Horner, after hearing of
his victory in the race for governor,
broadcasts his greetings and words
of appreciation to the voters of
Illinois. Chicago Daily News photo.

Judge Horner, governor-elect, chuckles over the election returns. Herald and Examiner photo.

Governor-elect Horner and his secretary, Arthur P. O'Brien, as they leave the former judge's Madison Park home on their way to the inauguration in Springfield. Herald and Examiner photo.

James Fieser of the American Red Cross, General E. M. Markham, Governor Horner, and Harry L. Hopkins, arranging for a cleanup of lower Illinois flood areas. Chicago Daily News photo by Russell V. Hamm.

Governor Horner with the casket of his long-time friend Mayor Cermak.

Governor Horner with Franklin D. Roosevelt and Senator William Dieterich of Illinois. Wide World photos.

Governor Horner, back from Washington on the Capitol Limited, tells a reporter how he was denied government assistance for relief in Illinois by the president and Relief Administrator Hopkins. Chicago American photo.

Governor Horner, arriving back from a second trip to Washington with Patrick Nash, Cook County democratic leader. Herald and Examiner photo.

Illinois Day at the Century of Progress Exposition. Left to right: Henry Horner, the incumbent; Edward F. Dunne, who was governor from 1912–16; Joseph W. Fifer, 1888–92; Len Small, 1920–28; Charles S. Deneen, 1904–12; and Louis L. Emmerson, 1928–32. Chicago American photo.

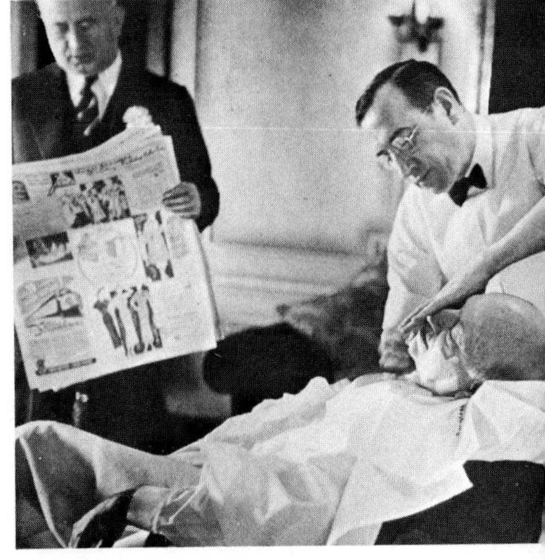

Governor Horner listens to the news as read by his private secretary, Arthur P. O'Brien. Chicago American Candid camera photo.

Governor-elect Horner, with Governor Louis L. Emmerson and other dignitaries, on his way to the inauguration ceremonies.

Governor Horner, Edward Barrett (left), state auditor, and John Stelle, assistant state treasurer, in conference in Springfield. Herald and Examiner photo.

Governor Horner with County
Chairman J. M. Arvey.

Governor Horner with J. M.
Arvey and Scott W. Lucas.

Governor Horner, Patrick Nash,
and Mayor Kelly.

Governor Horner and Mayor Kelly.

Back to back, with no sign of
recognition on the face of either,
Patrick A. Nash (extreme left),
Democratic national committeeman
from Illinois, and Governor
Horner pass in the lobby of a
Philadelphia hotel, where both
have gone as Illinois delegates
to the Democratic National
Convention. International News-
photo by Herald and Examiner.

Governor Horner in Florida,
where he went to recuperate
after being stricken
while in office.

Governor Horner strolling on the lawn of the Executive Mansion in Springfield after returning from a rest in Florida. By permission of Field Enterprises, Inc., Newspaper Division.

The Horner funeral cortege.

Members of the Horner Memorial
Commission conduct an official
pre-dedication inspection
of the Henry Horner monument
erected in Burnham Park:
Senator Raymond T. O'Keefe,
Oliver R. Barrett, Senator A.
L. Marovitz, Richard J. Daley,
Robert E. Straus, and
General Julius Klein.

James Levy, the governor's brother, and Judge U. S. Schwartz with the portrait of Governor Horner in The Standard Club.

month more for relief, Uncle Sam would turn off the federal spigot.

Within a few weeks it was necessary not only to continue the sales tax but to raise it. Governor Horner advised the new legislature that President Roosevelt was now pursuing a policy of finding work for the employables but was turning back to local communities the responsibility of caring for the unemployables, other than the aged and blind. Cash relief replaced disbursing order relief. Illinois also began making its first old-age "pension" grants (under the 1935 federal Social Security Act), widely supplemented by general assistance for medical care. Horner emphasized that he remained strongly opposed to restoring the property tax. Still there were about one million unemployed in Illinois who "through no fault of their own are denied the opportunity to labor for their daily bread. They cannot wait while we seek to perfect or adjust an economic system which will assure a job to every employable person and livelihood to each wage-earner."

With Mayor Kelly's backing, the administration sponsored legislation raising the tax rate to 3 per cent. The governor used his personal persuasion on legislators who cringed under anti-tax pressure from home. Paul Powell, a young Democrat from Vienna in southern Illinois, where the folks were "thinning out the soup a little more," showed a stack of telegrams to Horner. The governor thumbed through the telegrams, and anger flashed in his beady eyes. "That one cost a buck! That one cost 75 cents! I'm interested in the people who don't have a buck, who don't have a nickel!"

But, ever the dignified judge, he could not bring himself to the sordid practicality of swapping jobs for votes. Ben Adamowski, his House leader, reported that he could dredge up three Republican votes in exchange for twelve patronage jobs. Horner's mustache twitched with indignation. "How can they . . . when human misery is involved . . . put this on that level?" Leaving the governor's office, Adamowski mentioned his problem to Mayor Kelly, who was waiting to see Horner. "Will they take city jobs?" the mayor inquired. The leader checked and, finding city jobs acceptable, was able to chalk up three more Republican votes.

Despite the governor's persuasiveness and the mayor's patronage generosity, the bills failed miserably in both houses. They fell again and again, along with companion measures extending the sales tax rate to public utilities. The prevailing mood in the legislature was illustrated by Representative Lyons' advocacy of a bill to restore public aid administration to the townships. "There are," he suggested, "three political parties in the United States—Republicans, Democrats, and the Social Workers party, which is subsidized by the Democrats."

"For selfish, partisan motives," fired back Horner, "the Republican organization in the House, allied with the very active lobby of the public utilities, have voted to abandon to starvation and misery the families who cannot provide for themselves." For partisan political reasons, the governor charged, these Republican leaders were as careless of human life as the leaders who brought on the Civil War.

On April 18, Hopkins cut off federal funds until Illinois raised taxes. But the Republicans maintained their opposition, on the contention that waste and extravagance dominated relief administration. Representative Lyons called Horner's statement a "silly symphony." He said he had received no mail response to the speech, "proving that Horner is dead. Deader than Cermak. He is a political corpse." The legislative stalemate dragged on. Compromises were tried and failed. Horner pleaded, "If you do not like the method that is before you, then choose some other method of raising relief funds. Only do not leave the needy of Illinois without food." By May 18 the last food orders were exhausted. Transient relief stations in Chicago for fifteen thousand residents of other states closed. Horner took to the radio again, warning that every twenty-four hours without legislation would bring an additional twenty thousand families face to face with starvation. He called the Republicans "obstructionists." In conclusion, he said "the hearts that had remained indifferent to the pleas of the hungry beat in ready response to the call of the officials of the power companies of the state."

Hopkins explained in Washington that "I've got to see $3,000,000 a month on the line before Illinois will get any further federal allotments." Horner arranged an emergency conference with Hopkins in Cleveland, and on May 24, $5,000,000 in federal funds were released to end the crisis at a time when the Illinois Emergency Relief Commission had virtually ceased operations and shut down its relief stations.

With the pressure finally off, the legislature passed the sales tax increase on the sixth roll-call vote. The crisis had been averted, and, stewing silently at the lack of help from Washington, the governor was confined to bed with what was described as a bad cold. Actually, Dr. Nathan Rosen, Horner's Springfield physician, had been alarmed by his rising blood pressure, racing heart beat, and the appearance of a metallic sound in his aortic region. A nineteen-year-old graduate nurse was brought in to enforce the doctor's rules, which included another try at a low-protein, reduced-salt diet. The patient balked, of course, at being bedridden. "You tell me what I should do and then I'll do as I damn please," he instructed the nurse. "No slip of a girl is going to give me a bed pan." The arrival, at long last, of the federal relief check in the amount of several million dollars was deemed by the governor an occasion worthy of celebration. He popped the cork on a bottle of imported champagne and shared it with the young nurse. She recalled many years later that, inspired by the champagne, the governor forgot his blood pressure and chased her about the mansion later in the evening, a clear violation of all the doctor's orders and a startling experience for a damsel fresh out of nurses' training. The governor lost the foot race and soon recovered.[12]

In the months ahead there were more crises, more pleadings for the hungry, more opportunities for the "loyal opposition" in the legislature to look on bemused as the governor pressured the New Deal legislation through in Illinois and then engaged in periodic controversies with Hopkins over WPA and relief matters.

Meeting in special session in October of 1935, the legislature passed the required county welfare administration law so that Illinois could participate in the new federal aid programs for old-age pensions, blind relief, and aid to dependent children. After the usual amount of legislative resistance, Illinois also decided to take part in the new unemployment insurance program. Horner said, "It is neither socialistic or communistic, nor is it a form of charity —it is a measure of social security and justice which has a direct effect upon industry and affects the entire economic field. Our experience teaches us that employers and employees, as groups, succeed or fail together."

In January of 1936—an election year—the sounds from Springfield resembled those of a cracked record. Horner announced that no federal money would be available to provide the necessities of life to the unemployed and their families—"a crisis of the gravest import." He said immediate action was necessary "to prevent starvation and suffering among the needy and the helpless."

CHAPTER EIGHT

Eyedrops and Carol Sanders

Strolling down State Street in Chicago on a bright, cheery day in April of 1933, Dr. Louis Mann, the rabbi of Horner's temple, happened upon a rumor that distressed him profoundly. The governor, so he was informed, had decided to veto the eyedrop bill. Without a moment's hesitation, Dr. Mann turned into the nearest drugstore, purchased a toothbrush, and hastened with his single piece of luggage to the railroad station.

It will be recalled that the rabbi had caused his friend some political embarrassment in 1931 by his failure to appreciate the public service qualities of the Democratic organization's candidate for mayor, Tony Cermak. It is also familiar history that, only a few short years before, the Ku Klux Klan had reigned in southern Illinois. White-robed Klansmen had mustered in the state fairgrounds and paraded through the center of the state capital on the backs of state militia horses, a shocking public demonstration of the insolence of their bigoted legions. And now, on the force of its backlash, the nationwide economic protest vote of 1932 had swept a Jewish governor into office in Illinois for the first time. His beginning months were a difficult period of adjustment, and he sometimes found the burden almost overwhelming.

The forces devoted to the prevention of blindness had been campaigning for many years for a state law to require the placing of drops of silver nitrate in the eyes of newborn babies as a preventive for ophthalmia neonatorium, gonorrheal blindness. In the ten years prior to 1931, 77 babies had been blinded and 1,294 others hospitalized by this disease in the Chicago area. The names of candidates for the six beds in the ophthalmia ward at the State Eye and Ear Infirmary in Chicago were entered on a long waiting list.

Support for the bill was by no means universal. On religious principle, Christian Scientists opposed any form of compulsory medical treatment. In 1931 the bill finally squeezed through the legislature, only to be vetoed by Governor Louis Emmerson on the basis of the attorney general's opinion that it infringed on personal liberties. Thereupon Jewish women's clubs took up the cause in the 1932 campaign, extracting pledges from a number of candidates, including the Democratic nominee for governor.

Remembering Horner's pledge, the rabbi went directly from the train to the Statehouse, where he was promptly admitted to the governor's office.

"You promised that you would sign this bill," he said. "You cannot go back on your word."

Horner pointed to a large cardboard box in a corner, piled high with telegrams.

"I have no choice," he explained. "The weight of these protests from influential people in their communities, some from almost every hamlet in the state, people acting out of deep religious conviction, cannot be ignored. I'm sorry, but that's how it is."

"What about your integrity?" the rabbi asked. "Remember that some people do not yet accept vaccination. Would you bring smallpox back into the world? I'm afraid this is the most tragically inhumane act you could perform. I wish you could put yourself for an hour in the place of these blind infants. I doubt if you could sleep another night if by your veto you thrust even one baby into perpetual darkness."

"But what would I be expected to do, Doctor, if the legislature passed a law contrary to the teachings of our faith?"

"You ought to know that the Talmud, which carries on the teachings of the Old Testament, says the law of the State must be obeyed."

Then the rabbi recited a prayer he had used in his inaugural sermon at Sinai Temple on Rosh Hashonah Eve in 1923:

> Give me the power to labor for mankind;
> Make me the mouth of such that cannot speak;
> Eyes let me be to groping men and blind;

A conscience to the base;
And to the weak let me be hands and feet, and to the
foolish, mind;
And lead still further on such as Thy Kingdom seek.

The weary governor looked at the clock and told the rabbi he would miss the last train back to Chicago. The lines in his forehead and around his eyes had been deeply etched in the last few weeks, and his pasty jowls sagged with fatigue. Horner's fleshy, olive-toned face and heavy gray mustache accentuated the dark eyes that flashed with awareness and emotion behind the pince-nez bifocals perched on the broad bridge of his nose. His thick pelvis and heavy legs made his small narrow feet look even smaller.

"Go home to your wife," he said softly. "I won't disappoint you."

The last train to Chicago was detained at the station while the governor's car hurried to the station with the rabbi. On the next day Governor Horner signed Illinois' first eyedrop law.[1]

II

A few short years later, a seven-year-old girl, visiting the Executive Mansion, climbed onto the governor's lap, squirming and jumping gleefully about with her arms clasping his neck. When he spoke or laughed, the child placed her hands on his throat and her head to his chest.

"All that I have, all the power, the prestige, is nothing," he told a friend in the room. "This is the only important thing in life. A child."

On February 28, 1932, this child, then five days old, had been abandoned at the front door of the Cook County Hospital in Chicago. An eye infection caused the destruction of both eyeballs. She also suffered from a chronic ear infection, which left her partially deaf. Because of these double sensory handicaps, her speech development was retarded. For the first four years of her life, the child, whom we shall call Carol Sanders, remained in the hospital, a totally dependent lump, unable to do anything for herself except tear off her clothing.

A psychology professor at Northwestern University, Dr. Robert H. Gault, interested himself in her case during the course of his duties as director of the American Institute for the Deaf-Blind. In the mid-twenties, as a research assistant at the Carnegie Institute in Washington, Dr. Gault had demonstrated the possibilities of enlarging the usefulness of the sense of touch and vibration to help the deaf-blind learn to talk. Hearing of the girl and Dr. Gault's theories, Governor Horner ordered the Department of Public Welfare to use $5,000 a year from its contingency fund to support Carol Sanders in a foster home during the training period.

The concentration of attention from Dr. Gault and other teachers at the institute changed Carol from a biting, scratching, animal-like child with nervous, purposeless movements into a civilized, reasonably quiet, and composed girl. Her hearing appeared to be partially reawakened, picking up now the lower pitches of sound. She loved riding in a bicycle basket or rocking in a swing —much as a puppy might—and by 1938 her vocabulary had grown to fifty words. Her facility for feeding herself was that of a three-year-old, her motor learning and memory span that of a four-year-old. The child feared touching and handling unfamiliar things. Seated on the ground, she first learned the word "grass." But after the first contact she kept her hands in her lap and refused to touch the grass again. Her only real contact with the world remained touch, smell, and taste. Whatever knowledge she would ever possess would come from what she could learn of hardness, texture, and movement, mainly through her organs of touch. Because she had never experienced seeing and hearing, her handicaps could never be adequately explained to her. Nonetheless, by 1936 the welfare department bulletin predicted hopefully that "there is every reason to believe that with the aid of modern methods she may develop to be even greater than Helen Keller."

The governor continued his active interest in Carol's case. He visited her regularly in her Evanston foster home, and she made weekend trips with her teacher to the Governor's Mansion in Springfield. He gave her a radio with a special attachment which she could hold against her face and thereby "hear" music. He took a personal hand in the many fund-raising programs which Dr. Gault conducted in a difficult effort to raise enough money for the maintenance of his costly institute program.

Playing with his young visitor in the huge mansion where he lived with all the splendor and dignity that the state of Illinois could provide, the tears streamed down Henry Horner's cheeks and into his mustache as this pitiful youngster without eyes frolicked on his lap, fingering his ears, chuckling at her beloved "guh-ner," and holding her head to his chest to pick up the vibrations of his vocal apparatus.

Although Carol Sanders would never see, during the six years after the signing of the eyedrop bill only two babies were blinded from the disease in Illinois, and the ophthalmia ward at the Eye and Ear Infirmary closed down for good.[2]

CHAPTER NINE

The Lonely Man in the Mansion

At holiday time—the season for families—Henry Horner suffered most keenly the dreaded loneliness of a public figure who lacked a close family life. It was then that he drew closer to a new friend, James Aloysius Griffin, the Roman Catholic bishop of Springfield. In the neighborhood around Lincoln's home, a husky man in black cape and square-cornered hat hastened away many a lonely night from his austere brick house adjoining the cathedral and on through a back door of the Governor's Mansion two blocks away. There, in the company of a bottle of Old Belmont bourbon, which they jointly admired, the Jewish governor and the Catholic bishop talked politics, theology, and life into the small hours. Both were native Chicagoans; the bishop had lived in a poor shanty-Irish neighborhood back of the stockyards, where boys usually pursued careers as politicians, policemen, priests, or thieves; the governor had come from the more affluent surroundings of South Michigan Avenue.

Horner shared the handsome black-haired Irishman's gift of blarney and wit. Both were outgoing but moody men who sometimes strolled alone at night in downtown Springfield, peering into store windows—behavior nearly as odd for a bishop as for a governor. The governor had a standing invitation to Christmas dinner with the clergy of the deanery after the bishop said mass in the cathedral. Horner never failed to send poinsettias at Christmas, lilies at Easter, and gifts on the bishop's birthday. Some of the governor's gifts were impromptu and spontaneous. For example, since the two men patronized the same Swedish masseur, Horner thought it appropriate to "bring the mountain to Mohammed"—by means of the gift of an electric steam cabinet—"although I don't want you to think that I am trying to have you follow Mohammed in other respects." The bishop later donated the cabinet in Horner's name to the St. John's Crippled Children's Home in Springfield. Another gift from the governor, a rare fifteenth-century Latin text, was donated by the bishop to St. Mary of the Lake Seminary in Mundelein. One Sunday in May Horner dispatched three dozen snapdragons to the bishop's residence. Griffin implored him, in return, to "please remember that we always have a snack in the icebox and whenever you feel so inclined the distance between the mansion and the bishop's house is not so great." In another note the bishop referred to "your lovely friendship and kindly disposition." At Christmas, 1934, Griffin confided in his letter of greeting that "I marvel at your ability to enjoy anything and everything from a prize fight to a theological discussion. You are many-sided and fit nicely into any and every picture."

When Horner fell ill, the bishop inquired whether "there is any possibility of loaning you my fine physique? I have what God gave the Irish—brawn. He was not so generous with the brains."

The governor did not restrict his thoughtfulness to Roman collars. He once sent flowers to the pastor of the First Methodist Church as a token of appreciation for the chimes that sounded a block away from the mansion.

II

In large measure these deeds served to offset his loneliness in Springfield. Horner rejoiced in the company of a few friends like the bishop who he could be assured were not playing him for political advantage. Springfield society, dominated by a few old-line families with names like Herndon and bloodlines traceable in the community back to the time of Lincoln, made no effort to welcome the Jewish governor, nor did he cultivate such company. He went to absurd lengths, though, to avoid being alone in the mansion. One Sunday morning the state historian, Paul Angle, worked for a couple of hours in the library and was walking home when the governor spied him passing the mansion. Horner insisted that Angle stay for dinner. So the state historian, unshaven and wearing an old flannel shirt, was served Sunday dinner by the black-coated butler in the mansion dining room. Sandburg also visited often at the mansion and, according to Horner's correspondence, "we talked goats a good deal." [1] After hearing from Sandburg about the nutritional qualities of goat's milk, the governor threatened some of his semi-alcoholic friends with an executive order placing them on such a diet. Robert Sherwood and other literary lights also were mansion guests, although Horner tended to tire of visits from celebrities rather quickly. Sandburg's visits, on the other hand, were always entertaining because of his offbeat antics; once he bellowed in the rotunda of the Statehouse to hear how his voice would echo under the huge dome.

Political cronies would frequently be invited to "come over to the mansion and get potluck." But their visits seemed less than satisfying. Dr. Nathan Rosen, the governor's physician, was under the impression that "he was not a very happy man, especially when he was alone. He wanted someone near him to talk to and discuss the things that were depressing him. His political friends were not too close to his heart. They were a ruthless bunch, interested only in power and profits. He craved the friendship of intellectual people to whom he could talk about literature, drama, art, music." [2] The doctor's assessment reflects the many sides of Henry Horner. He was a diligent worker and a stickler for detail —with an enormous capacity for mastering that detail. He was generous to and beyond a fault. He was devoted to children as only a childless, selfless bachelor could be. He was a terribly lonely man, a gluttonous neurotic at the dinner table, a seeker of vicarious adventure in the motion picture theater.

Alone in the rambling old mansion, but for Clarence the butler, the governor would lie propped in his upstairs bed, wading through the legislative bills, bulky reports, and correspondence that were stacked in a book truck beside him. For all the staff assistants paid to handle the routine tasks of his office, Horner could not bring himself to delegate responsibility as any good administrator must do. Any bill that he signed into law, any report that carried his signature, any letter written over his name would be his ultimate responsibility, a thought that gnawed constantly at his judicial mind. Long past midnight he worked in bed trying to keep up with this impossible work load.

Under the youthful likeness of his mother which hung on his mansion bedroom wall, the governor struggled to follow the doings of 232 legislators and the many thousands of state employees under his jurisdiction. Clarence Liggins, a stately, silver-haired Negro from Paducah, Kentucky, visited the bedroom regularly on refueling missions with ice water and cigars. As he worked, the governor's sense of time grew fuzzy, and he sometimes phoned one of his cabinet directors at 2 A.M. Along about that time, too, he would hie downstairs for the pickled pigs' feet in the refrigerator, or perhaps the kosher dill pickles or salami that were kept segregated in his personal closet, along with other goodies he had paid for himself. Or maybe he would send out for chili and tamales for his bedtime snack.

If his chores permitted, Horner would then devote a couple of post-midnight hours to Lincoln. Clarence, assuming the new role of librarian, hauled books from Horner's large collection back and forth from the sun porch library, which had been specially braced to bear the excessive weight. On most nights Clarence would sneak into the bedroom at about 3 A.M. and find the governor asleep surrounded by his books and papers.

Beginning on Inauguration Day, his old Chicago friends scolded Horner for overdoing. But he believed that a really close tab on the state's operations required tedious personal inspection; and on Sundays the governor did precisely that. Accompanied by one of his aides—often Insurance Director Ernie Palmer—Horner set out on his Sunday tours without notice of any itinerary. Instead of using state limousines, Van Diver piloted the governor's own Buick, which had been supplied by his brother Jim Levy.

On a typical Sunday sortie he would stop at a mental hospital, a fish hatchery, a teachers college, and at the homes of several Democratic county chairmen. At the hospitals he poked in the kitchen corners and looked under the beds. Palmer carried a notebook in which his companion's running comments were recorded. Emerging from a hospital, the governor's pockets would be stuffed with miscellaneous notes from the patients. One would ask, perhaps, that he inform Aunt Tillie back home that the patient was feeling much better and that she was not to worry. Willingly, the governor would include the letter to Aunt Tillie in the stream of correspondence that he would dictate on Monday morning. Through his desire to discover all the workings of state departments, Horner not only learned what was going on but also came to know downstate Illinois and its people, an advantage which would stand him in good stead later.

By nosing into dark corners, the governor found out where the tax dollars really stopped. He fired off little notes to O'Brien—"Arthur, watch this and see that we do the right thing." Doing the right thing was important, no matter how minor. The governor's files are full of notes like "Mr. Bowen, how can this disinfector cost $2,300?" One incident involving the welfare director illustrates the point:

Summoned into the governor's office one morning, Bowen was shown a voucher for $58.50 for one walking cultivator for the hospital farm at Peoria. Horner asked the director if he saw anything wrong with the voucher, but Bowen detected nothing out of the ordinary. "Well, I see something wrong, Arch," the chief executive asserted. Whereupon he whipped out a catalog from his desk drawer and pointed to the price of $56 that had been quoted to the state for this type of cultivator. "Where does the other $2.50 come in?" Horner wanted to know. Checking with the hospital, Bowen discovered that a pair of fenders had been added to the cultivator at a cost of $2.50. "Okay," said the governor, "but the voucher should show that. Don't let it happen again." And on his next trip to Peoria hospital, Horner visited the farm and asked to see the cultivator, just to satisfy himself that the fenders were there. By spot-checking vouchers personally, the governor let it be known that any state expenditure, no matter how trivial, might be subject to his scrutiny and the perpetrator of an irregularity bounced out of work. On a visit to Menard Penitentiary, the governor was distressed to find rats eating holes in the flour sacks. He instructed the warden on how to stack the sacks differently in order to stop the damage, a bit of knowledge gleaned from a family grocery business background not possessed by many governors.

The judicially desirable trait of demanding perfection added many hours to the work of the governor's office. Drafts of letters by assistants had to be triple-spaced; and in the end Horner usually made so many penciled revisions that the original version proved to be a waste of time. Nevertheless, the presence of the gubernatorial nose in many ordinarily inaccessible compartments of government shook up some of his underlings. Horner interested himself, among other things, in the complicated details of public utility rates, bypassing the commerce commissioners and going directly to their staff engineers for information that he wanted. When sixteen cement producers submitted identical bids, they were warned that unless the prices were reduced by true competitive bidding the state would begin making its own cement in its own plants. Despite his First Ward indoctrination in years gone by, the governor could not stomach the enterprising angles that some of his troops thought up. Welfare Director Bowen, Simeon Leland, Ernie Palmer, and others—some of them Republicans, others worse than that, reformers—disagreed continuously with Stelle and others on questions of patronage and the distribution of other spoils. Regardless of his political sponsorship, any hospital attendant fired for abusing a patient was blacklisted from future state employment. Without exception, Horner stood behind Bowen. The welfare director had a big, difficult job to perform, and his replies to petty political requests were often curt. But the grievances aroused by such rebuffs caused Stelle and his associates to transfer their increasing displeasure to the governor.

Many downstate Democrats wanted Horner to play down the social reforms of the New Deal. In spite of his troubles with Washington, the governor believed fervently in what the New Deal was trying to do and never faltered in his devotion to Roosevelt's objectives. He corresponded regularly with the president's wife, whom he admired. He sent Mrs. Roosevelt flowers, and the official White House invitations to social functions were usually accompanied by a personal note to him from her. Word of her soft heart circulated through Illinois, and she forwarded a series of requests to Horner from women throughout the state. Mrs. Roosevelt followed up on these cases with letters such as this: "Thank you so much for looking into the case of Mrs. William Ritchey of Vienna, Illinois. I am glad to know that she has a job, and I do not feel there is anything more we can do in the matter at the present time." [3]

Although he had never lacked feminine companionship before coming to Springfield, the governor's activities were now necessarily circumspect, especially after he was criticized by some newspapers for having two well-known women singers as overnight guests in the mansion. When he paid a sympathy call on the widow of a friend, rumors circulated that he was courting her—rumors that, he wrote another friend, were "unfortunately false."

Horner was a fastidious dresser, sometimes going through two or three shirts a day. In the summer he wore a double-breasted Palm Beach suit, boater straw hat, white shoes, hard collar, carnation in his lapel—and he carried a cane. While enroute to a meeting, he took some extra clothing along in the car and often changed in the back seat. He sometimes shaved in the car, too, using lotion and shaving cream. Not having a family waiting at home, it is not surprising that Horner lacked the homing instinct. He loved parties and hated to see them end. When bleary-eyed friends wanted to call it a night, his orders were to pour another drink and deal another hand. He played poker and bridge, for money, at regular mansion parties to which his political cronies were invited. Not only did the governor like to stay up all night; he disliked getting up in the morning. Upon arising, Horner started the day in the right frame of mind by smacking a punching bag that hung in the hall outside his bedroom, a therapeutic whack at his enemies and his problems.

But the punching bag did not help him overcome what (in politics) is considered a serious flaw: basically an impulsive sentimentalist, he needed to be liked. During a brief period of payless pay days at the University of Illinois, some of the employees threw their pay-substitute tokens at him as he rode through the streets. For several days he was deeply despondent. His mansion staff even remembers his bringing home a stray dog one night with instructions to feed it and maybe "it will like me." Disappointments pierced the hard outer shell which most successful politicians develop. He wanted to believe that people were on the square, and it hurt him to discover that men who had slaved for his election were now lining their pockets. Extremely conscious of his Jewishness, Horner was quick to assign anti-Semitism as the reason behind any hostile act against him.

To compensate for this emotional instability, he ate compulsively and in gluttonous quantities. Ordered again and again to diet because of his high blood pressure, the governor would sometimes devour a six-course dinner and then direct Clarence to bring in the melba toast in order to honorably fulfill his obligation to Dr. Rosen. He would travel forty-four miles to the Peculiar Cafe in Pana for a bowl of chili. A roadside hot dog stand and a supper club equally attracted his fancy.

As a movie-goer, the governor was an embarrassingly noisy popcorn muncher who guffawed and poked his companion in the ribs when something amused him. On auto trips from Chicago to Springfield he usually arranged to stop at a movie in one of the small towns along the way. His traveling companions, who were anxious to get home to their families, tried to detour past the theaters, but Horner kept an eye on the advertising signs to learn what films were playing in Braidwood or Chenoa or Pontiac. He especially liked Will Rogers movies and cowboy and gangster shows with lots of gunplay. When the governor settled back into his theater seat he was carried away with Tom Mix to the badlands, unaware of anyone else in the theater. One night, after seeing *A Tale of Two Cities* with *Tribune* reporter Percy Wood, he brought Percy back with him to the mansion where the sleepy reporter was conscripted to read to the governor from the book of the same title until 3 A.M.

Another indication of Horner's emotional identification with the movies is that he wrote fan letters to cinema stars at times of stress in his own life. After seeing Bobby Breen in *Make a Wish,* he was so moved with boyhood nostalgia that he wrote: "Keep on soaring, my boy, on fame's wings—but pause sufficiently on your journey to drink deeply and joyfully of the playtime of boyhood and the recreation of youth, for youth never pays a second visit to man." [4]

But even more satisfying than his moments at the movies or the dinner table were the hours he spent with children. As he grew older, the emptiness in his own life, his disappointment at not having a family, seemed to increase. He never missed an opportunity to remind friends that their children represented the only genuine treasures of life and that they should never lose sight of this. He once begged a political associate visiting in the mansion to stay half an hour longer so he could watch the man's youngsters asleep on the couch.

Old friends from Chicago, many of them Republicans, visited the mansion with their children. When this happened, Horner put all else aside. He conducted the children on a tour of Springfield and invariably they went home with a book (*Biff the Fire Dog* was a Horner favorite) to read in the car on the return journey. Luncheon at the mansion ended with taffy apples and peanut brittle.

Circuses and children go together, and Henry Horner loved both. Whenever the big top came to town, the governor passed the word through the appropriate channels that any child who did not have the price of a ticket should meet him at a certain gate. He always bought tickets and refreshments for the gang. If the governor noticed in the newspaper that a Springfield Boy Scout troop was planning a wiener roast on a day when he was free, the governor would go along. Two newsboys who delivered papers to the mansion were sometimes invited in for a chat and a snack by the governor. One day they showed up at the Statehouse to announce that they were returning the favor by taking the governor to lunch. The three went to a hamburger stand in the governor's limousine and sipped pop from a bottle with three straws.

Early one December Horner received a letter from a six-year-old Elkville girl, asking if he would use his influence to have Santa Claus bring her a doll and a toy piano. He replied that he would see to it that Santa did not forget her. One of the Christmas cards he received that year carried the mother's inscription: "Thanks for the joy you've given one poor little girl."

Money seemed to mean nothing to Horner except for the pleasure it brought others. The canceled checks preserved in his personal papers remain a vivid record of how he spent his money: payments to book stores, florists, candy stores, cigar stores, churches, synagogues, and charities. He gave $19 worth of marshmallows to a 4-H club camp; $500 for furnishing a room in St. John's Hospital; $275 for three rare volumes—*America on Stone* by Harry T. Peters and two volumes of *Currier & Ives, Print Makers to the American People*—which were gifts to Harry Hopkins. On an impulse he bought a $2,000 sapphire ring for a woman relative. Once, after V. Y. Dallman, the Springfield newspaper editor, had joined him at the state fair and admired a British keeshond in the dog show, the express company delivered a crate to Dallman containing a keeshond, which Dallman appropriately named Governor.

In the mid-winter of 1934 the State Arsenal burned in Springfield. The fire was banner news the next morning in the Springfield newspaper. Stuck away on the back page was a one-paragraph item about a tiny shack occupied by a widow and her children that had burned the same night. Horner sent Art O'Brien to find the woman and bring her to the mansion. Then, although Democratic county chairmen were beating him relentlessly with patronage demands, Horner arranged for her to have a state job.

CHAPTER TEN

C'mon, Governor, Get Mad

In December of 1933 the country's sorry social experiment designed to repress mankind's attraction for alcoholic beverages finally ended, fourteen years from its inception and several months too late for Tony Cermak. Illinois needed only fifty-five minutes to ratify the repeal amendment by convention on July 10. By December 5 enough states had followed to officially bury Prohibition.

In the vacuum left by the repeal of Prohibition, the states had the responsibility for prescribing the rules governing the sale of liquor. In Illinois, this would be the difference of opinion that would separate Governor Horner and Mayor Kelly. Because he had forfeited his claim to party leadership, and because he had had a hand in the creation of Mayor Kelly (by signing the act enabling Kelly's special election by the city council), the governor never was distracted by any pangs of subservience to the Chicago leader. Kelly, on the other hand, thought of Horner as the same malleable party servant who had always bowed before the domination of the Kennas, Harrisons, and Cermaks. In effect, Kelly believed that he had inherited Cermak's control, a concept that failed, however, to register with the governor.

Irrespective of this misunderstanding, the old familiar collision between Chicago's School of Personal Liberty and the contrasting social forces, largely of a regional nature, that had begotten Prohibition in the first place could probably not have been avoided in the special session that was called for the imposition of state liquor controls. Repeal had been brought about, Horner said, chiefly because liquor regulation was properly recognized as a function of the states. "We are now about to enter upon a new experiment," he continued, "to ascertain whether a large measure of personal liberty may be restored to the individual under such regulations as will promote the good order of society and protect the general welfare. Only forward-looking legislation can accomplish the two ends which are of paramount importance—obedience to and regard for law and self-control and moderation." With actual repeal but two weeks off, he considered prompt action by the legislature imperative. Recalling that both party platforms had been explicit in their opposition to the return of the old-time saloon, Horner said it would be unthinkable to bring back liquor without state controls of any sort.

After a Chicago alderman shot a policeman at an all-night drinking party attended by the mayor and the county sheriff, Dick Finnegan's Chicago *Times* mounted a crusading campaign for the strongest possible state controls. "The old saloon," his editorial declared, "was a political saloon. The saloon and politics must be separated. The governor knows that; so does the mayor." Finnegan demanded guarantees that government agencies would be protected from the domination by saloon interests that had characterized Cermak's era. Liquor licenses, the *Times* felt, should be permitted neither for public officials nor for those holding offices in political parties. "Sad, but true," the editorial asserted, "there is not in Illinois a conspicuous public man who sees the liquor problem as President Roosevelt sees it. . . . He personally asked the Chicago City Council and the Illinois General Assembly to remove those evils of the liquor traffic which 'harm good government, law and order.' " [1]

When Finnegan telegraphed the editorial to the governor's office, Horner fired back this answer:

"Dear Dick: The amendment you refer to in your telegram today has been introduced in the senate even though your editorial writer seems to think there is not 'a conspicuous public man in the state who sees the liquor problem right.' You ought to know that no one desires the divorce of politics and the liquor problem more than I do. Please read the bill and the amendments proposed. Et Tu? Henry Horner." [2]

Another editorial followed the next day, and Horner wired another comment:

". . . I am at a loss to know what your editorial means by its reference to a Horner-Kelly program. Do you know of such a program and are you familiar with the Horner program? I assume you have read the editorial, but I can't believe you wrote it. My heartiest felicitations to you and your lovely family."

"The editorial writer was myself," Finnegan confided in a letter to the governor. "I do believe that before the legislature gets through something is going to come from getting you thoroughly aroused." He said he hoped to see Horner not just as a judicially-minded executive conscious of public sentiment on the saloon question, but as a protagonist so zealous "that sparks will fly if any selfish interest monkeys with the buzz saw." The editor wrote:

> You may be surprised to hear it, but a lot of folks have the idea that you and Mayor Kelly may be shadowboxing and that you have an agreement to do some feinting. . . . You are the Gibraltar on which the people of the state tied their anchor lines a year ago in November—you and President Roosevelt. It was not the Democratic Party as much as you may think. Or at least as some of the Democratic leaders still think it was. The party in this state is going around in a fog. If you don't lead the donkey where he may not want to go, but where his health may be better, there just isn't going to be any grass for him after a while. As to the Horner-Kelly program—whether there is one or is not is not so important as the fact there are 8,300 places spilling liquor in Chicago, that some of them are terrible joints, selling terrible booze, and that this is what the legislature, Horner, and Kelly have let come upon us. . . . It hasn't made you as angry as I thought it might. I may have the wrong idea but I think I am doing my small part to steer you away from withering criticism later on, if you let the pressure slip you back a few notches. You are young enough and have enough young friends to appreciate what new ideas are permeating social, industrial, legal, educational, and legislative thinking of the country in this metamorphosis from a dying philosophy. The old men don't see it. Even some of those with young physiques nowadays are old men. Unfortunately, the ideas of old men have too much weight. Heaven protect you from the hang-overs. Heaven send you some colleagues who are not hang-overs. My holiday wish for you is one of such sentimental personal regard that I can endure even your temporary displeasure, and if I can arouse you to the understanding of what I have told you personally and written you—namely, that Henry Horner must look out for Henry Horner. Nobody else will look out for him. To do this properly, he must have very close to him folks that are aware of

> far more than routine. I still think you need some idea hunters, men that aren't in politics. My wish for you this eventful Christmas is that you can find some. Certainly I hope that the surging affairs of 1934 will see a lightening of your personal burdens by a small corps of progressive horsemen who can ride with you anyplace and tell the professional politicians to go to blazes.[3]

Whatever shadowboxing might have been going on soon turned into real slugging. Kelly wanted the state to keep its hands off Chicago liquor control, licensing, and regulating, for the sake of home rule. The governor insisted on enough strings in the law to be certain that the "old saloon" could not return. His bill provided that a tavern must serve food too. To do that, Kelly jested, would be a farce; taverns could comply with the law by serving rubber sandwiches.

"We might as well face the facts," summed up Harold Ward, Kelly's Senate leader. "We've got high-brow wets and low-brow wets. The low-brow wets are in the majority and they want the saloon." At a Democratic conference in the governor's office Horner asked the Chicago senator to "come up front, Harold." But Ward answered, "I'm sorry, Governor, but this is one time I take a back seat."

Consequently, repeal went into effect in Illinois without a state control act. Chicago newspapers assigned reporters to log the old familiar police radio calls—"Intoxicated man causing a disturbance on second floor at 5426 Augusta"; "Drunk lying in the street at 1484 Milwaukee." Just before Christmas, Horner demanded publicly that Kelly release his bloc of votes. "I'm growing tired of having the administration obstructed by personal and private interests in matters affecting the welfare of the entire state," he said. Kelly, who was licking his chops in anticipation of the political advantage that would go along with the unfettered control of thousands of liquor licenses, defined their differences as a question of "territoriality." "I don't know," the mayor said, "whether it's the governor or the downstate dries around him who are trying to kick Chicago all over the lot." He clung to his demand that Chicago be allowed to make its own liquor rules and complained that Horner's plan would bring back the "snooping era of Prohibition." The governor reflected that it had been a mistake to repeal Prohibition at all until a concrete plan of liquor control had been worked out.

Not until May of 1934 did Illinois finally get a compromise

liquor control measure. Regulatory powers were shared by the city with a state agency, and most public officers were forbidden to hold liquor licenses; but there were no restrictions on party leaders or legislators, as Finnegan had wanted.

In the midst of the liquor control disagreement, Mayor Kelly dispatched his 1933 Christmas greetings to the governor: "I want you to know that I am thinking of you and remembering your fine friendship which has been and is a real privilege to me. Life would be rather drab if it were not for the friends we have—those who fulfill the real meaning of the word and who are willing to carry out every obligation it implies."

That cryptic last sentence might well have set Horner to wondering about what obligations it *would* imply.

II

An unhappy reality that eventually confronts any high-minded idealist in public office is that besides having to resist the greedy instincts of many of those surrounding him, he is also doomed to disappoint many of his old friends who lack any understanding of how things do or do not get done. Shortly after he took office, Horner began receiving letters like this from old acquaintances: "Is it possible that one of the finest men who ever sat on the bench or assumed a high office is becoming 'a bit political'? God, I hope not!"

A few months later, the Chicago *Times* published this column by James Weber Linn, a noted liberal at the University of Chicago:

> Henry Horner, the keenest intellectual and the most sympathetic idealist to hold the office of governor of Illinois in the present century . . . is getting the worst "press" of any governor in my memory. Worse even than that great idealist, John P. Altgeld. Hardly a paper in the state is willing to pay the slightest attention to the innumerable good things Horner has done. Eighty-five per cent of Illinois papers are either fanatically Republican (downstate) or fanatically anti-Roosevelt (in Chicago). . . . This effort to discredit him goes as far as picturing him as a "dictator" and even worse. A Springfield dirt agency has sent everywhere paragraphs of innuendo regarding his personal life in the Governor's mansion. Insinuations were made regarding the Governor's luncheon at which the Duncan sisters were present.
>
> Lies about the Governor of Illinois, even a failure to do

justice to him, are of national concern. This particular governor happens also to be a Jew, in a period when anti-Semitism is being eagerly encouraged by a certain type of politician all over the world. Horner, a Jew with genuine nobility of character, becomes, therefore, incidentally a figure for those who despise anti-Semitism to rally round and point to. Yet many Jews of my acquaintance are deceived by misleading press accounts.

To anyone who knows the facts, Governor Horner's mistakes are open and palpable. He "kills himself by inches" by unwillingness to delegate details. He spends fourteen hours a day at work. A judge by training accustomed to familiarizing himself with every detail of every document, he has consistently refused to organize a group of fact-finders around him at Springfield who could acquaint him, as Roosevelt is acquainted, with all such details in summarized form; and so, some of his decisions and appointments are delayed.

Made irritable by his fearful industry, he is called "not cordial" by newspaper correspondents in Springfield, and even by old friends who go to see him at the mansion and are kept waiting. And finally, eager to put four-fifths of his time on matters of social welfare, in which he always has been primarily interested, he has permitted himself to be distracted into giving social welfare matters less than a twentieth of his almost endless working time.

But these (except for his passion for detail) are picayunish matters. In comparison with his grasp of the principles of state legislation, with his determination for economy and efficient spending, with his inherent sympathy for the underdog, with his power of statement when he allows himself to be concise, with his constancy of purpose and fineness of character, these things are as dust in the balance. Yet a hostile press has maneuvered to get his accomplishments minimized, his acts misinterpreted even by school teachers, his political diplomacy called "dictatorship" by one group and "subservience to an organization" by another, and his unshaken devotion to the service of the state defined as "fussiness." Well, I can't do anything about it. He could. But he won't. I wish he would.[4]

It seemed especially difficult for the governor to please his old Jewish friends. One of them, Jennie Purvin, complained that he was hedged in by so many "self-seeking politicians, some of them unfortunately Jews,"[5] that he was unable to see through to the world outside. Horner wrote back that he was hedged in not by politicians "but by the many problems that are constantly bearing down on me." He told her that he worked seventeen hours a day seven days a week.

On a Saturday afternoon in 1934, seven hundred Jewish precinct captains, roughly one-fifth of the total Chicago Democratic organization, met in the Morrison Hotel at Alderman Arvey's call. Harry Fisher talked about the collective interests of Jews and said that there were unlimited possibilities for any Jewish precinct captain who really applied himself to his duties. Then Barnet Hodes mounted the rostrum. He agreed that it was a good idea to try to build new Jewish personalities, but reminded those present that two years earlier they had been instrumental in the election of the greatest Jewish personality in the state to the governorship. Hodes went on to say that Horner no longer enjoyed the enthusiastic support of Jews and had even been under open attack by his own people. He suggested that Jews should think twice about abandoning their Jewish hero.[6]

By the following year, however, Hodes had been disappointed by Horner's strict demands upon the men in his administration. He switched his allegiance and his flair for promotion to Mayor Kelly. Even Colonel McCormick's *Tribune* exhibited little enthusiasm for a genuine Republican fight against the Democrat in the mayor's office, and Kelly piled up 799,060 votes to 167,106 for his opponent. This tremendous achievement impressed the White House. FDR now looked with new awe upon the mighty Democratic machine in Chicago. Figures of such proportions struck a responsive chord in this thoroughly practical political leader. Thereafter, there could no longer be any doubt that when Illinois came to Roosevelt's attention, his antenna would be turned first to Ed Kelly. Kelly now could go to Washington and deal with authority on subjects like the distribution of Works Progress Administration largess in Illinois. The impression that the mayor, not the governor, was the man to see in his state was helped along by the junior senator from Illinois. Bill Dieterich and Henry Horner were entirely different political types and hit it off badly. While Dieterich was a downstate judge, he had spent most of his tenure as a visiting jurist in Chicago. He fitted the stereotype of the Chicago politician much more closely than did Horner.

Then too the governor's clashes with Barrett and Stelle became more frequent. Once, after he had a few drinks, Horner explained, "Well, you see, those boys are on the other side of the fence. They think it's greener on my side. And whenever they reach their hand over the fence, I slap it." It distressed him that some of those who had been responsible for his election could not be put in positions of public trust. In one letter he said, "Most of my friends have been loyal and understanding, although I have had a few shocking disappointments in this respect." Once while the governor was talking with Paul Angle about appointments to the Federal Writers' Project, the historian noted that many of the jobs had gone to political hacks. "You talk as though all politicians are crooked," Horner retorted angrily. A few minutes later, after the conversation had changed course, the governor suddenly returned to the topic with the after-comment: "You know, you *are* goddamned near right at that."

The strength to stand up under these pressures was missing in a man who was still adjusting to the loss of Tony Cermak. During an especially depressing period, Horner referred to the "constant and tremendous pressure on me. There seems to be no letup in the work that is continuously heaped on the governor's desk. Everytime I leave my desk for a day it means that I must spend two evenings far into the night to catch up with my work." Endless demands for favors from old acquaintances in the name of friendship drained his energies still further. Lloyd Whitman pestered his former law partner with unsolicited advice and requests for jobs for himself, his sons, and others. One of his letters referred to Horner as a "cold-blooded efficiency machine." He wanted a commerce commission appointment, which, if granted, "would constitute that recognition by you, the lack of which has now a long time been a definite professional handicap to me." Whitman also represented a convict seeking executive clemency and sent a stream of vitriolic letters in his client's behalf. Another time, after his political advice had been ignored, Whitman informed Art O'Brien:

> Nuts to you and the likes of you, say I. You so-called practical politicians haven't the brains to know brains when you meet them, and of course don't appreciate that this is a day of ideas, not of mere flat, stale and unprofitable so-called practical politics. . . . A really great mind would recognize and seize upon a man of my intelligence and enthusiasm as a pearl of great price. One might infer that you and your boss think that while you were growing up these past 25 years I stood still and today am not good enough to manure your roots, let alone sniff the blossoms of your greatness. Go to h——! [7]

Ella Cornwall confided in a note to a co-worker that "Mr. Whitman's letters are getting to be the bane of my existence." The times made men desperate, even those devoted to Horner. To one job seeker, the governor wrote, "One of the banes of my life is to try to find positions. I have, however, no difficulty finding work for myself."

Still the pressures persisted. The Rockford *Daily Journal* reminded the governor that "last fall when [you] were a candidate, the Rockford *Journal* was the only paper that gave the Governor its wholehearted support. Now that the state fair is about to start, the *Journal* is the only paper that has been left out of the advertising program. Would you call this reciprocity?"

One of the highest officials in his administration wanted to sell the state a building he owned in downtown Chicago. Even Jim Levy, the governor's brother, wired—"I sincerely hope you can see fit to favor me on the nine trucks and compressors for highway division."

The governor gave his personal attention to letters like this: "As usual, I am looking for something. My thinking is that the Number One license plate would make me very happy, and whoever you intended to assign this number to would be just as happy with Number Four. Also, if there is another number somewhere under the hundred figure I would like very much to have it for my son George." Horner took great delight in answering that, although he would be only too glad to accommodate, the authority for license number allocation rested with Secretary of State Edward Hughes, to whom the correspondent should direct his perfectly reasonable request. The fact that low-number license plates were carefully dispensed to big campaign contributors and that the Roman Catholic archbishop of Chicago, a personality of some political significance, had a rather secure grip on Number One, did not detract from the governor's satisfaction in shunting one of his many appeals to another public official.

Not all the pressure bearing upon him could be considered so lightly. Horner's official papers document his attempts to resist influence. Among the governor's Christmas gifts his first year in office was a beer mug from "an old pal" in the American Concrete Expansion Joint Company of Chicago. Such familiarity nettled the governor and, upon checking, he discovered that the firm had received some $400,000 worth of highway contracts because no competitor had been able to meet the specifications. Horner ordered the specifications broadened to permit bidding by others. Subsequently, a former political associate, a Chicago Democrat who had been helpful during Horner's political apprenticeship, organized the National Road Joint Manufacturing Company. To his friend's astonishment, however, the governor appointed a committee of civil engineers from the faculty of the University of Illinois to conduct road joint tests. When the committee found National's joints lacking in performance, Horner's former associate responded with the following letter to the governor, dated July 28, 1937:

> Delay in obtaining approval of the joint in Illinois . . . has crucified us in other states. Upon your assurance and positive promises given me several times that the joint would be approved, I invested not only every dollar I had, but also the money Mrs. ______ [his wife] saved up, and was even obliged to secure loans which are coming due and I shall stand to lose all. In view of what I have done for you during the many years, I cannot believe you will bring about my financial destruction.[8]

As an aftermath of the entire experience, the governor became fond of W. C. Huntington, the engineering professor who served as chairman of the committee, and presented him with the gift of a personally engraved watch.

The methods that were used by some of his old family friends distressed the governor. At the annual New Year's Day receptions it was not unusual for a mother to walk through the mansion receiving line with a son, ask for a state job for him, and stubbornly refuse to move on until a promise had been extracted. Friends bothered him with personal matters, such as recommendations for private employment, most of which he refused. An especially steady torrent of ideas and requests came in from his own area of Chicago, Hyde Park. Letters from merchants suggested ingenious ideas for leasing various parcels of their real estate to the state. Patronage brokers demanded that some state employees be "viced" and others "placed" in their jobs. Somebody was always after a contract for this or that. Pressure for judgeships never ceased.

Would-be big-time operators (seemingly always coming or going from "the Coast") bombarded the governor with tips of all sorts, trying to give the impression that all they did was dash about the globe telling people what a great governor Illinois had. One such operator was Julius Klein—promoter, public relations man, confidant of important people. Wires (invariably signed "Your Pal") flowed into the mansion. "Like to see you as soon as possible to tell you what's what . . ." Or, from Minocqua, Wisconsin, "Spending the weekend with Ed Kelly . . ." Klein specialized in "the Jewish Question," his correspondence seemed to indicate, and he appeared to be forever proposing joint Lehman-Horner statements ("You will speak as an American governor, not only as a representative of our people"). After Joe Louis disposed of the German Max Schmeling in their second boxing encounter, Klein excitedly wired Governor Horner from ringside: "Cannot tell you what this Louis victory means. It is the greatest asset for our cause. I am so happy." Klein suspected, however, that some of those around the governor did not appreciate him, and one year this letter to Ella Cornwall followed on the heels of a telegram—"I sent the governor a telegram on Thanksgiving Day and am wondering if he ever received it or whether or not some 'well wishers' kept the wire away from him. I see that he acknowledged telegrams from a lot of other people and although it isn't necessary to acknowledge mine I am curious to know if certain people around the governor are still poisoning him against his real friends." [9]

III

Horner did not qualify as a "professional Jew." As early as July of 1933, Samson Horn wrote in the Jewish magazine *Opinion* that the governor had not been doing all he could to combat anti-Jewish propaganda in the United States. Horn pointed out that Horner's causes had never included Zionism, the movement to establish and preserve a Jewish homeland. To him, said Horn, an American Jew differed in only one respect from his neighbors—his religion. The writer recalled that the Jews of Chicago had held a meeting "when blood shone on the moon over Germany" and that Horner had delivered one of the shorter speeches, with Governor Paul McNutt of Indiana making the principal address. Horn correctly characterized Chicago, which Bill Thompson had once called the sixth German city of the world, as already a focal point of the Hitlerian infection.

In 1937, when President Roosevelt journeyed to Chicago for the dedication of the Outer Drive bridge, a committee of prominent Jewish citizens asked Horner to prevail upon the president to speak out soon for assistance to the Jews in Poland. After Roosevelt's return to Washington, Horner wrote Marvin McIntyre, the president's secretary, saying that the bridge dedication visit had not been the time or the occasion to make this suggestion. "Would it be asking too much of you to submit the subject to the President when you can get his ear, that he may consider the propriety of mentioning the subject in some proper way?" Horner wrote. "It is important to humanity generally that the minorities, including Jews, of all countries be treated with the tolerance and respect that is due them from understanding Nations . . ." The hesitant tone of his letter reflects the governor's uneasiness about linking his public office and his faith.[10]

He paid especially close attention to state purchases from Jewish vendors. When a Springfield merchant supplied an inferior grade of caps to a state welfare institution, he exploded with rage. "You have disgraced me and you have disgraced our people," he screamed. "If you don't replace this merchandise I'll get you in the courts." The same happened to a produce merchant who was a friend and a campaign contributor. On that occasion the governor personally accompanied the purchasing agent to Jacksonville when the freight cars were unloaded to reveal half-full cases of inferior fruit.

It would be erroneous, though, to conclude that Horner closed either his mind or his heart to the persecution of his fellow Jews in Europe. In 1934 he refused to participate in a Lincoln's Birthday program because the German ambassador would be on the program. "The Hitler flag to me is a flag of hate," he explained. He did his best to help Jewish refugee doctors from Europe find medical positions in state institutions. As an example of the desperate times, an unemployed former University of Illinois professor persuaded Eddie Cantor, the Hollywood celebrity, to request that the governor give him a job as an attendant in a mental institution.

A few anti-Semitic letters arrived in the governor's office, but not many. One, signed by a Pat Kelly, insinuated that Horner had been responsible for the removal of Father Coughlin's broadcasts from a Chicago radio station. "When it comes to insulting our priests," Kelly declared, "it's time we are up in arms against you and the Jewish people. Hitler was too foxy for them but they can make a sucker out of the U. S. . . . We will never stand for another Jew governor."

During Horner's governorship forty-three men and one woman were put to death in the electric chair. The execution of the first of these, Morris Cohen, on October 13, 1933, brought a cry of protest from the Jewish community because the electrocution of a Jew was permitted to occur on a Jewish religious holiday. Later, Bishop Griffin called the governor's attention to another execution scheduled for Good Friday. The object of this death penalty happened to be a woman, Gertrude Puhse, forty-four, who had helped another man do away with her husband. A woman had not been executed in Illinois since 1845, and Horner decided to commute Mrs. Puhse's sentence to ninety-nine years.

Understandably, this responsibility for rendering final judgment on death penalties weighed grievously on so sensitive and humane a man as Horner. However, he also retained his judicial objectivity and, in spite of his personal opposition to the death penalty, insisted on factual legal grounds before exercising his power of executive clemency. He read the court record in death cases, looking for some legal justification for commutation. "I have an oath to enforce the law," he often explained. "I don't make the law, nor do I pass judgment on it. Why this responsibility on me?" Prior to the Puhse case and many times thereafter he worried over death cases that involved women. "How could I permit a woman to be executed?" he asked himself and others. Several other execution orders were commuted after the Puhse case, one on the strength of a psychiatric examination showing the prisoner to be "of a disordered mind."

But in 1936 a mother of four, Mrs. Marie Porter, thirty-eight years old, was sentenced to death for killing her brother after having taken out an insurance policy on his life. The judge remarked from the bench that Governor Horner had said publicly that no woman would be executed while he was governor. Nevertheless, Horner concluded that "if there was ever a perfect case against a murderer, this is it." He decided, therefore, not to intervene. "Notwithstanding my views as to the death penalty as punishment for murder," he said, "it is the law of this state and a law which we are bound to observe. I have searched the record of this case and have been unable to find any circumstances to mitigate the heinousness of the crime."

On January 28, 1938, the governor went to an early evening movie with a friend. At eleven o'clock they returned to the mansion and waited nervously as Mrs. Porter was prepared for the walk to the electric chair in Menard Penitentiary. Phone calls came in from lawyers in other states who offered to act as appeal counsel. Beads of perspiration covered Horner's bald head and jowls, and he walked up to his bedroom to gaze at the picture of his mother over his bed. At one minute after midnight a flash of electricity killed Marie Porter. The governor retired for a sleepless night.

In 1937 the son of a rabbi, Joseph Rappaport, had been sentenced to death for killing a government informer who was to have testified against him in a narcotics case. A stay of execution was first granted because the electrocution date fell on a Jewish holiday. Despite extreme pressure from rabbis and an ancient curse cast upon him in a Chicago railroad station by Rappaport's sister Rose, Horner permitted the young man to be executed after a lie detector test removed any doubt, the governor thought, of his guilt. "I can't afford to be a sentimentalist in this job," he said. The experience upset him, his blood pressure shot upward, and his heart rate became fast and arrhythmic for weeks afterward.

IV

As if in one tremendous never-ending waterfall, the reverses, pressures, and disappointments cascaded down upon the governor's head. The Chicago *Tribune* turned on him with a vengeance when Roosevelt's NRA compliance provisions were introduced in the Illinois legislature. A *Tribune* cartoon labeled "To the Highest Bidder" showed the state on an NRA slave block being offered for sale by the legislature in return for a bag of federal patronage from Farley. To the *Tribune* it was always the "NRA tyranny law." A short time before, Colonel McCormick had sent Horner a copy of a long rambling speech he had given to a Northwestern University audience on "The Prospect for America." A note was enclosed. "When I return [from a southern trip]," it said, "I want to meet with you and have a long talk. I believe that between us we can save this country and that if we do not no one else will. We have an opportunity and a duty." The colonel shipped gifts of sides of beef to the governor from the *Tribune*'s experimental farm. Near the end of his first administration Horner said he asked McCormick if he had been a good governor, and that the colonel had answered in the affirmative. "Then why do you attack me?" the governor asked. "Because I want to get Roosevelt and the only way to do that is to defeat such officials as you who uphold him and help him," McCormick is said to have answered. There is an amusing postscript to the governor's relations with the powerful Chicago publisher. John B. Davis, McCormick's chauffeur and bodyguard, had been issued a state police star and identification card as a courtesy. The state police discovered, though, that Davis had been taking his law enforcement prerogatives too seriously and had been stopping errant motorists and reprimanding them for traffic violations. Horner directed the state police to demand the return of the star, and one evening the badge was dropped off at the Executive Mansion, without comment, by an unidentified messenger.

Unlike a true professional, Horner did not develop enough protective armor to prevent barbs from persons whom he respected from pricking his conscience. When old friends criticized him, he grieved. In the thirties there was indeed a ready supply of concerns to excite liberals. Two of the most obvious examples were bills before the legislature to investigate alleged Communist activity at the University of Chicago and to require loyalty oaths of school teachers.

One morning in a stack of letters served along with his breakfast Governor Horner opened this one—marked "personal please" —from Dick Finnegan: [11]

> Dear Henry:
>
> Have you or haven't you a brain to think with? Have you a fist to double? Can't you raise some Cain? Don't you know what is happening in this country? Injustice is happening. Slavery is happening. Every conceivable kind of cruelty and crookedness is happening.
>
> School houses are closed and school teachers are going hungry. Patriotism and reverence are rotting. Why?
>
> Because you don't get mad.
>
> C'mon, Governor, get mad. Who is responsible for this cruelty, this crookedness that is destroying men and patriotism? Why you are, Governor, because when it comes to getting right down to brass tacks, you're just not there—you don't get mad. You have no heart throb. You don't double your fist and you don't raise Cain.
>
> Strange as it seems, Governor, you're indicted with the rest of us. But since we can't convict you, we're going to stand by and see the school teachers and the schools and the universities convicted. Attaboy, Governor, get out the old Simon Legree whip and drive the school teachers up to take the oath of allegiance. Chase the Communistic dogs off the college campuses. Then we'll restore patriotism in the United States and there won't be any injustice. Slavery will disappear. Cruelty and crookedness will slink into their ratholes. The millions of men who are standing in the breadlines rotting will again believe in themselves, in their God, in their country and their fellow men. Their pride, ambition and their self-respect will return and this will be a wonderful world. Our vast nation will be beautiful and free again, proud and strong.
>
> Ain't it something, Governor? If you don't believe it, I seen it

in the paper and I hope you ain't one of those guys who don't believe nothin' he reads in the paper.

Take a look, Governor. C'mon, get mad!

Henry Horner's reaction to this remarkable communication from his old Skeeter pal is not recorded. He did not answer the letter. It can be assumed, however, that he was shocked and dazed and set to thinking. For soon after, Horner's heart would indeed throb, his fist would double, and he would raise a fair amount of Cain.

CHAPTER ELEVEN

...And Two Cents for the Jew

In the state of Illinois the normal instincts which are supposed to direct the quest for public office are qualified by geography. Illinois sweeps down from the shore of Lake Michigan all the way to the Ohio River. Its dominating metropolis is perched at the top, as though on a throne. Regional differences in history and in social and cultural background have combined with the dynamics of political power to produce this general rule: the controlling political force in Chicago ordinarily cannot be expected to work smoothly with one of its own men in the Governor's Mansion *if* the leader of the local government and the governor are forceful individuals each intent on fulfilling his leadership responsibilities to the constituency he represents. The mayor of Chicago and the governor of Illinois have always seemed to run on different tracks, and until Chicago obtains the measure of home rule it deserves they probably always will. In 1871, after the Chicago Fire, the mayor went directly to the federal government for troops to help restore law and order. This irritated the governor, John Palmer. At the time of the railroad strike of 1894 the mayor disregarded Governor Altgeld's wishes and appealed to the federal government for troops. Thus, even without their policy disagreements, it is questionable whether Horner and Kelly could have pulled in harness for long. As the leader of the party, Kelly thought Horner should telephone and "check in" when he came to

Chicago. "Why should I call him?" Horner would reply. "I've got nothing to say to him. I'm the governor of this state." In his personal conversation with other Irish politicians Kelly sometimes referred to Horner derisively as "The Goose," underworld jargon for "The Jew." Horner became impatient with Kelly's attitude and with the dubious projects that he tried to ram through the legislature without much regard for the rest of the state.

The sharp instrument with which to lance this festering boil appeared at the 1935 session of the legislature. Casting about for new ways to pay its teachers and police, the Chicago city administration proposed that horse racing handbooks—bookies—be licensed by the city and therefore operate openly under regulation, as taverns did. The number of such establishments would be "limited" to twenty-five hundred in Chicago. Half of the licensing fee revenue would be used for schools, half for the city's general corporate fund.

Compared with this proposal for a vast system of legalized gambling dens, with its invitation for control by the remnants of the Capone mob and their political partners, the gang warfare during Prohibition might have resembled Sunday school musical chairs. But of even greater anxiety to the Protestant world downstate was the "moral issue." Horner's old Masonic acquaintance, Louie Lewis of Christopher, for example, had been brought up as one of eleven children in a Baptist farm family where father lectured at the supper table on the sinful evils of "chance taking." In Chicago, where the heritage of Tony Cermak remained strong, such attitudes were not as prevalent. However, operating out of the office of the Speaker of the House, and helped by Treasurer Stelle, Mayor Kelly won over some of the downstate votes by agreeing to eliminate the downstate area from the coverage of the bill and by pleading for revenue assistance.

Early in the session Horner told Kelly he could never "go for" a bill that provided public sanction for gambling. There are several signs that at this point in the governor's career the prodding from Dick Finnegan and his other old friends had started to sink in. But he did not assert specifically that he would veto the bookie bill if it passed. He remained silent while the bill rolled through the House, 89 to 53, and through the Senate, 31 to 14.

As to the possibility that the governor might not sign the measure, Kelly remarked on a number of occasions—clearly intending his words to get back to Horner—that "if he vetoes this I'll veto him right out of his job." Lewis and the other downstaters were shocked by such talk, but the governor kept his silence, both to Kelly and to the public.

From downstate church groups in particular, the protests poured into the governor's office. To avoid mansion telephone calls, Horner fled to an unlikely scene for contemplating the legislation before him—the state fairgrounds. On July 10 Attorney General Kerner rendered a favorable legal opinion on the bill's constitutionality. On July 11, just four hours before the measure would have become law without his signature, Horner vetoed it.

In judicial tones he first explained the possible constitutional objections to the act, all of which had been found to be invalid by the state's chief legal adviser. Horner did not dispute Kerner's legal conclusions. Then he proceeded to analyze the measure:

> I know of no other piece of legislation passed by the 59th General Assembly which can affect so immeasurably, for good or ill, the people of this state. It is revolutionary in that we abandon definitely an attitude toward public gambling which has been fundamental since laws have been written for this state. This policy finds expression in the spirit if not the words incorporated in the present Constitution of this state:
>
> > "The General Assembly shall have no power to authorize lotteries or gift enterprises for any purpose, and shall pass laws to prohibit the sale of lottery or gift enterprise tickets in this state."
>
> It may be traced back to the Constitution of 1848; to the laws of the Northwest Territory before this territory was carved into states and even back to the common law which gave birth to the great legal principles which animate our jurisprudence.
>
> I have weighed fairly and carefully the arguments advanced for and against enactment of this legislation. I recognize that merely because it is an innovation, a change in long-established policy, it is not necessarily wrong or harmful. Changing conditions do warrant changes of customs and habits, of thought and action. But if we have fallen into conditions which are not what we may think they ought to be, this does not justify the lowering of standards.
>
> The principal argument for House Bill 1045 seems to be that the desire to gamble is inherent in human nature, that it cannot be suppressed or eradicated and therefore it should be permitted, regulated and legalized with a portion of the profits accruing to government.
>
> It is readily admitted that the desire to gamble is found in most persons—perhaps in some form and to some extent in all

persons. Its prevalence, however, does not stamp it as a virtue. Nor do I concede that public and commercialized gambling cannot largely be suppressed; even it if cannot be entirely eradicated. Because there are violations of a law, it does not follow that the law should be repealed. If there is any justification in legalized bookmaking, there is equal justification in legalizing all other forms of public gambling now prohibited.

One of the arguments used in favor of licensing bookmaking is that there are only occasional instances where results to the public are disastrous. Unfortunately, we have no statistics from which to draw our facts, but surely there are many instances where the lure of public gambling has led to embezzlements, prison sentences, mistreated and broken families.

We need not concern ourselves so much as to persons whose self control can hold their desire within bounds, but society must supply the protection for the weaker members who cannot resist practices which result disastrously.

So far as I know, licensed bookmaking has been proposed for no other state or city in the United States. No such law has been adopted for any other state or city. It will be without my aid if our state becomes the pioneer in legalizing public and commercialized gambling such as is proposed in this bill. It is a hazardous experiment for a state to legalize a business which is now illegal everywhere in the country.

House Bill 1045, as first introduced, authorized all municipalities to license, tax and regulate bookmaking. In order to secure its passage, its proponents amended it to apply only to Chicago. It is of interest that the General Assembly living outside of Chicago permitted for that city what they would not tolerate for their own communities.

The fact that the proceeds of the municipal licensing of bookmaking under the bill go to city revenues and schools does not justify our approval of the bill.

After careful consideration of this question, I am convinced that the consequences of the adoption of this law would be inimical to the best interests of the people of Chicago, and I therefore veto and withhold my approval of this bill.[1]

Horner's coolly reasoned veto message smacked the faces of the Chicago Democrats like a pail of icy water. In later years some of them claimed their anger stemmed not so much from Horner's veto as from his keeping them in suspense, allowing them to go through the motions of passing the bill—"making us look like a bunch of second-story men," as Kelly himself once expressed it. Another bill, which had failed to pass by a straight party-line vote, called for permanent voter registration. The Chicago Democrats were horrified by the idea that signatures would be maintained to help establish the eligibility of voters.

Most surviving contemporaries agree that Kelly's threat to veto Horner out of his job had been, at the time, little more than a tactical bluff. The mayor knew that the governor could be shoved around by Cermak, so why not by him? Surely a governor could not be denied renomination just because he had refused to swallow a controversial piece of legislation, especially when the White House was occupied by a strong president of the same party who had been helped immeasurably by that governor. Or could he?

II

One day, on a trip to Chicago, the governor stopped for lunch in one of the many small towns along the way. In his accustomed fashion he ate heartily, and a full stomach usually brought out his most jovial mood. When it came time to pay the check, Horner guffawed loudly and asked, winking at his companions, just what the extra two cents added to the price were for. "Oh," remarked the poker-faced and less than alert restaurant owner, "that's for the Jew in Springfield."

As a matter of fact, throughout much of the state a grumbling grocery store dialogue had become stylish, the housewife muttering "and two cents for the Jew" when she plunked down the extra two pennies in sales tax. John Stelle and his associates capitalized on this discontent, organizing delegations of downstaters to carry the message to City Hall that downstate would never retain in office a governor who had slapped them with a sales tax.

Horner knew about all this but was not impressed. With an almost haughty air he laughed and said, "They've got to take me and my record. They have no choice. The White House will see to it." Homer Mat Adams, superintendent of sales tax investigations, supplied his sizable force of investigators with material to answer the tax complaints. The state was not only paying its way now but had paid its debts. If the state had been compelled to depend only on a property tax, the public welfare institutions would be closed, the roads full of holes, the public schools closed, the needy in revolution, the state government $50,000,000 deeper in debt. "Which is better," asked Adams, "the spending of money for relief or bullets? If our millions of unemployed were left without relief or work of some kind, there would be bloodshed and revolution."

Horner devoted his Governor's Day speech at the state fair primarily to a defense of President Roosevelt, jabbing at the Republican legislators who "offered only a stone when we asked them to provide bread for the starving." He said he stood ready to lead the party in 1936. This proposition evoked a lack of response from the other speakers on that occasion. Mayor Kelly not only did not attend; he did not even send a telegram.

While the governor persisted in remaining aloof, his troubles piled higher. The Young Jewish Lawyers' Association resolved in Chicago that "for the good of the Democratic party and conscience-bound as Jews," they could not support Horner for re-election. Among their reasons the lawyers cited the governor's refusal to grant a stay of execution to the Jew electrocuted on Yom Kippur, pointing out that he had postponed the execution of a man with an Irish name on the same day.[2] A Democratic state senator from Collinsville, James Monroe, made public a letter to Horner, which he had written on October 3, 1935, asking him not to run:

> It may turn out that the party leaders are stupid enough or sufficiently lacking in interest to permit you to run without making any effort to prevail on you otherwise. I sincerely hope this will not be the case for it amounts to defaulting on our control of state government. And it will entail heavy losses to our whole ticket throughout the state. That is the thing that concerns me. . . . I estimate that you would run from 300,000 to 500,000 votes behind the ticket, and hurt everyone else besides. . . . I feel it is my duty to speak this bluntly and emphatically to you in the hope that you will put the welfare of Illinois above any ambitions you may have to continue in high office.

Another Democratic legislator, Representative Frank McClure of Galesburg, presented a different kind of indictment:

> Three years ago the people of this state said they were dissatisfied with the administration of the affairs of the state of Illinois. They said they wanted a Democratic administration. The people didn't say they wanted a Democratic governor and a Republican assistant. They didn't say they wanted a Democratic governor and a Republican in charge of the motor vehicle policies of the state. They didn't say they wanted a Democratic governor and a Republican director of public welfare. The people didn't say they wanted a Democratic governor and a Republican in charge of all the road work, building 'em, maintaining 'em and planting trees on 'em from hell to breakfast. No, the people wanted a Democratic administration, and I believe that

> means Democratic from the governor's office down to the smallest feist of a motorcycle cop that yaps at you from some remote crossroad.

Perturbing reports reached Horner, too, from his few scattered friends in Washington. Senator Dieterich, he was informed, had been funneling misinformation into President Roosevelt's ears about the situation in Illinois. All the while, the governor's work load strained the limit of his energy. He detailed a typical workday during that period for a friend: Most of the day was spent trying to distribute state coal bids so as to give maximum employment for miners. Then he had to deal with three insurrections—strikes in Wood River and Kewanee and organized milk dumping on the highways in northeastern Illinois. Instead of doing their jobs, complained the governor, local officials were constantly clamoring for the National Guard whenever trouble threatened.

Not long afterwards, the conversation among Democratic politicians swapping rumors at Clark and Randolph Streets ran along these lines: "The big fat Jew is going to take a judgeship; the Jew won't run again." Or "the yellow sheeney won't fight back." Consternation also mounted among the governor's payrollers in response to speculation that Horner would succeed another Jew, Samuel Alschuler, soon to retire from the United States Court of Appeals.

One important link in this chain of events has been rusted by the years. It seems likely, though, that the one who convinced Ed Kelly that Horner would not fight back was Ben Lindheimer, the governor's commerce commission chairman and trustee of a family friendship going back nearly fifty years. Lindheimer had left the administration after a disagreement with the governor. There are conflicting versions of the reason for their disagreement, but none are capable of verification now, and therefore it is not worthwhile to speculate.

In these trying days the governor did not lack for uplift from his genuine friends, his "non-political" friends. Bishop Griffin wrote him that "on your record you certainly should be re-elected. . . . Everybody wants the poor taken care of through the emergency relief but nobody wants to pay the taxes." Carl Sandburg apologized for not making a promised visit, explaining that he "had a case of neuritis not worth taking to Springfield." He wrote that "your record will not be dimmed by that peculiar sort of opposition you are now getting and the methods it is employing. This era, these times, are going to be slow in settling into the sort of pace they knew before the Crash. Who can read anything like tranquility following whatever outcome we see next November?" Down in Franklin County, Louie Lewis stopped by for a porch-swing chat with J. R. McDuffy, an itinerant Baptist preacher who, among other things, had tried without success to land the patronage job as chaplain at Menard Penitentiary. McDuffy couldn't believe that the Chicago organization would dump Horner. He and Lewis invited a group of farmers and coal miners to a meeting where the first southern Illinois Horner Club came into being. More than eleven thousand names pledging their backing for the governor were collected on petitions in that depression-ridden county.

In the midst of all this reconnoitering occurred one of the more comical conflicts in Illinois history: the Battle of the Baby Books.[3] Dr. Herman Bundesen, a physician, had been second only to Horner as a Cook County vote-getter in the 1920's. He was born in Berlin, Germany, of a Danish father and a German mother and had been brought to Chicago by his penniless widowed mother. At age fifty-two he was showman, promoter, exhibitionist, and flamboyant health maniac. He wore a monocle and pounded his abdomen with his fists to demonstrate the firmness of his muscle wall. In 1931 he had been a serious rival of Cermak's for the mayoralty and was placated with the city health commissioner's job. In this post he scored significant advances, reducing infant mortality, improving milk sanitation, and curbing diphtheria and smallpox. In later years Bundesen was bewitched by venereal disease control and during World War II boasted that Chicago was the safest city in the world in which to have sexual intercourse.

As a politician the doctor carried the art of baby kissing a step beyond. Baby books were prepared, partly at city expense, and copyrighted by Bundesen. Using city birth records, they were distributed to new Chicago mothers and sold to insurance companies. The health commissioner proclaimed himself the "Savior of Babies, Friend of Mothers, Builder of Health." The election of a Democratic governor opened up an entire new vista to Bundesen; he saw no reason why his three baby books—*Our Babies, Before the Baby Comes*, and *The Growing Child*—should not be distributed all over Illinois. His friend Barnet Hodes approached Horner with the suggestion that the Illinois Department of Public Health, to which statewide birth records were submitted, distribute the Bundesen baby books. But Dr. Jirka, Cermak's son-in-law and the health director, also had a fair share of political astuteness. Why should Horner help build up Bundesen throughout the state? The governor stalled off the matter, against Hodes' urging, until early 1935. Then Jirka convinced Horner that, instead of advertising Bundesen, the state should print and distribute its own baby books promoting Horner—and, of course, Jirka. Naturally, Bundesen disliked this development and complained that Horner was "being unfair to the mayor," although the governor had promised that the state books would not compete in Chicago with Bundesen's literary handiwork. Nevertheless, although the state's machinery for processing addresses of mothers was slower than the city's, two million books were printed in the autumn of 1935. Entitled *Our Babies—How to Keep Them Well and Happy,* the books were almost identical in appearance to Bundesen's, down to the smiling cherubs on their covers. The books cost about a nickel apiece and the addressograph slugs a dime. Before long, however, the venture proved too repulsive to Horner's sense of economy and instead of being foisted on all new mothers, the books were merely distributed to local health departments and hospitals.

III

Against Pat Nash's better judgment, Ed Kelly reached a decision by mid-autumn that "we're going to take that son-of-a-bitch out of the mansion. We're going to drop him down the chute and there's nothing he can do about it." [4] Nash considered it a mistake for a party to repudiate its state administration. But the feeling of Democratic security in Illinois seemed unassailable. Kelly's verdict was final.

In Washington, Harold Ickes noted in his diary that "Horner was not notable for his courage. . . . Horner is an honorable man and an able man, but he is a poor politician and he certainly lacks guts." The governor never waivered from his certainty that Roosevelt wanted him re-elected and would make his influence felt at the proper time. On November 27, two days after Horner's unconditional statement of candidacy had been announced, Jim Farley said, nonetheless, that the national administration had not requested his renomination; the governor and his associates were dumbfounded. Horner still could not believe that he would be denied a second term by the leaders of his own party.

Democratic leaders from many sections of the state, among them Horner's friend Dallman from Springfield and Jacob Arvey of the Twenty-fourth Ward, met early in December at Kelly's house to begin pondering who the replacement candidate should be. Both men insisted later that they had resisted the dumping of Horner but were outvoted. In his Statehouse desk the governor still kept the telegram he had received from Arvey and Hodes after his New Year's Day radio speech in 1934—"You may count on us to join your legion of devoted followers." But Hodes had since departed the state administration to join the Kelly legions, and Arvey now served on the committee on candidates that sealed Horner's doom.

One of the most pathetic scenes in the annals of the Illinois Democratic party occurred at a luncheon on December 9 at the Stockyards Inn in Chicago. Horner had received a form letter of invitation to the luncheon honoring President Roosevelt, who would be addressing the National Farm Bureau Federation convention that afternoon. Attached to the governor's invitation was the routine notification that his letter must be presented at the door as means of identification. As they waited for the president's arrival, Kelly and Nash stepped into Horner's limousine in front of the inn and informed the governor that the sales tax issue made it impossible for him to be re-elected and that he would therefore not be endorsed for renomination. His puffy face pale and lined, Horner made an uncharacteristic response. "I'll beat the hell out of both of you," he said in a shaky voice. "I've got more friends over the state of Illinois than you realize. You'll find out." [5] Moments later, Franklin Roosevelt dragged himself on his crutches into the Stockyards Inn, Kelly on one side of him, Nash on the other. Horner straggled in alone and sat by himself far down at the head table, now, in full public view, relegated by his party to oblivion.

The next day, Kelly, Nash, and Horner all accompanied Roosevelt on a train ride to South Bend, Indiana, where the president received an honorary degree from the University of Notre Dame. FDR offered the governor a federal judgeship—and even mentioned the vague possibility of a Supreme Court appointment. The realization of what had happened finally started to sink in. He had been ditched by his party with the full approval of the president of the United States. His fighting words in the car at the stockyards now seemed far off, and he lapsed into a state of emotional shock, bewildered, hurt beyond belief, and overcome with self-pity. On the following day the deal was sealed as the leader of the mighty Kelly-Nash machine rode with Roosevelt back to Washington and dined with him that evening in the White House.

There were, to be sure, misgivings from many Illinois Democrats who considered it political suicide to publicly jettison the party's own governor in such graceless style. Ickes recorded in his diary that Roosevelt told him he did not think Horner could win with Kelly and Nash against him. If he were in Horner's place, confided the president, he would be satisfied with a judgeship or some appointive federal job. Ickes said he warned Roosevelt that Kelly was Colonel McCormick's man. "The trouble is," Ickes explained to himself, "he [Horner] has played with that gang right along, and it is going to be difficult for him to stand up to it now."

The reaction of the Decatur *Herald* to these events was typical of the view of downstate Democrats:

> Mayor Kelly has invited the Democratic Party in Illinois to cut its own throat. . . . No surer way could be found to insure the return of Illinois, normally a Republican state, to Republican control. Mayor Kelly, of course, is fully aware of that and perhaps is prepared to accept such a result, counting upon his own intimate Republican connections as a means of doing business with a state government of the opposite party. Before now, a Republican machine in Springfield and a Democratic machine in Cook County have operated almost harmoniously, yielding crops of new millionaires in both camps alike. No matter how pleasant such arrangements may be for Chicago politicians, however, it is a little hard to see how downstate Democrats can be enlisted for such a scheme.[6]

CHAPTER TWELVE

"Who Is to Be Trusted?"

On his dreary retreat by sledge from Moscow to Paris after the military misadventure of 1812, the Emperor Napoleon had ample opportunity to ruminate about the obscure men he had raised to prominent positions of trust and who had then betrayed him when his fortunes were reversed. His military companion, Armand de Caulaincourt, recorded in his memoirs the unburdening of his master's mind about the perverse nature of political patronage. When rumors of Bonaparte's death in Russia reached Paris the emperor's followers scattered for their own survival.

De Caulaincourt wrote:

> He [Napoleon] mentioned several notable men whom he had employed in very responsible situations, adding that he did not trust them, that they were capable of betraying him at the first opportunity when they considered it in their interest to do so, although they owed everything to him. According to the Emperor, the binding nature of an oath, fidelity in the execution of the functions of service in which one is employed, the sense of honor that makes it impossible to betray the man one serves, meant nothing to these men; religion and fidelity were sentiments wholly lacking in their natures.
>
> Even patriotism, he went on, is a word that conveys nothing to them if it is not consonant with their own interests. . . . When certain people meet with the slightest disappointment,

such as the refusal of a post they have requested for some rascal who happens to be a relation, they turn against me; some are even ready to plot against me if I put a stop to their peculations and open pillage.

Not only does Frochot owe everything to me, he has also sworn fidelity. Yet, when he believed that I was dead, he was faithless to me and to his oath—and still thought himself an honest man thereafter. . . . Such are the men and the notions begotten by the times we live in. Who is to be trusted?

. . . It is well known that I should show no mercy on swindlers, still less to officials who did business on their own account. Never has the Treasury been in such good order. It has been necessary to make examples. Sometimes the delinquents have been men who were connected with prominent personages, but I have stopped for no considerations of that sort. Feeling myself strong enough to do what was right, I have gone on to my goal allowing nothing to turn me aside, paying no heed to the outcries of various cliques.

Who makes an outcry in France? A few salons; a few people who have soon forgotten their debt to me for the position of fortune they now enjoy; others whom I have brought back from exile and restored to their property, which they would never have recovered but for me; a few obscure lordlings who are discontented at no longer being sprinkled with holy water on Sundays; a number of self-centered shopkeepers who are under a cloud at the moment because they can find no scope for speculation; some army contractors, veritable bloodsuckers whose ill-gotten gains I have made them disgorge. These are the people who cry out against me. The great mass of the nation is just. The nation sees that I am striving for its good fame, its happiness, its future.[1]

II

The timeless quality of Napoleon's insight struck the bishop, and he sorrowed at the depressing reality of political life. The book tumbled from his lap and slid onto the floor, and the bishop slumped in dejected but helpless concern for his neighbor and friend. In any age and in any nation, under any political system, the disappointed seeker of jobs for some rascal who happens to be a relation would indeed be ready to plot against his benefactor. Good men would flee upon hearing rumors of the death or the impending demise of their leader.

On that very morning, Ben Adamowski, the Democratic leader of the House, had dropped by the bishop's study, as he often did, after early mass. The young Polish-American was a devout Catholic who attended mass almost every day while in Springfield.

"What happens now? What do you do now, Ben?" inquired the bishop. "What is the dogma that applies in a situation like this? What do men like yourself do when the party, the almighty party, decides that a good public servant, an honorable man, must be turned away like this?"

"If the individual can hold himself above the organization," Adamowski replied, "then there is no organization. It means nothing. It has been shown a great many times that a political organization must operate by orderly procedures if it would hope to succeed. I may not agree, and this time I don't, but it has to be that way."

"Ah, I see, something like mayoral infallibility, is that it?"

"You know that the church or any other institution has to have leadership if it expects to be strong."

"But Henry has been a good governor. Anything he has done he has had to do. You above all know that. Is there no right and wrong to be considered in this? How can you turn on this man after all the times you stood on the floor of the House and defended him?"

"I'm sorry," Ben answered, "but I'm an organization Democrat. The governor lived by these rules, too, until they no longer served his purpose."

Just as Bishop Griffin and other friends of Horner's were dismayed by the course of events culminating in the party's decision to jettison the incumbent governor, so the governor himself wavered between table-pounding fits of defiant anger and a terribly despondent, unbelieving philosophical daze. Could this actually be happening? As he waited forlornly in his suite at the Congress Hotel in Chicago, a procession of political "friends" called to express their sorrow and to notify him that, regrettably, they could no longer be with him. It was like a wake, the mourners praising the attributes and good deeds of the politically deceased, although in this case the body had not yet been deposited in the coffin. That, the mourners uniformly believed, would be an unpleasant but necessary technicality that would be taken care of on primary day, if Horner stayed in the race. Pat Nash made a final visit, at which tears are supposed to have been shed by the old war horse. Nash hoped their long friendship could continue, though their political ways must part.

Arch Bowen, the public welfare director, wrote the governor on

January 14 that the trite saying "Whom the gods would destroy they first make mad" never had a more appropriate meaning than now in Illinois. "There is revolt in both parties," Bowen told him, "against the very obvious effort that is being made in Cook County by the *Tribune* and the mayor of Chicago to dictate both the Republican and Democratic nominations for governor of this state." The *Tribune* had commented editorially that "Governor Horner is a party burden because the New Deal is a party burden in this state."

There were, in fact, signs of what seemed to resemble madness in the governor. At times his behavior bordered on the classic emotional disorder of manic-depression—hyperactivity followed by extreme depression. First, bravado, the emperor will prevail, the emperor must prevail; then sad confusion from a man who had little stomach, seemingly, for the struggle ahead. It is probably because of the latter response that some of his contemporaries, many of them political allies, have maintained the impression that Horner initially was resigned to defeat and had to be goaded into combat readiness. The letters that Horner left behind do not substantiate this interpretation. Most likely, the governor's sensitivity, his inability to understand *why* his old Fourth Ward pal whom he had helped to secure the mayorship, *why* his friend Pat Nash had to do this to him, reinforced the impression of hesitation about waging the battle. Some time later, Horner wrote a letter to a college student whose grandmother had been a friend of his mother's and who was contemplating quitting school: "No one gets enthusiastic over a quitter," the governor advised him. "The world has little place for a quitter in its strenuous twentieth-century civilization. The world wants men with courage and stick-to-itiveness."

Participation in the wake by his Jewish political compatriots grieved the governor most of all. Jacob Arvey, the boss of the Twenty-fourth Ward with its legions of Russian Jews and the leader of the Jewish Progressive League, the trade union of Jewish Democratic precinct captains in Chicago, explained that although he had done everything in his power to prevent the decision, he now had to stand with the organization.

The experience made a wiser man of Horner. He sent a telegram to the political leader who had organized the road joint enterprise, stating matter-of-factly that he assumed he would be on his side. The man replied that he was sorry, but he too had done all within his power to have the governor reslated, "notwithstanding that I have been knocked around and deliberately and willfully subjected to a lot of trouble and unnecessary expenditures" in connection with the road joint venture.

The son of another of Horner's long-time Jewish teammates, Harry Fisher, had been recommended by Pat Nash for a position as attorney in the office of public administrator of Cook County. But the governor had taken his time about making the appointment. Now Horner telephoned Judge Fisher in Florida to advise him that if a letter of endorsement were not forthcoming the next day, David (the son) would be unemployed. Fisher's letter from his vacation residence in Hollywood, Florida, has been kept in the Horner papers:

> . . . This [involves] a friendship that I prized for nearly a quarter of a century. Now you ask me to choose between that friendship and what may mean the future happiness of my family, and you propose to make yourself, in your present frame of mind, the sole judge.
>
> We are all human, my dear Henry, and when forced with the back to the wall by an act which we regard as a clear injustice we often find that the most powerful will is insufficient to restrain the desire to seek personal shelter.
>
> You say our accounts are even. Since 1914 I labored in every one of your campaigns, did I not? Did I ever ask reciprocity? Can you recall a single speech on my behalf in any of my campaigns? Search your memory for a single letter written publicly for me.

Then Fisher went on to claim that his long hours working in the 1932 campaign had been the reason for an unfavorable candidates report by the bar association. He said "they" had insisted that he accept the nomination for state's attorney in 1932 but that he had refused because it would have required the elimination of a second Jew as the candidate for governor.

Fisher continued:

> You say our accounts are squared, we owe each other nothing, and I take it you mean that David's appointment was in full payment—granted—but do you know that he has not drawn a single dollar out of it and that if he surrenders his position now it will be at an actual loss? What, in that event, will have been your compensation by which you claim our accounts were balanced?
>
> . . . Your opponents . . . seem to regard my actual participation of great value. You might say that an idealistic sense of

> public duty would give me an excuse, but have you not destroyed that by putting the whole matter on a plain, blunt, political patronage basis? You leave me no alternative except to decide on the sordid ground of personal advantage and unfortunately, in these circumstances, the decision is simple.
>
> Should this unfortunate circumstance result in the loss of your friendship, please believe me that will be by far the greater hurt than any you could possibly inflict by an irrational blow struck during the madness of a violent political battle.[2]

During the governor's period of brooding and self-doubt, Ed Kelly made a serious blunder. Downstate Democrats loyal to the Kelly-Nash machine had been led to believe that a downstater, the popular Bruce Campbell of Belleville, who had run well in the 1932 primary, would be Horner's replacement. Reports vary as to precisely how firm Kelly's promise had been, but there is little doubt that Campbell for one considered the commitment sealed. With Kelly-Nash delivering the vote in Chicago and a highly regarded downstater on the ticket, how could Horner hope to survive?

At the last minute, however, Kelly cast aside Campbell and tapped that erstwhile friend of all mothers, Dr. Herman Bundesen. Barnet Hodes had something to do with selling Kelly on the health commissioner, although his influence has probably been exaggerated. Bundesen had attracted over a million votes in his race for country coroner in 1928, and his unique baby book appeal to mothers did rate as a successful political gimmick. Nevertheless, Kelly's motives for selecting Bundesen must be examined with suspicion. Two days before his death from leukemia in 1962, John Stelle told the author that Kelly had no real desire in 1936 to see a Democrat in the governor's chair. Kelly had learned his lesson from Horner: that a Democratic mayor of Chicago has a smoother time with a Republican governor than with a governor of his own party who poses the constant threat of rivalry for party leadership. There is a sizable body of thought, therefore (confined by no means to Mr. Stelle), that Kelly wanted to "put Bundesen to sleep" (Chicago political jargon) in the 1936 election. Although Kelly thought Bundesen would whip Horner easily in the primary, there is reason to believe that he wanted to arrange the fall election so that C. Wayland (Curly) Brooks, the Republican candidate put up by his friend Colonel McCormick, would win and that coincidentally one of his potential rivals—the inestimable doctor with his unpredictable following of mothers—would be anesthetized for good.

To complete the ticket, the regular organization slated Stelle for lieutenant governor, John Martin (who had been treasurer before Stelle) for treasurer again, incumbent Ed Hughes for secretary of state, incumbent Eddie Barrett for auditor, and incumbent Otto Kerner for attorney general. Horner had regarded Martin and Kerner as close friends, and their continued loyalty to the machine disappointed him.

However, the unexpected selection of Bundesen had a reviving effect upon the governor and jolted him out of his stupor. "Bundesen? Bundesen?" he exclaimed after hearing of the choice. "Why he's nothing but a nonentity. I can beat him. Of course I can. They call me a dead fish. Well I'm going to be the livest dead fish you ever saw. Watch and see."

In January, an intermediary from the White House brought up a federal judgeship again. The representative, Robert S. Hunt, pointed out that Alschuler soon would be retiring from the federal court of appeals and "what is more logical than the belief that he should be followed by one of his own race?" And the Supreme Court, Hunt added, was not beyond reach in the future.[3]

In the meantime Horner had tried without success to persuade the president to supplement the state's federal relief allocation. All Roosevelt could do was to increase the Illinois WPA quota by twenty-five thousand jobs. Faced once again with an empty relief till, Horner had no alternative but to reduce monthly payments by half and to call yet another special session of the legislature. Stelle, who was entranced by the immenseness of the WPA program, proposed that the relief commission be replaced by a state road building program that would provide jobs for the poor. Horner suggested that Stelle's plan had been "inspired more by a desire for publicity than by any willingness to contribute anything constructive. . . . Unhappily, Stelle is not familiar with either the problem of relief or the problem of state financing."

Stelle's American Legion activities had given him contacts with influential people throughout the state, and now he took the lead in organizing WPA workers into a functional auxiliary arm of the Democratic party. Horner exploded when he learned of this conversion of the federal assistance program that he had implemented in Illinois into a weapon that would be turned around and fired against him. The governor discharged two relief commissioners who were friends of Kelly's, accusing them of "trying to play politics with relief and with WPA jobs for their own and Kelly's selfish ends." Horner charged, moreover, that WPA workers all along the line had been intimidated.

About this time the national Democratic chairman, Jim Farley, explained in a letter to L. P. Bonfoey, head of the state aeronautics commission, that "very frankly, I will get into trouble if I start to interfere in local state affairs. Every state organization has a right to administer their affairs without interference from the National Administration." [4]

When he was informed of this message, Horner wrote Bonfoey:

> Farley's letter is typical. If it were true that he were not "interfering in local state affairs" I would agree with him that it was all right to keep out of the state primary controversies. However, the national administration is interfering and has instructed the people on the federal payroll to go along with the "crackup" machine. If he really had kept out of state affairs it would have been better for the national administration and President Roosevelt's chances—but he has not nor is he fooling anyone into the belief that he is keeping out of state affairs. However, we are going to win and we are going to make Roosevelt win too. For what I have done for Roosevelt in Illinois others are reaping the reward. However, there will be judgment day soon.[5]

Along the same lines, the governor informed Senator Lewis: "Kelly has been making the people believe he and Roosevelt are sipping from the same spoon and many who believe in Roosevelt are surprised to be told, without any denial from Washington, that he is 'ganged up' with the Chicago machine. However, notwithstanding all this, I am quite sanguine about the campaign." [6]

Along with the chronic relief financing headaches, Horner confronted the special session of the legislature with a timely subject in which he had now acquired a personal interest: permanent registration of voters. "Our government," he explained in his call, "is based upon democratic principles. The people are their own rulers. This right to rule must be jealously protected to retain this form of government. Unless elections are honestly conducted to prevent frauds, the will of one person or a few is substituted in place of the majority." Organization Democrats were whipped into line and the bill failed, after Pat Nash made what seemed like an unduly frank public declaration that "permanent registration would cost us two hundred thousand votes." Adamowski, for one, had been in favor of permanent registration until Nash convinced him that it would harm the organization. The defeat of the bill gave Horner a good issue. "Do any of you think President Roosevelt would care to be elected in Illinois by crooked votes?" he asked. "They are still trying to vote butterflies, fence rails, and ghosts, but it is not going to work this year. The people of Illinois are aroused against bossism and they are going to see that Boss Kelly won't rule Illinois." Thus, the overriding issue had been drawn—bossism.

III

By any standards, the primary campaign of 1936 was as costly, as vicious, as destructive, as unilluminating, as mud-spattered as any in Illinois history. Many political campaigns among understanding professionals are rhetorical exercises in which large war chests are raised but are not necessarily invested altogether in the war. In this struggle, though, about $3,000,000, an enormous sum in that pre-television era, was expended. Nearly two-thirds of the total was spent on the governor's campaign, to which the taxpayers made a major involuntary contribution. His hastily formed organization consisted of men and women on the state payroll. One hundred bonded collectors oversaw the assessment of contributions deducted from state paychecks at the rate of $1,000 a day. Suppliers of goods and services to the state government were clouted again and again for contributions. One observer watched the distribution of $500,000 in cash to downstate campaign leaders the day before the election. State police guards were assigned to accompany the leaders back to their communities from the distribution point at the St. Nicholas Hotel in Springfield.

The only Chicago ward committeemen on Horner's side were three who had enjoyed the benefits of favoritism—Art O'Brien's brother Martin, the Cook County public administrator; and James L. Whelan and Al Horan, who were called the "Gold-dust Twins" by Bundesen. Horan handled state surety bonds, and Whelan had state trucking contracts.

Robert Straus, the governor's cousin and a Chicago bank executive, collected campaign funds from businessmen and the Jewish financial community. Standard Club members, the Skeeters, and the wealthy contacts that Horner had made during his years on the probate bench also came to his financial aid.

Here was a contest that pitted the once gentle judge, fortified now by all the power emoluments of an incumbent, against the invincible big-city political machine. Although Horner may not have fully appreciated all the ingenious ways in which his office could be used to reward and to punish, there were men at his side who did. Chief among his political strategists was roly-poly Dan Sullivan, a former Chicago *Tribune* employee who had the disconcerting habit of falling asleep in the middle of a conversation.

No one in his right mind could discount the cold efficiency of the Kelly-Nash machine. On the West Side Jacob Arvey supervised a service organization that did favors legally or otherwise for the voters. The party ran its own charity system, with one full-time employee assigned to that project alone. In this haven of Jewish immigrant residents, the science of merchandising votes probably reached its ultimate refinement.

Jake Arvey, a short, gnomelike man of forty, had inherited the ward from Moe Rosenberg and had made a strong Democratic district even more solid for his party. In organization politics the leader who can control a big vote in an important election swings a big stick in the party councils. But what would be the reaction of the Jewish masses in the Twenty-fourth Ward to the attempted political lynching of the first Jew to reach the highest office in Illinois? Horner's social contacts had been largely limited to the wealthy German Jews at the Standard Club. Their reaction obviously would be one of resentment. But what about those on the West Side who knew only that Horner was a Jew and that there were other Jews, Jake Arvey and Judge Fisher among them, who were instrumental in the plans for his destruction?

Late in January, Rabbi Solomon Goldman of the conservative Temple Anshe Emet at Pine Grove and Grace Streets on the North Side spoke of the dilemma to his congregation. If Jewry had been united behind Horner, he said, the party leaders would never have dared to dump him. The rabbi recalled that in 1932 all of the Jews of Illinois had wildly supported this man, rabbis had extolled him from the pulpits, and Jewish mystics had prophesied great things for him, some of them even finding in the Book of Daniel allusions to prophecies of his glory. In "one of the great Jewish clubs of the city [the Standard Club], one not ordinarily noted for its Jewishness," the rabbi sarcastically recalled, citizens consumed quantities of food and cigars and quietly contributed thousands of dollars to advance the cause of Henry Horner. Henry Horner did not then meet the qualifications for a "real Jew," according to the rabbi. A real Jew is one who is first and last for his people, not one who avoids mentioning his ancestry as though it were something of which to be ashamed. He related how the governor, as toastmaster at an assembly of Jews at which a professor from the University of Jerusalem had spoken, had not once mentioned Jerusalem or Palestine. He revived the story of the execution of Morris Cohen on a Jewish holiday and reminded the audience of Horner's refusal to be honorary chairman for Jewish Day at the World's Fair. What Catholic official, the rabbi wanted to know, would play false with his fellow Catholics? The great English statesman, Benjamin Disraeli, who was born a Jew, once retorted to a slurring reference to his ancestry by saying that when his critic's ancestors were roaming the fields with the wild animals his forefathers were advanced to a high degree of civilization in Palestine. That, the rabbi boasted, is the spirit a Jew should possess, not a "low, cringing manner." But on the other hand, he admitted, since Jewish prestige hung in the balance, each Jew must arrive at his own careful decision.

Julius Klein, who had been working in Hollywood as a story writer for RKO Studios and was now running for congressman-at-large on the Republican ticket in Illinois, wrote identical letters on this subject to Arvey, Fisher, Hodes, and other Jewish leaders of the Democratic party:

> To you, one of the Jewish leaders in the Democratic party of my native state, I am addressing this letter in this hour of great need. As a Jew I cannot remain silent. As a man I must express my opinion, and as a former Chicago native son, I must send this appeal to you. I have been watching the political situation in Illinois very carefully, reading every Chicago newspaper. Many prominent Chicago citizens and public officials have been guests at my home here and at the studio during the past few weeks, so that I have a pretty accurate low-down on the political situation in Illinois.
>
> Never in the history of modern times have the Jews of the world passed through a more serious crisis, and never in the history of American Jewry have we gone through more dangerous conditions as right now.
>
> Hitlerism began in Germany when Jewish public officials were accused of monopolizing public office, using it for personal gain. Jewry in Germany was divided with the result that when the crisis came there was not a united front. Hitlerism has won out in Germany. Now Hitlerism has invaded our country, spreading its poison in America. The city treasurer in Chicago,

> Gustav Brandt, was made president of the German Day Committee with the help of the Friends of the New Germany. Chicago can boast of a first public official, the city treasurer, who respects the swastika as we do the Stars and Stripes.
>
> American Jewry has been well and honorably represented in public office. Men like Governors Lehman and Horner, judges like Brandeis and Cardozo, have been a credit to Jewry. The election of Henry Horner in 1932 in a state with nearly a million German votes was hailed as a tribute and credit to the patriotic and conscientious American Jew. It was the proper answer to sixty million Nazis that we in America accepted their challenge.
>
> . . . Horner has made a good and honest governor. He is a credit to our race. What can you tell your constituents against him? How will you explain this to Chicago and American Jewry? What will you tell the thousands of German refugees who are all over the world now, and who have lost their rights as citizens? How will you justify an honest public official being driven from office with the help and without the protest of the people of his own faith? Political expediency yielding to a political machine is dishonorable.
>
> . . . Do you realize what will be the effect all over the world if Horner should be defeated by someone of German origin? It will be heralded as an Aryan victory everywhere. Streicher's paper in Germany, *Der Stuermer,* and Goebbels', *Voelkischer Beobachter,* will have headlines: "It's Beginning in America; America is Cleaning House; Jews are Being Driven from Office Back to the Ghetto Where They Belong." No, I do not subscribe to the injection of racial issues here in our beloved land—but I do know what Goebbels' press will say. . . . My friend, this is an historical occasion. For your own self-preservation, you must act and fight. In the eyes of the bosses and of the common enemy, you're not Democrats; you're not even Americans; you are just JEWS and stooges for a machine.[7]

The task of unselling this Jewish hero to the Jewish masses fell to the two leaders of the Jewish Progressive League, Jake Arvey and Harry Fisher—Arvey who could not qualify for the Standard Club because he was not a German Jew; Fisher, respected and loved by the throngs of West Side Orthodox Jews because of his long record of service to the cause of Eastern European Jews. The brainwashing had to start with the Jewish precinct captains. A series of Sunday afternoon meetings at the Morrison Hotel was staged for the four hundred and fifty Jewish precinct captains. Over and over, the captains listened to the theme of the hour: as

Jews we must not rely on clannishness; we have to depend on the organization.

Typically, Ed Kelly sounded the keynote. "When Horner was nominated in 1932 all the Irish in town got on the firing line and battled side by side with the Jews to elect him," said the red-headed Irishman. "Now we're fighting Horner, not because he's a Jew, but because he is fighting the organization. We expect the Jews to fight for us now. I admire the man who declares his religion. Why I would kiss the cardinal's ring at State and Madison Streets in broad daylight. But no Irishman is going to tell me to vote for an Irish candidate just because he's Irish. He can't use me that way."

Then, as the captains clapped uncertainly and mumbled to one another, Artie Elrod, the secretary of Arvey's Twenty-fourth Ward organization, strode down the aisle yelling, "Make room for the governor! Make room for the governor!" Hands clasped overhead like a prizefighter, Herman Bundesen jogged behind Elrod and skipped up to the platform.

"When I was in an orphan asylum as a boy," Bundesen said, straining for some identification, "my mother was able to take me out because of the job she got from Jews." Again, mumbling in the audience.

Pat Nash then came on with the doctrine that religion and politics actually should not be mixed, a rather absurd thesis for this crowd. "I am ready to help a good precinct captain when he delivers," Nash explained. "I want you people who benefited through this organization to get this ticket in. I helped to put many Jews on the ticket, and in doing so turned down a lot of Poles and Irish. But I was glad to have them in. Arvey knows that. I want to help the race." Again, mumbling.

For clean-up speaker there was Harry Fisher—the same judge who had told Horner during their telephone conversation from Florida that his doctor had ordered him to remain there throughout the campaign because of his heart condition. Now at least Fisher's vocal chords were in robust order.

> This organization [the League] is a child of my own brain. We need security for the Jew who is engaged in political activity. Horner was not endorsed because it was the practical thing to do. Shall we endanger the jobs of thousands of Jews in public life in this state just to go in and support an irresponsible bachelor? Horner made his own bed. Let him lie in it. But don't

let him endanger your future livelihood. We've offered him a job on the Federal Court of Appeals and offered him many honors if he would retire gracefully. But that was not good enough for him. The re-election of Roosevelt means more to Jews than a million Horners. I raise my voice for Bundesen because I can trust him. Arvey must carry his ward for Bundesen. We owe Horner nothing. Don't be accused of voting for a Jew because he is a Jew. Mayor Kelly has told you what is in the minds of others. Let us take heed.

We saw the downfall of Horner sixty days after he took office. He tried to build up a machine of his own by appointing chairmen of each county against our advice. We knew nothing. He knew it all and we saw the storm coming.

He kept Republicans in major offices. We pleaded with him not to look for Republican votes and warned him he would have to get Democratic support.

Six months ago he said they wouldn't dare throw him off the ticket. At that time Arvey told him the only chance he would have to get the endorsement was because he's a Jew. Talking to him was like talking to a stone wall. Maybe it's the result of his unfortunate condition of being a bachelor and having no responsibility. He imagines he's a great man because he's surrounded by a lot of yes men. We tried to get the endorsement for Horner, but not one of the twelve leaders who met to decide it said he deserved it. In spite of my eloquence before that committee in behalf of Horner, they convinced me that he could not win. What a terrible thing it will be if the Democratic party turned against us Jews and refused to employ us in public office! Isn't there plenty of discrimination in this world today without this? If Horner has a personal controversy with Kelly, let him go out in the alley and fight it out. It would be more dignified that way.

An enterprising reporter obtained and printed a transcript of Fisher's remarks, so the entire state shared the judge's plea to his fellow Jews. Not all reacted favorably. In the downstate city of Rockford, Rabbi Abraham H. Feinberg attacked Fisher's line of reasoning in a sermon. It was, he said:

the outline of a policy which, if carried to its logical conclusion, although benefitting the Arveys and the Fishers, would in the end lead to shame and disaster for the Jewish people. It is plain to see that what Fisher is trying to do is to create a Jewish political machine. Its main purpose in being thus organized is to give the Jews engaged in political activity security. We are observing this week the Feast of Passover. And just as we were

> once delivered from the Egypt of bondage, so may we also be delivered—Jew and Christian—from the Egypt of political chicanery. Set us free from political shysters and aldermanic ward heelers! [8]

The injection of religion into the campaign was probably an unavoidable consequence. Arvey claimed later that the Horner people had started it by pointing out to any Jews who would listen that Bundesen had been born in Berlin, certainly an unpleasant association during this period. In a St. Patrick's Day speech at Pontiac, the governor said he would be content to drive just one snake, the boa constrictor Boss Kelly, out of Illinois. When the firing had ended, the Board of Managers of the Chicago Bar Association expelled Fisher and three other judges for unethical involvement in partisan political activity. The other three, all Kelly backers, were James J. Kelly, Oscar F. Nelson, and John J. Sullivan. Sullivan signed a letter calling on the Irish to vote against Horner.

> Self respect and pride in the honor and accomplishments of our race prompt this letter. The fair name of Edward J. Kelly, mayor of this great progressive city of ours, has been viciously traduced. Henry Horner, as a candidate for the Democratic nomination for governor of this state, has seen fit to pour forth a torrent of abuse and vilification of the mayor. . . . The same arrogance and egotism characterized Horner's entire administration that actuated him to go to the extreme of proclaiming on St. Patrick's Day that he was going to assay the role of St. Patrick and drive that Irish snake, Mayor Edward J. Kelly, out of Chicago. Horner's only purpose in slurring Mayor Kelly has obviously been to cater to the prejudices of that small group of voters downstate who have an inborn hatred of the name of Kelly or any name like Kelly.[9]

Most of the Lindheimer family, so important in German Jewish circles, opposed Horner. Ben had resigned from the governor's administration "to devote my entire time to personal business affairs." Horace Lindheimer was Kelly's candidate for Cook County treasurer. Art was an executive in the Material Service Corporation, which provided paving and other materials for the city, county, and state. Only Horner's good friend, Maude Lepman, whose husband Horace had been given a job as state superintendent of foods and dairies, stuck with Horner.

Bundesen's campaign was unusual, if not ridiculous.[10] He toured downstate wearing spats and a monocle, passing out his baby books and exhorting the voters to eat an apple a day and drink plenty of milk. The Horner woman's organization of one hundred thousand, put together by the assistant director of public welfare, Blanche Fritz, circulated the story among women that besides the spats and monocle Bundy wore lace on his underpants. The candidate referred often to his six children and jested that he wanted to live in the Executive Mansion because of his large family. Although Kelly had reasoned that Bundesen's identification with good health would help, he failed to reckon with the dislike dairy farmers had for the man who had put through pure milk ordinances in Chicago, forcing many of them to destroy their herds. Personally, the doctor radiated good health. At downstate party rallies, often held in local courthouses, he hurdled the courtroom railing and engaged in platform calisthenics to demonstrate his athletic vigor. "Whenever you see a man who is aggressive," Bundesen lectured, "you will find a milk drinker." Coal miners in southern Illinois who were weaned on a shot of whiskey and a beer chaser blinked at this advice. The candidate's cronies were compelled to drink milk, a substance most of them considered distasteful enough on oatmeal. When the urge struck the doctor, he would insist on walking a mile or two down a country highway, both for the exercise and to shake hands with farmers in the barnyard or surprised motorists whom he would flag down. On one occasion he grabbed a pitchfork and spent the afternoon helping a farmer extinguish a haystack fire instead of seeking votes. To many downstate politicians he seemed plainly daft.

"One thing I prize above all material things is the more than a million letters which have come to me from mothers," he said. "I call as witness to my devotion to the public good those thousands of mothers and babies whose lives and health I have guarded." Horner's attempts to label his opponent the "Milk Bottle Kid" didn't daunt Herman, and some of Bundesen's helpers reciprocated by calling Horner "Henry the Pawnbroker." "I'll keep on talking about babies when I get to the Statehouse," he promised. "The babies of today are the men and women of tomorrow." After this unassailable revelation, he advised the voters to drink a quart of milk a day ("milk puts the rouge in your cheeks") and told them also to eat lots of vegetables, those grown both above and below the ground.

Two Horner men trailed the Bundesen caravan in their state car, sending back intelligence reports of his weird antics. Spike Hennessey, Bundesen's press agent, "threatened to punch us in the mouth," one of the reports mentioned. Another time the Bundesen staff threw rocks at the spy car, and when the spies got out to survey the damage their vehicle got stuck in the mud at the side of the road. Perhaps the zaniest Bundesenism occurred in Sterling, a conservative, God-fearin' downstate community of folks highly suspicious of Chicagoans. To this audience, Bundesen declared: "Try and get a bet on Horner! Just try! See what the odds are. The bookies in Chicago are quoting three to one. If anyone wants to call my bluff, please come up here after the meeting is over." His listeners, of course, were much too shocked to call his bluff. None of this much bothered the Kelly-Nash leaders who were virtually ignoring downstate in their confidence that the huge Chicago primary vote would overwhelm Horner.

Senator Dieterich made speeches for Bundesen downstate, charging that Horner had committed "political larceny by annexing New Deal achievements" to the record of his administration. Another speech prepared by the senator seemed anti-Semitic to some of those who read it in advance, among them Jake Arvey. Arvey told Kelly that if Dieterich went through with his speech, Arvey would jump to Horner's side. The speech was junked.

The president, meanwhile, managed to stay out of the controversy, although Mrs. Roosevelt and Ickes were rooting for Horner, and Hopkins, of course, assisted Kelly in any way he could. The relief director was an accomplished poker player and more than willing to stake the political use of the WPA in Illinois for the good of the Kelly-Nash machine. Farley, the national chairman, said he "wouldn't touch it with a ten-foot pole. It's purely a local affair." Although Farley was grateful to Kelly and Nash for helping to pay off the Democratic National Committee debt, he is supposed to have told Ickes that it would be better for the president if the governor won. Ickes continued trying to convince Roosevelt that the Illinois developments were playing into the *Tribune*'s hands. Once, when FDR was reminded that he had started his own career fighting the Tammany machine in the New York Senate, he replied, "What was proper for a state senator does not apply to the president." According to Ickes' diary, Mike Igoe, who was by then United States attorney in Chicago and on Horner's side in this primary fight, told Ickes he resented Cardinal Mundelein's involvement in Kelly politics.[11]

Horner, who had been known as Gentle Henry during his placid days on the probate court, stunned the party with the vehemence of his attack on the "greedy boss" Ed Kelly. Dan Sullivan had recognized the mileage in the bossism issue. Furthermore, many of his Chicago friends had offered advice similar to James Weber Linn's statement that "your only vice is being too high-principled and . . . your only fault is lack of political arrogance." The governor instructed his followers to "call Kelly any goddamn name you can think of but go easy on the old man [Nash]." On a state-wide radio hookup, Horner defined the issue as "the Democratic voters of the state against Boss Kelly. The voters of the state know that I could have had my party's nomination without a contest had I chosen to be subservient to a political boss." The only excuse for dumping him, the governor insisted, was that he "wasn't a politician." "If to play politics with human misery, to drive men who are dependent upon relief into line for a candidate whom they do not even know is to be a politician," he declared, "then I am not a politician."

Horner often referred to the occupants of the organization headquarters in the penthouse of the Morrison Hotel as "the Penthouse Pirates." His tongue also slipped when he had reason to attack the "Nelly-Kash machine."

"My biggest mistake," the governor confessed, "was when I made Kelly mayor of Chicago. I will tear off his mask and with the people's help I will purge Illinois of bossism and sinister influence." In another speech he said "there would not have been any shouting if I had put my slim figure in a straitjacket and given Boss Kelly the key." He told his followers that "in the thirty-eight months of my administration I've done a damn good job for this state." Explaining the bookie bill veto, Horner said, "Why I even take a chance [gambling] myself when I'm sure. But I told Kelly the people of Chicago won't stand for it. He would be in charge of giving out licenses and what a soft thing that would be. What a racket to put on the legislative books. I would veto the bill again and again. The boss is the only thing I want to reform." Bearing down to the nerve with his personal assault on the mayor, Horner said Kelly had "stopped just short of jail" when he was forced to pay $105,000 on unreported income of $450,000 in 1926, 1927, and 1928. Stelle and Barrett—the "two cherubs," Horner called them—also came in for their share of denunciation. When, in one of his speeches, Stelle had mentioned the surplus that existed in the treasury, Horner suggested that "he's not worrying about a surplus so much as he's worrying because he can't get his hands on it." Another time, the governor described the two as "self-serving politicians who are unfit for any office." To the citizens of

Stelle's home town of McLeansboro, Horner confessed that one of his worst misjudgments had been to make their fellow townsman state treasurer.

By defining the issue—Chicago bossism—and then pounding it home day after day in his dignified, cultured, caressing style, shaking his finger in a rhythmic, hypnotic gesture, the governor gained ground. His Sunday travels downstate, all the funerals and civic affairs he had attended, his knack for fitting in instantly at a high-brow cocktail party or a low-brow bull session with farmers in overalls seemed now to be paying off. In small towns all over the state the voters were somehow getting the message that the sinister big city bosses in that penthouse were trying to do in a fellow who was honest and had done the best job he could for the whole state. "Boss Kelly," Horner told them, "is trying to ride on the coattails of Franklin D. Roosevelt. But he will be shaken off in the great ride we are arranging for him in this state."

The mayor did not, of course, sit back quietly while all this was going on. He made the rounds of the Chicago ward rallies, ripping into "this lily-white governor, this self-styled reformer. Horner's against betting. He's against everything a liberal man wants or likes. He would like to make a Sunday school town out of Chicago." Shades of Tony Cermak!

"He vetoed the [bookie] bill and made himself a high church member and made us a bunch of porch climbers. The handbooks are still with us, but the grafters are getting the two million dollars that should go to the city of Chicago.

"Do you suppose if Ed Kelly were governor two degenerates would be allowed to have private baths [Richard Loeb and Nathan Leopold at Joliet penitentiary], conduct a school, and play poker for $1,500? Henry Horner thinks that he is the czar of Illinois. He feels that Chicago wants to ruin him, and he thinks he'll ruin Chicago in return. But we're not going to let him. We'll take him out of there before he has a chance. I've told him repeatedly, 'Governor, you don't belong. You're just like a bull in a china shop.' "

"As a governor he is a good hod carrier," the mayor judged in another speech. "I'm told that he has put ten thousand on his payroll where there is no work to be done." Referring to the permanent registration issue, Kelly expressed grief for the poor fellow who might be unable to write his name with a cramped hand on a cold day and would therefore be deprived of his vote. Why, Horner is always for blue laws, Kelly complained. Instead of allowing you to patronize plain old bars, he makes you have a sandwich with your drink. Ridiculous. The working man won't be denied his glass of beer. Decent citizens can't put down a buck on a nag, Kelly said, but handbooks are being operated in the penitentiaries. Trying to fight fire with fire, Kelly disparaged Horner's "autocratic attitude" and accused the governor of wanting to set himself up as apostle of the entire state, just as he had done in probate court.

Kelly drew dire inferences from the support Horner received from parts of the "anti-Roosevelt Press." Actually, Kelly's city ordinance establishing permanent daylight-saving time had resulted in the elimination of one financial edition of the afternoon newspapers, thus benefiting Bertie McCormick's morning *Tribune* but making enemies of the afternoon papers.

Bundesen took his cue from the mayor and digressed more frequently from his health lectures to attack his opponent. "Can we forget that Loeb and Leopold, two degenerate murderers whose families are lifelong friends of my opponent, have been allowed to direct the policies of the entire penitentiary, teaching the prisoners, getting work assignments for them at will, conducting gambling operations, and being provided private baths?"

Dick Finnegan's *Times* scolded both candidates for accentuating the negative aspects of their own programs. Unexpectedly, considering Finnegan's moral outcry during the liquor control battle, his newspaper had approved of Kelly's bookie bill with the flimsy excuse that the city needed revenue desperately. There were reasons other than ideological for Finnegan's faltering friendship with the governor. He had wanted exclusive rights to publish the lists of delinquent state property taxpayers in Cook County, but Horner divided publication between the *Times* and Hearst's *Herald-Examiner*.

Horner was helped during the campaign by an unofficial advisory committee of past or present newspapermen. In this group were Milburn P. (Pete) Akers of the Associated Press, Tod Sloan of the Chicago *American*, Lloyd Lewis of the *Daily News*, and Julius Klein.

Egged on by his campaign advisers, who kept telling him that he was running far behind in the race, Horner increased the ferocity of his personal attack against the "crooked" machine leaders. The campaign grew more and more intense. The state superintendent of lodging house inspections resigned, charging that public health inspections were being used to intimidate innkeepers into supporting Horner. Bundesen said that printing shops in the state penitentiaries were being used to crank out Horner campaign literature. Reacting to the difficulty he was having in getting publicity in downstate newspapers, Bundesen accused Horner, accurately, of placing downstate newspapermen on the state payroll. Through it all the governor drove himself until he nearly collapsed from exhaustion. In the latter weeks he was bothered by a persistent hacking cough and a noticeable diminution of his vitality, until he seemed like an automated creature spewing out a mechanical barrage of charges at his adversaries.

Regardless of the outcome, Henry Horner could never be the same man. His party had tried to turn him out of office for what he regarded as unconscionable reasons. He had learned, and could never forget, the meaning of Napoleon's maddening experiences on the way back to Paris. He had learned, and could never forget, the "perverse nature of political patronage," the antics of "veritable bloodsuckers" who were ready to plot against him for putting a stop to their "peculations and open pillage." Such are the men and the notions begotten by the times we live in. Who is to be trusted?

CHAPTER THIRTEEN

Pay-off Day: The Machine versus the Statehouse

A bent-over old man with a long, scraggly gray beard leaned on his cane and glanced up from the steps of the synagogue on this 14th day of April, Achron Shel Pesach, the last day of Passover, and primary election day in the state of Illinois. The boss of the West Side Twenty-fourth Ward, whose guidance on matters political seemed at times to assume divine proportions, stood watch in front of the precinct polling place next door to the synagogue as the Jewish voters filed by to perform their civic responsibility. The old man limped up to Jake Arvey, the calm, confident, masterful representative of the machine. "You did a terrible thing to me today," the old man said wearily. "A terrible thing. You *made* me vote against Henry Horner, *our* Henry Horner." The 14th of April was a supreme test in Jake Arvey's political lifetime, but he would remember the old man with the beard for the rest of his days.[1]

II

Throughout Chicago the masterful machine turned out the vote. Holding the ethnic components together and making the apparatus purr were the 50 ward committeemen, the 3,164 precinct captains (each supplied with $25 to $100 to carry out his election day functions), and some 15,000 precinct workers. In addition there were 50,000 metropolitan area public jobholders, not including 10,000 police and firemen, and 76,000 WPA workers who generated auxiliary power. Quite a machine.

Pay-off day had arrived, the time for squaring the ledgers. Now all the favors that the organization had dispensed—matzoth and noodles and shoes, and the illicit dispensations granted bookies and call girls and after-hours tavernkeepers—would be called for votes. Election day was also known as "resurrection day" in Chicago, because of all the dead in whose names votes would be cast. The polls opened at six o'clock. In the darkness a precinct captain shepherded thirty flophouse bums into a polling place and rewarded them with 50 cents apiece and a slug of rye.

Downtown in the North Side Forty-second Ward the captains under George Brennan's protégé Botsy Connors went to work. In this one ward could be found all the vivid contrast of the metropolis—the Gold Coast, swank Michigan Avenue shops, Bertie McCormick's throne at the Tribune Tower, rooming house transients on Clark Street, Romanians, Negroes, Yugoslavs, Germans, Swedes, Sicilians, Little Italy, the Oak Street beach, Holy Name Cathedral, railroad yards and warehouses along the Chicago River. Botsy's captains were deployed—the literate well-dressed Gold Coaster; the resident of Little Italy who sported a diamond shirt pin and operated a year-round legal aid bureau for voters who got in trouble with the law; the agents down by the river who handed out favors, maybe a ton of coal or a meter reader's job with a utility.[2]

On this day Henry Horner, the gentle judge who had gotten too big for his breeches, was a marked man. He had lived by the code of the machine, and on this day he must be destroyed for ignoring that code when it served his purpose. Because of his organization upbringing, the governor was aware that votes would be stolen. He sent five attorneys to the office of the board of election commissioners where they watched the ballot boxes being brought in. He hired a detective agency to observe the counting in the suspect precincts. Of more practical importance was Horner's realization that County Judge Edmund K. Jarecki, who had administrative control over the election machinery, had also been having his difficulties with Kelly; the governor took advantage of this situation to win Jarecki's friendship. It was Jarecki who had once boasted that "less than 10 per cent of Chicago votes were fraudulent." Throughout the day Horner's workers manned the strong organization wards to protect as best they could against the traditional shenanigans.

Horner awaited the verdict in the Congress Hotel. Kelly and

Nash stayed at their headquarters in the Morrison. A pattern began developing in the early returns: the first downstate precincts showed big turnouts that heavily favored the governor, as Kelly and Nash had expected; in Chicago the organization produced, but not as spectacularly as the machine had anticipated.

The governor was in a vile mood that evening and cursed in Yiddish at Dan Sullivan. When Horner shouted obscenely at Sullivan about the big vote margin in the Chicago machine wards, the astute Irishman answered simply: "Believe me, Governor, they've got to steal 'em faster than that to beat us. We've got 'em."

He was right. Realizing the standard machine practice in such a situation—to hold back the reporting of vote returns from enough organization precincts until it became clear how many stolen votes were needed to win—Horner and Sullivan retaliated by shutting off the reports of downstate returns and dispatched detectives into the tardy city precincts.

"Well, Doc," groaned a tired Pat Nash in the Morrison suite, "it looks like your brigade of loyal mommies has deserted."

They had, and no amount of shenanigans could undo the fact. Horner pulled off a stunning upset, winning by 161,092 votes. He beat the supposedly invincible machine. The governor carried every downstate county (including Stelle's Hamilton County) and amassed a plurality outside Cook County of 317,105. Although his downstate feat was impressive, it would not have been enough had the machine rolled up the Chicago margin of which it was capable. Bundesen won Chicago by 159,301, Cook County by 156,013—less than half the 350,000 Kelly had thought he could realistically bank on.

How did it happen? Inside Chicago the governor carried eight wards. Three of these were South Side wards with substantial numbers of German Jewish residents. Charles K. Schwartz, a member of the state tax commission, had assembled an organization for Horner in the largest ward in the city, the South Shore Seventh (which happened also to be Bundesen's home ward), and won it for Horner by 2,300. Horace Lindheimer's Fifth Ward—Hyde Park—fell to Horner by almost 1,000 votes. The governor also took the Woodlawn Sixth Ward, where Jimmy Whalen was committeeman and on his side. But Horner narrowly lost his own ward, the Fourth. Despite the religious sentiment for Horner in the Twenty-fourth Ward, there were enough voters like the old man with the cane to enable Jake Arvey to come through for Bundesen by 5,000 votes. Al Horan and Marty O'Brien delivered for Horner, though, in the Twenty-ninth Ward, an Irish and Italian section next to Arvey's ward, by 10,900 to 6,200. The other wards taken by Horner were the Thirty-ninth and Fortieth in Albany Park on the Northwest side; and the Forty-eighth and Forty-ninth on the North Side near the lake.

An examination of the ward figures helps to explain how ethno-religious thinking influenced Jewish voters in this election. Jewish voters tended to respond to their religious identification with Horner in direct proportion to their position on the economic scale. Arvey and the Democratic machine exercised a more secure grip over their economically deprived Jewish constituents than over the less needy Orthodox Jews who lived in Albany Park. The prosperous German Jews, on the other hand, clearly tended to vote as Jews for Horner. Other Jews of lesser economic status were responsive to the appeals of their party leaders to disregard Horner's Judaism and vote the organization line. The voter who depended on, or thought he depended on, the Democratic precinct captain to have his relief application processed and approved gave less weight to ethnic considerations.[3]

It is well known that the machine always does its most effective job in a boring election when the turnout is small. This time, however, the total Democratic gubernatorial vote showed an increase of 691,361 over the 816,773 who had voted in the same election four years before. The increase in Cook County alone was 405,087. Many Republicans undoubtedly had crossed over into the Democratic column in both Cook County and downstate as a way of registering their vote against Democratic party bossism in Chicago. In Horner's old ward, the downtown First, he was steamrollered by more than 6 to 1. One First Ward precinct counted 292 for Bundesen, 3 for Horner. The South Lawndale Czech wards gave huge pluralities to Bundesen—5 to 1 in the Twenty-fifth Ward, for instance. Negro wards, with a high proportion of relief cases, also came through for the machine as might have been expected. Botsy Connors carried the polyglot Forty-second Ward. In the more prosperous outlying wards at the fringe of the city, however, where his role as an underdog probably had some appeal, the governor chipped away at the normal machine pluralities.

John Cassidy, the governor's running mate against Stelle for lieutenant governor, lost 544,215 to 500,347. Two Chicago city hall patronage clerks, Isaac Epstein and John L. McCormack, were also entered in that race by the machine and split a decisive 225,431 votes between them. Cassidy carried every downstate county but Hamilton. For the Republicans, C. Wayland Brooks, who had prosecuted the murderers of *Tribune* reporter Jake Lingle, beat seven opponents for the gubernatorial nomination. Chief among his foes was the familiar figure of Len Small. J. Hamilton Lewis was renominated for the Senate to run against Republican Otis F. Glenn. Eddie Barrett beat Horner's candidate, Homer Mat Adams, for auditor. Martin and Kerner were renominated without Horner faction opposition for treasurer and attorney general.

III

On the next day a band played "Home Sweet Home," and ten thousand Springfield citizens turned out at the railroad depot carrying torchlights to welcome home and escort to the Governor's Mansion the victorious Jew from the big city.

Jim Farley sent a wire of congratulations: "If I can be of any service in any way, please command." Roosevelt was said by Ickes in his diary to have been satisfied with the outcome, although Ickes pointed out that Hopkins had "played very open and flagrant politics with WPA for the benefit of the Kelly-Nash machine." Arch Bowen wrote his leader that "it seems that the lion in your character is fully as perfect as the lamb." Bishop Griffin added in his congratulatory note: "In my wildest dreams I did not realize your capacity when challenged. That you have culture, personality, and winning ways was known to me. I frankly feared that the injustice would weight heavily upon your sensitive nature and might even affect your health."

Henry Horner, the gentle jurist whose intestinal quotient had a short time earlier been open to doubt, had indeed worked a miracle deserving the national attention it now received. Against unbalanced odds he had challenged and conquered a big-city machine with enormous patronage resources at its disposal. He had beaten the machine without help from the national administration; indeed, the political weight of the Works Progress Administration program had been made available not to him but to the opposition. In the height of the depression he had waged an aggressive campaign that aroused public interest; he had milked every ounce of sympathy out of the old familiar image of the poor little lamb battling its executioner; he had used what patronage he did have in Chicago to maximum advantage; he had raised a large campaign fund in the city and established a metropolitan beachhead in the Jewish wards that had been such an important part of

Cermak's coalition against the Irish. And, of course, he had started with an extraordinary base of support in the downstate counties.

Ed Kelly took it all rather philosophically. "Oh, well, we wouldn't have had him anyway," he rationalized. "This was the chance we had to take and we really didn't have anything to lose." On the other hand, it is probably not at all strange that the experience produced a profound change in Horner. The lion that Bowen had mentioned almost devoured the lamb. He became a strong hater, believing now that he had been blessed with a latecoming insight into the jungle laws of politics. It was kick or be kicked. "I certainly was pretty soft for three years," he is said to have told Ickes. Now Horner took on a new sheen of unnatural toughness. He swore and pounded the table. At French Lick, Indiana, where he vacationed after the primary, he told John Cassidy, "I'd cut off this finger if I could get Stelle out of that office."

But Stelle remained. And Horner's only chance of rewarding Cassidy with a place on the ticket depended on a federal appellate court appointment for Otto Kerner, who frankly preferred a judgeship to his present job of attorney general. But Kelly, who still had control of the Democratic State Committee, insisted on Mike Igoe instead of Cassidy, and the disagreement finally caused Roosevelt to avoid the controversy by giving the judicial appointment to an Indiana judge.

The ordinary American politician is capable of turning his emotions on and off according to the needs of the moment. One day he will question the morals and the ancestral lineage of the opposition. On the next, with the election over and anger serving no practical purpose, he reverts to the role of the calm, businesslike operator thinking more of tomorrow's alliances than yesterday's betrayals. Not so Henry Horner. The transformation that had possessed this quiet, cultured man left him with an afterthirst for revenge. He became a thorough political bookkeeper determined to pursue the Kelly-Nash machine and crush it.

Consequently in May the governor called the legislature back to Springfield for another try at permanent voter registration "to protect the sanctity of the ballot box." An election is only free and equal, he said, when each person entitled to vote is allowed to cast his ballot according to the dictates of his own conscience and to have his vote so recorded and counted. Mindful of the defeat of the last permanent registration bill, Horner noted, "Another election has been held which has again demonstrated the necessity for such a law."

This time, helped along by the momentum of the machine's primary election loss, the bill passed. The signature of each voter would thereafter be on file, and each voter would be required to sign his name in the polling place. Going into effect for the November election, permanent registration would presumably screen out voters in the very wards where Horner stood to gain the most support, such as the West Side Twenty-fourth with its Jewish residents, the downtown First Ward, the Twentieth and Twenty-seventh with their many transients and unemployed relief recipients.

That the punitive methods invoked during the primary campaign were slow to be rescinded is indicated by a letter to the governor from Jake Arvey dated July 28, 1936. "I wish," Arvey wrote, "you would bear in mind my brother who operates the Crown Office Supply Company and who has been shut out of all [state] [4] business for the past three months. He has found it impossible even to obtain a tabulation of bids."

Horner was not so harsh with lower level state employees, taking the position that "they figured the machine couldn't be beaten. It would have meant their jobs. We have poor slobs who are blind and obedient. That blind obedience keeps the political machine rolling. Now they will be loyal to me and do better work for the state. They are experienced. Replacements would waste a lot of time learning the routine."

Efforts to bring about a reconciliation between Horner and Kelly, initiated by a variety of individuals ranging from Jim Farley to Bishop Griffin, came to naught. Horner did not seem especially anxious for a *rapprochement*. In a letter to a friend in May, he said, "I would do anything to bring about harmony if I could do it without losing my self respect. That is important to me and I would rather sacrifice the governorship than lose it." At the Democratic state convention in the Fairgrounds Coliseum the Cook County delegates booed the governor and cheered the mayor. A short time later, Horner wrote in another letter:

> These bosses have been seeking to extend their octopuslike stranglehold on the whole state. . . . Their efforts in our state convention were a disgrace to the party and their subsequent conduct has only emphasized to the people the dangers to our state. And so the arrogance of bossism continues. . . . Gibbons prophetically says "against stupidity the Gods themselves con-

> tend in vain." The only thing Roosevelt need worry about would be blundering like the WPA in Illinois. The purposes of WPA are basically all right but the bosses have had control of it in Illinois.

The use of the WPA by his opponents in the primary seemed particularly to stick in Horner's craw. He forwarded to Farley a letter of complaint about the WPA, saying it was "typical of a thousand other letters I have received. If you want the WPA to continue smashing the President's chances for carrying Illinois that is up to you. We are working diligently here to prevent it." Another letter to Farley asserted that the "WPA in Illinois has done the national administration more harm than good. This would not have happened if Washington had consulted those who knew the state outside of Cook County instead of those who used the patronage to help themselves personally and *not* the national cause." [5] He urged Senator Lewis' support for legislation that would make WPA state directors responsible to the governors and reminded him of his understanding that participants in WPA projects were to be chosen only according to need. He said:

> Not only was the administration of the WPA political, but it was partisanly political. The entire administration of the WPA was active against the Governor in the primary battle, employing every known device of terrorism for that purpose. Any self-respecting Governor would not permit partisan political control, even for his own political advantage. Nor did it stop there. Demands were made upon the WPA workers for contributions to political campaign funds. Those on WPA projects were herded to political meetings, compelled to wear campaign buttons, and in other ways subjected to political slavery.

Prospects for harmony deteriorated still more when the governor vetoed a special session bill sponsored by Ben Adamowski to use half instead of one-third of the state sales taxes for relief. Without the new legislation, Chicago needed to raise $1,400,000 a month from local tax resources for public assistance. "Further diversion of needed state revenue," Horner warned in his veto message, "will inevitably wreck the finances of the state." In response, Kelly placed the responsibility for Chicago's plight on the governor's shoulders. "There is no other way to raise the money," he said. "We are not going to raise taxes on the people of Chicago."

A reconciliation between Horner and his old friend Pat Nash

was achieved more easily. But the governor sneered at newspaper reports that he and Kelly had buried the hatchet. "Kelly would love to bury the hatchet," he confided in one speech, "right in this bald pate of mine." At the national Democratic convention in Philadelphia, the Horner and Kelly delegations sat separately and messages were carried between their leaders by emissaries. Horner tried unsuccessfully to replace the national committeewoman from Illinois, Elizabeth Conkey, with Blanche Fritz, a downstater. Nash stayed on as national committeeman, too. Kelly objected to Horner's designation of Lynden Smith of Pontiac as downstate campaign manager for the Democrats. But Horner insisted on Smith, and the lumber merchant who had toiled so diligently for him in the primary kept the title.

Shortly before the state fair, Senator Lewis relayed a curious message to the governor requesting that Senator Dieterich be permitted to speak at the Governor's Day program. "There are existing in the state," Lewis explained, "some who regard Senator Dieterich as a German in his political views, and since there are those who feel the issues as prevailing in certain parts of Europe in racial questions apply to Illinois, it is a very intelligent move to have Senator Dieterich appear to be supporting the candidate whose nomination he had opposed." Horner replied coldly that the speaking time had all been allotted and regrettably none could be found for Dieterich.

Late in August President Roosevelt and his national chairman, Farley, decided the Illinois feud had passed the danger point. Fresh from a brief vacation in the Wisconsin North Woods, Horner spoke to Kelly for the first time in nearly eight months at a conference with Farley in New York City. "Everything is harmonious and that's no bunk," Pat Nash informed reporters. Kelly grudgingly announced at a party rally soon after that, "I'm for every man on the Democratic ticket from top to bottom. Personalities have no part in this campaign."

Roosevelt visited Illinois himself in September to dedicate the Mark Twain Bridge at Hannibal, Missouri, to inspect drought-stricken farms in Pike County, and to talk with the governor and the mayor at the Governor's Mansion. A special ramp was constructed so that the president could be wheeled up to the front door by one of his sons. Kelly assured FDR that the Cook County organization could carry Chicago heavily for Roosevelt in his bid for a second term against Alf Landon. But the mayor told the president that he was not sure Horner could be re-elected because he was running as a downstate candidate and had antagonized many Cook County Democrats.

There is little doubt among surviving contemporaries that Kelly considered selling out Horner as a favor to his old friend Colonel McCormick. Some who claim to have first-hand knowledge say, however, that Kelly finally had to tell the colonel that the stakes were too high. The Roosevelt landslide had gained momentum, and it would simply be too difficult to try to "brake" the machine for one candidate. In the meantime the Horner forces were devising a strategy of their own. The Horner Papers contain a letter dated June 3 from Witt K. Cochrane, a Chicago advertising executive who had quit the Horner organization because of some personal differences with the governor's other aides. Part of his letter read: "I am closely allied to Big Bill Thompson and am preparing a scheme that will knock Brooks into a cocked hat and make your election certain. Big Bill can't be elected and he knows it, but he will kick hell out of Brooks and Kelly and Nash. Don't worry, I wouldn't double-cross you for ten truckloads of gold dollars. But, by the living Gods, that can't be said of every member of your organization. You are too trusting." The scheme was, of course, a simple one. Thompson would enter the race as an independent and drain off enough Republican votes to cripple Brooks's chances —thereby gaining some measure of revenge against McCormick. A Democrat who said he was in on the transaction told the author that the Horner campaign fund contributed $25,000 toward Thompson's "campaign expenses."

Brooks worked energetically at his campaign. Bishop Griffin advised his friend in the Governor's Mansion that the Republican had requested a meeting and that he wanted to head off word of the "scandal." "Sometime you might let me know of the terrible trimming he is going to get," the bishop wrote. "Should I put this figure at 400,000 or 500,000? . . . You might offer up a silent prayer that I land on my feet after the interview."

In keeping with standard Illinois campaigns during that time, this one generated more heat than light. Brooks concentrated his fire on the "tax gouge." "The only thing I hear about is taxation," Horner replied. "You can go out to the poor farms and talk about taxation to these poor souls who haven't a penny to their names and they'll get excited about taxation." Horner charged that the *Tribune* wanted to run the state and that Brooks operated only as a "fountain pen" for the newspaper. Brooks promised to reduce the sales tax and remove it from food altogether. Horner said this was ridiculous; the sales tax could not possibly be cut, no matter who the governor was. Although the ordinary expenses of government had been reduced 16 per cent during his administration, public aid and education had necessarily risen. Brooks combined his pledge to cut taxes with demands for new government programs that Horner insisted would more than double over-all costs. Harold Ickes delivered a speech at Northwestern University about Brooks's two qualifications for office: he had been an assistant state's attorney at the time of the Lingle murder case; and he had curly hair. Ickes referred sarcastically to the two colonels—the Sunrise Colonel, McCormick of the *Tribune;* and the Sunset Colonel, Knox of the *Daily News,* currently the Republican vice-presidential nominee and no longer a friend of Horner's. Incidentally, although Horner despised the *Tribune,* its publisher, and many of its workers, he remained on good terms with one of the paper's legislative reporters, the gentlemanly Percy Wood. It was Wood who had guided *Fortune*'s magazine writer in his research for the definitive article it published in 1936 on "The Kelly-Nash Machine," and when the governor heard of it, he wrote Wood—"While I may bark at you occasionally, my affection for you has never and will never abate."

Campaign funds flowed in nicely as the governor's cousin, banker Bob Straus, again performed yeoman's service in Chicago. Abel Davis, Horner's long-time Republican friend, gave several hundred dollars. Just before the election, Horner wrote to Skeeter Paul Steinbrecher:

> You're a brick and always a devoted friend. It was mighty good of you to write me as you did and also to enclose your generous check. The other personal work you are doing I appreciate also. With your child wife spending so much time at the Women's Independent Headquarters, I hope to allow you a little time to stay home and bake the cookies and direct the housework. Edith is doing a splendid job, and as she neglects you during the campaign I hope you will forgive me.

The Democratic landslide of 1936 that swept across the nation is familiar history. In Illinois these figures were left in the rubble:

Roosevelt	2,282,999	57.7%
Landon	1,568,393	39.7
Others	102,329	2.6
Horner	2,067,861	53.1

Brooks	1,682,685	43.2
Thompson and others	141,426	3.6

Roosevelt's plurality of 714,606 compared with J. Ham Lewis' 597,717 and Horner's 385,176. FDR carried Chicago by an incredible 555,492, winning 65.1 per cent of the vote. In the city Lewis won by 485,504, and Horner by 319,690. That Horner had, in fact, been "trimmed" by some organization precinct captains is shown by these comparative figures for four North Side precincts in the Forty-seventh, Forty-eighth, Forty-ninth, and Fiftieth Wards, all with large Jewish populations:

Horner	*FDR*
181	231
185	267
184	348
202	292
752	1,138

A tired Henry Horner, his blood pressure up, his breathing labored, nonetheless had reason to be pleased. After a succession of crises, he had persevered and walked out of the political jungle alive and upright. A year earlier, few of his most devout believers could have thought it possible. At the end of the year, Charlie Wheeler, political editor of the Chicago *Herald-Examiner*, gave way to his exuberance:

"Horner fell upon the Chicago Philistines with several jawbones, reviving and dramatizing the oldest bromide in political slugging—'smash the bosses.' Rejoicing in a leader as intrepid as Joshua and ready to march seven times around the Chicago city hall with his blasts from the ram's horn, the downstaters flocked to Horner in great hordes."

Shown Wheeler's copy in advance, the governor commented only that Joshua would surely cancel his subscription were he compared to Henry Horner.

CHAPTER FOURTEEN

Exit the Gentle Judge... Enter the Tough Pol

On the day Henry Horner was inaugurated for a second term as governor of Illinois, his portrait inexplicably plummeted from the wall of the Jersey County Circuit Court and struck ninety-one-year-old Uncle Joe Page on the cranium. The stunned editor of the Jersey County *Democrat,* who doubled in brass as master in chancery for the court, looked up and proclaimed that the fallen picture must have indeed been a message from on high. Surely it must signify that Henry Horner was destined for the White House in 1940.

The inaugural itself was less dramatic. The new armory building across from the Statehouse was sufficiently near completion to accommodate the ceremonies, although women guests snuggled in their furs against the cold drafts, and water dripped onto the stage from the unfinished roof. A mounted detachment of the 106th Cavalry escorted Horner to the armory, where the oath was administered by Chief Justice Lott Herrick. Mayor Kelly led a Chicago delegation of about a thousand. Mercifully, the governor read only fifty-two minutes of his fifteen thousand word address. In this comprehensive recapitulation of all the many problems of the state, he asked for a constitutional amendment permitting an income tax and called the system of local responsibility for dispersing state relief funds a "direct encouragement to waste and inefficiency." Through a transposition of letters in the text of his speech, the governor was put in the infuriating position of lauding the WPA, which he detested, and of not mentioning Ickes' PWA, which he admired. Horner dashed off a written apology to Ickes and explained that if he had read proof on the speech personally, as he should have, the error would not have occurred. That evening a rather perfunctory inaugural ball was held in the first and second floor rotunda halls of the Statehouse.

At this juncture, with the governor moving into his second four-year term, it is appropriate to concentrate for a moment on how the events of the past election year would affect Horner and his supporters. Beneath all the hoopla and ritual, politics is little more than collective human nature applied to public affairs. A governor had been told by the powers in his party that he was finished. Just as in Napoleon's time, many of those who had been lifted to positions of trust in the governor's administration deserted their benefactor, who was in deep trouble. But a few in Chicago, and more downstate, remained loyal to their leader—some out of principle, more (downstate especially) because there was no other more practical place to go. Having chosen to sink or survive alongside the governor, these individuals knew they could be blackballed when the regular party passed out rewards in the future. In his anxiety not to sink, the governor had resorted to some campaign devices which were out of character. Faith was deposited in people who could produce large numbers of votes, because the candidate desperately needed every vote he could muster. But now that the election was over, those who had gone through the war and survived seemed to feel less constrained about wringing whatever riches they could from state government than they did in the first four years out of respect for, or fear of, "the judge."

By the same token the engineers of Horner's triumph now expected and received positions of power in the second administration. James Slattery, who had been Cook County campaign manager, filled Ben Lindheimer's place on the commerce commission. Charlie Schwartz, who had worked the miracle in Bundesen's own ward, took over as patronage chief in Chicago. Lyn Smith, formerly business manager of the highway department, was promoted to the position of public works director as the reward for his downstate campaign direction. And the little haberdasher from Belleville, Sam Nudelman, who had been wished on Horner by Lindheimer, found himself at thirty-five years of age the new finance director.

The transformation in the governor himself can hardly be exaggerated. His traumatic campaign against Kelly and Nash had left its imprint. Horner now appreciated practitioners of political deeds whom he had regarded before as cheap and sordid and un-Lincolnian. He became vindictive, vain, revengeful, easily annoyed by little things, a hater. To emphasize a point in office conversation he struck the side of his hand hard on the top of his desk. He devoted great energy to trying to punish his enemies. When a congressman who had incurred his wrath was proposed for a federal judgeship, Horner assigned the research resources of one entire state agency to find material that might be used against the man at his Senate confirmation hearing.

As vacancies occurred on the Supreme Court, Senator Lewis and others suggested Horner's name. But with Stelle in the lieutenant governor's office now, the governor knew that all his friends would lose their jobs if he changed his. At the time of the Cardozo vacancy, Horner wrote to a friend: "Personally, I do not think the suggestion will get any further than to enable my biographer—if I have any—to say that I was 'also mentioned.' I feel now my duty to the people of this state is to finish my work as governor, as there is much to be done."

Early in his second term Horner could not avoid being drawn into a controversy that disturbed the nation. Frustrated by the Supreme Court's tendency to discard what he considered vital New Deal legislation, Roosevelt tried a drastic method of changing the attitudes of the court. He proposed to enlarge the court with additional members of his own choosing, an excessive suggestion that backfired in public opinion and is remembered as FDR's "court-packing scheme."

After their respective re-elections, the president had written this friendly note: "My dear Henry—I need not tell you how happy I am in your re-election. As you know, I am a strong believer in close cooperation between Washington and the various states, and I look forward to a very pleasant association." [1] The pleasantness ceased during the court-packing furor, however, when the president arranged a meeting in the Chicago Stadium to counter a series of regional rallies that had been sponsored by opponents of the plan. Horner was called by the White House and asked to preside at the stadium affair. Genial Henry said he would be glad to cooperate, but of course he would have to make known his own position on the question. And what was that? That he very emphatically opposed Roosevelt's court reorganization proposal and would have to say so. The rally went on without the governor.

Harold Ickes and Governor Gene Talmadge of Georgia both came to Springfield for a Lincoln's Birthday program during the dispute. Ickes argued that Lincoln too had been accused of "scuttling the Constitution, squelching the judiciary, setting up a dictatorship." New Deal critic Talmadge disagreed. Lincoln, he said, would never have approved the "wild orgies of spending" and the "oppressive taxation." "Would that we had a man like Lincoln in the White House today," he asserted. "[He] would never allow a braintruster's creed of teaching the doctrine that you can boondoggle your way back to prosperity." Horner considered this an insult to the president and dispensed with the usual courtesy of inviting a visiting governor to the mansion. Although Roosevelt's plan failed, one of his staunchest Senate allies had been Dieterich of Illinois, who would be up for re-election in 1938.

Right at this time another federal appellate judgeship opened up in Chicago, another opportunity to elevate Attorney General Kerner and thus substitute Horner's friend John Cassidy. There were more complications though. According to Ickes' diary, Cardinal Mundelein wanted a judgeship for his lawyer, and District Attorney Igoe was also interested. Horner pressed his demand on Senator Lewis with this telegram: "I should be more disappointed in the failure of Judge Kerner to receive the appointment than all the other disappointments that have unhappily come to me by action of Washington." The matter dragged on for months. Lewis wrote Horner that "the Poles have pressed strongly on the [Chicago Democratic] organization their rights and the President is opposed to naming someone freshly elected by the people." Horner's irritation increased. Again he wrote Lewis: "Naturally I am a little discouraged with the indifference shown in certain quarters in Washington to suggestions I make, but I ought to be used to it by this time." [2] In spite of his victory, the governor had not been able to follow up by blasting the Kelly-Nash forces out of party control, and both senators were aligned with the machine. In 1938, at the expiration of Dieterich's term, Horner would try to retire him.

All these complications notwithstanding, Horner remained on ideological grounds a believer in Roosevelt's New Deal crusade. He never allowed himself to be deceived when he scanned the over-all picture. Late in 1937 he wrote a friend in Spain: "The breach between the President and so-called big business—and the satellites of big business who joined with it—is widening and the unfair attacks upon the President by this opposition are becoming daily more vicious and unbridled. . . . While business may have much to complain about, yet it has much more to be thankful for, and the latter it has lost sight of. Sometimes I feel that business has lost its far-visioned leadership."[3]

Thanks largely to the governor's persistence, Kerner eventually landed the judgeship, and Cassidy became attorney general. Cassidy asked Horner how he would feel if he tried to clean out the slot machines that were operating openly in many downstate cigar stores. "John," Cassidy says the governor told him, "you can go over to that office and make a fortune. Some men have. If I thought you wanted to do that, I would not have appointed you. I'll never ask you to pull a punch. If I ever do, you can tell me to go to hell." The governor went further and pledged the use of state police for any gambling raids that the attorney general contemplated.

Although the new Horner had acquired a tolerance for raw politics, his personal standards were unchanged. In a 1937 convocation address at Illinois College, he said: "Politics is the science or the art of making government serviceable. There is no such thing as dishonorable politics any more than there is dishonorable physics or dishonorable chemistry. It is true that there are dishonorable politicians who have ambition to serve not their communities but themselves only." Another time, in a less scholarly pronouncement, he said:

> You're not going to find any saints on this earth and the last place to look is in politics. . . . It's amazing how many men there are in public life who think that every contact they have with public administration should mean an opportunity for graft. I have known Hinky Dink ever since I was a kid, and he has never asked me to do a wrong thing, but I know some holier-than-thou patriots who would steal this Statehouse if I let them get away with it. By watching every detail of the executive office I am going to make sure that however else the Horner administration may fail it's not going to have any scandals that I can stop.

In talking to his appointees the governor usually said something like this: "You owe only one guy for this job, and he'll never ask you for anything—because I'm that guy. Pay no attention to any other pressures, even Artie O'Brien's. And remember that if you ever do anything wrong, I'll haunt you to the grave."[4] So long as Horner remained vigorous, his helpers would have to weigh their desire for enrichment against the knowledge that the governor would tolerate no questionable practices. When his Skeeter pal

Bert Massee, the soap company millionaire who had gone broke in the crash, came to Springfield lobbying for an insurance bill, Horner promised his help, along with a warning that "if I find anybody bringing money in here on this bill, I'll turn against you."

But the governor had no more spare time at the start of his second term to reflect about his troubles than he had in 1933. While he was returning from the second Roosevelt inauguration, the Ohio River overflowed its banks and caused the worst flood ever recorded in southern Illinois. From Shawneetown to Cairo the rampaging river turned southern Illinois into a lake. In Eldorado, Harrisburg, and Cairo, Horner directed rescue operations from a rowboat, coordinating the efforts of the various federal and state agencies. Blankets were trucked from state hospitals and penitentiaries to help care for the eighteen thousand homeless people. The rebuilding costs exceeded $2,000,000.

This period also saw the birth of the sit-down strike. Workers used the new device of camping on the company premises and refusing either to move or work. In February of 1937 about one hundred sit-down workers defied a court ejection order at Fansteel Metallurgical Company in North Chicago. Union negotiations in Horner's office failed, and, with the governor's approval, the sheriff of Lake County used tear gas shells to forcibly evict the demonstrators. "There is," the governor said, "no warrant in law to justify a so-called sit-down strike," an opinion reached later and in more expansive language by the United States Supreme Court. Horner refused, however, to send National Guardsmen for the removal of strikers, explaining that bloodshed would result without the issues being settled. Labor strife persisted thereafter throughout his second administration. At Sterling, forty-one men were arrested, and one union member suffered injuries that required the amputation of his leg during a clash between the CIO and sheriff's deputies at the Northwest Barbed Wire Company.

II

When one of a succession of "action" committees filed into the governor's office, a social worker from Chicago named Jane Addams sought to pinpoint Horner's difficulty, as she saw it. "You're so busy watching the people around here so they won't steal," she said, "that when it comes to seeing through to the great problems of the day you don't have the facts or the vision."

Through New Deal program after New Deal program, the Great Depression hung stubbornly on. In the middle of 1937 there were still 427,400 receiving unemployment relief, 121,000 on WPA projects, and 115,000 on old-age assistance rolls. By the next year there would be more old-age pensioners in Illinois than in any other state.

The coal mine controversy refused to simmer down. Ray Edmundsen, president of District 12 of the United Mine Workers, demanded that the governor do something about poverty throughout the state. He charged that in Chicago hundreds of families had been evicted without any place to go and thousands of children were without clothing. Horner responded by inquiring which form of higher taxation Edmundsen preferred. As always, Dick Finnegan remained a burr under the saddle. In an otherwise jovial letter signed "Dick," the editor nettled the governor by adding the offhand comment that hundreds of families in Chicago were hungry. Addressing his frosty reply to "Dear Mr. Finnegan," Horner denied the hungry family statement, said an increase in relief appropriations would have to be met with additional taxes—and "I would be glad to have any suggestions you have to make for such additional taxes." [5]

Horner took the position consistently that the fact that the federal government operated a tax system which was more progressive than the tax system of many of our states was an argument in favor of more federal benefits for public assistance. But another point of view (expressed in *Collier's* magazine of July 20, 1940) saw the depression in Chicago as "one of the most glorious and successful in history." [6] The cynical author described how federal money had filtered through the politicians' hands. That the Chicago machine was fueled by federal generosity during these years is undeniably so. The governor struggled constantly to prevent the machine from gobbling up some of the many federal dollars. Relief and WPA jobs were tied in directly with the political organization. In many neighborhoods a contact with the precinct captain was a prerequisite for a foreign-speaking newcomer to obtain government help. Even internships in Cook County Hospital and jobs making jelly sandwiches in the school lunchrooms were sometimes politically sponsored.

In at least one instance the governor's loyalty to an old friend made him more than an interested party to a conflict with the federal government. The federal social security board paid close attention to how old-age pensions were being administered by the states. In Illinois the program was run by the former mayor of Kewanee, a kindly old man who always wore his straw hat in the office. He was not a very good administrator and before long an incredible mess had been created. A backlog of twenty thousand cases awaited processing, and the federal agency found that some people not entitled to aid were receiving it. Efforts to persuade Horner to replace the administrator were unavailing, and in August of 1937 federal grants for old-age pensions in Illinois were stopped. The governor finally brought in John Weigel, the welfare department's fiscal supervisor, to restore order to the program. He discovered that patronage had been abused. He worked his staff week ends, installed the state's first business machine system, and soon had the program working to Washington's satisfaction.

In order to gain the governor's cooperation on Chicago legislation, Kelly agreed that Horner could select the House speaker in 1937, and the governor picked his old Masonic acquaintance, Louie Lewis of Christopher. But later the governor lost an argument with the regular organization over whether his highway division or Ed Hughes's office of secretary of state should administer the new drivers' licensing law; evening the score, he won another battle over the tax levy for the Chicago Park District.

Near the end of the 1937 session Oliver Barrett wrote to Horner of his "hope that you have begun in earnest to cut down your hours of labor with a corresponding increase in the hours of good fellowship and recreation, not forgetting the movies." [7] Accordingly, the governor's friends rejoiced when, after the bill-signing period, he agreed to take a short vacation at Ross Woodhull's summer home in Land-o'-Lakes, Wisconsin. Their pleasure multiplied when Horner arrived with eleven suitcases, indicating that he really intended to stay long enough for a good rest. Every night, though, the light in the governor's room burned until quite late, and Woodhull's curiosity prompted him to peek in. Ten of the eleven suitcases had been filled with state work, and the governor was busily going through papers in his room on his Wisconsin "vacation."

III

Added to his official work load now were the duties of a political leader. Not burdened with the family responsibilities of his associates, Horner held regular Sunday morning strategy sessions in the Congress Hotel with his team of Tom Courtney, Al

Horan, Charlie Schwartz, Lyn Smith, Martin Kennelly (a Chicago businessman who was later elected mayor), and Ben Adamowski, who had now gone over to his side. These men were plotting, first, the downfall of Senator Dieterich, whose anti-Semitic tinge in the 1936 fight would not soon be forgotten by the governor. (Dieterich, whose parents were rural German immigrants, has been aptly described by Paul Y. Anderson of the St. Louis *Post-Dispatch* as "a large pink and white man, with a strident voice and a swelling shirt front.")

Although the governor had no immediate opportunity to break up the Kelly-Nash combine, it was a time of optimum prestige for him. But he harbored plans to try to beat Kelly in the 1939 mayoral election, with Courtney probably. At Governor's Day at the state fair, Courtney told the assembled Democrats that Horner's job "has been made more difficult by those who do not appreciate honesty in public service." Mike Igoe, who would soon receive his federal judgeship, praised the governor. "Problems greater than those encountered in the Civil and World Wars have been met and solved in Illinois," he said, "under the matchless efficiency and superb leadership of the man we acclaim today as the pride of our democracy, the protector of the common man."

In October Horner left no ambiguity about his feelings for Dieterich: "He is not the choice of the Democracy of Illinois, nor can he win. Senator Dieterich has never spoken to me about his candidacy nor sought our support. He knows he cannot obtain it." This left Kelly, Roosevelt—and Dieterich—in a quandary. The president and Farley were compelled to help Dieterich because he had been a regular supporter of administration causes. But could Kelly hope to beat Horner with a downstater of such dubious vote-getting pull as Dieterich? Consequently, the mayor advised Roosevelt that Dieterich could not win and would have to be scrapped. At this point, Farley, who was already preparing his own plans for the presidential nomination in 1940, threw his support to Mike Igoe with the expectation that Igoe could then control the Illinois delegation for him at the national convention.

The governor visited the White House for dinner and a musicale, after which he informed the president that a downstater and not Igoe would have to be the candidate. Dieterich, who had not given up hope, denounced Horner, saying the governor "has organized a political holding company for the purpose of commercializing politics and has had himself elected executive head of that company." "If he has any question as to how the people of this state view his services," shot back Horner, "all he need do is file his petition for renomination."

No longer a political novice, Horner's confidence hinged privately on his anticipation that Mayor Kelly would make one very important additional mistake. The mayor complied. Besides supporting Igoe for senator, Kelly decreed that Edmund Jarecki would be dumped as county judge. Born in Plzan, Poland, the son of a butcher, Jarecki had been a protégé of Stanley Kunz', the first chief of the Democratic Poles in Chicago. He went to the city council with Tony Cermak in 1911 and continued on up the ladder until he took over supervision of the election machinery as county judge in 1922. His endorsement of permanent voter registration prompted Kelly and Nash to demand his retirement. They ran another Pole, Circuit Court Judge John Prystalski, against him. In doing so, Kelly played into Horner's hands. Now the election machinery would be in Horner's control, not the organization's; moreover, Horner and Jarecki had an issue, the sacredness of the ballot box—and they had an appeal to the Polish voters of Chicago. This time it would not be strictly a Chicago-downstate fight.

Once it was certain the Jarecki dumping would stand, the governor chose Congressman Scott Lucas of Havana to run for senator. This did not please the president. Lucas had a conservative voting record in the House and had opposed the court-packing plan, the wages and hours bill, and many other New Deal programs.

Caught in the middle of this uncomfortable squeeze, Dieterich withdrew "in the interests of party harmony." The national administration understandably supported Igoe against Lucas, but without the president's direct involvement. For state treasurer Horner ran Louie Lewis, and Kelly and Nash put up Bruce Campbell. Dan Sullivan had died early in 1938, but Horner remobilized most of the 1936 organization and campaigned as though he were running himself. He flailed away at Barnet Hodes—"When Mayor Kelly takes snuff, Hodes sneezes. He sits on Kelly's knee and babbles like Charlie McCarthy. But even in Charlie McCarthy's wooden head is enough spunk to talk back to the master now and then." Hodes roared back in the same vein. History, he declared, would remember this as the Primary of the Five Conspiracies—hypocrisy, slander, confusion, misappropriation (of voter registration cards), and assassination (of the Democratic party). The conspiracies, he went on, were conceived by traitor Democrats, by hypocritical Democrats, by fake Democrats, and by Democrats suffering from swelled heads—in short, by the "mugwump and carpetbag ticket" Horner had conceived.

Religious identification played a part in this campaign too. Back in the 1920's Lucas' older brother, Allen Thurmond Lucas, said to have been a member of the American Protective Association and the Ku Klux Klan, had been accused of distributing anti-Catholic literature when Chicago Irishman Roger Sullivan campaigned in Cass County. This bit of history returned to haunt Lucas in 1938 and was widely used against him in Chicago Catholic neighborhoods. In some of these districts, over-imaginative precinct workers improvised further by suggesting that Lucas was actually a Jew who had changed his name, thus reviving more of the 1936 emotions.

On primary election night, while Horner and Lucas waited in the Congress Hotel and the governor's downstate leaders sat in the St. Nicholas Hotel in Springfield, Igoe scanned the Cook County returns and issued his radio victory speech. "They know something we don't," insisted the visibly perturbed Horner. Chomping on a cigar at the St. Nick, the governor's lieutenant Joe Knight did actually know something that Mike Igoe didn't. He knew he was sitting on a 300,000-vote margin downstate that he would not let loose until he was certain enough late votes could not be resurrected in Cook County to offset them. The governor's hard work, the extra influence of Jarecki in Cook County Polish districts, and the approximately $1,600,000 spent by the Lucas forces paid off. Once again Gentle Henry had knocked off the Kelly-Nash juggernaut. The final count showed a difference of only 75,284. The conservative Lucas outpolled Igoe 418,530 to 163,999 downstate —but lost by 179,247 in Cook County. This time Jarecki's strength in the Polish wards and Horner's popularity in the same Jewish wards he had carried two years earlier turned the trick. Without Jarecki (who also won) on his side, Horner could never have beaten the Chicago Irishman with a downstater—and he knew it. Louie Lewis beat Bruce Campbell, too, by about the same edge.

For most of the same reasons that existed after the 1936 primary, the governor could not consolidate his accomplishment by shoving the mayor off his throne. That chance would not come until 1939 and the next municipal election. So Horner took the national acclaim in stride. A friend who had sent him a newspaper clipping of a story booming him for the White House in 1940 was advised: "Don't get too excited about the Presidency. Politics is a funny thing. If we did not win at the primary, I might have been recommended as a Class A truck driver for the WPA."

Whatever his temptation to challenge the machine to combat, Horner had to temper his anger. There was a more immediate practical problem. Lucas had won the primary fight and now had the formidable challenge of running against Horner's foe of several years in the legislature, Richard Lyons of Mundelein, the Republican nominee for the Senate. There were alarming signs of Roosevelt's growing unpopularity in isolationist Illinois as international tensions drew tighter. How could the torn Democratic party elect a senator if the governor remained at odds with the source of most of its votes in Chicago? James Weber Linn, the University of Chicago professor who was running for the legislature, expressed one point of view. "I ask you," he wrote, "to remember 'I shall be content if I can drive just one snake out of Illinois.' If they are so keen on harmony let them harmonize by themselves while you and yours go on to victory. Personally, I would rather lose than harmonize with crooks and doublecrossers. The lion cannot lie down with the snake under the swastika." Linn also added a caustic and timeless postscript about his own campaign: "The damn university [of Chicago] people have come through for only about $350. I have to do it all myself. They make me sick."

When Senator Lewis was quoted in the press as having assured President Roosevelt that "political peace now reigned" between Horner and Kelly, the governor wired him forthwith: "I have just read your statement and am wondering on what source you based it. Any announcement to be made about my attitude on political differences I will make myself." The governor had a sarcastic postscript of his own: "I saw in the newspapers recently an account of your having determined to ask $10,000,000 from the federal government for relief aid for the state. I shall be pleased to know if you have made any progress along that line."

The arduous primary campaign sapped the governor's health. Dr. Rosen warned him that his circulatory system would not take such exertion and that he must slow down. His labored breathing particularly alarmed the physician. But when he was advised to rest in bed for a few days, Horner exploded. "I need something to relieve this nagging cough, not hugging the bed," he protested. "When this campaign is over, there'll be plenty of time for bed rest."

As Horner had feared, the fall campaign was fiercely contested.

Lyons, whose campaign literature portrayed the Statehouse with three balls on the top, suggesting a pawnshop, assailed high taxes but promised a $30 a month old-age pension if he were elected. The governor reminded voters all over the state that Lyons had fought old-age assistance down the line until campaign time. "They were but deserters in the depression," he declared. "They had no heart for the people. How could they? You can't grow a heart overnight. You can't wave a wand and develop a conscience. You can't acquire love for humanity in an hour."

Jake Arvey took the initiative in trying to restore some semblance of harmony to the party. The mayor was persuaded to appear at the state fair on Governor's Day and to speak glowingly of Horner, although Horner's Chicago ally Tom Courtney refused to appear on the platform with Kelly. Kelly promised Horner that there would be no "trimming" of either Lucas or Jarecki by organization precinct captains. But later in the campaign Courtney, recalcitrant again, disobeyed Horner's instructions and attacked the machine at a party meeting. Although it was not evident at the time, this was the end of the relationship between Horner and the man who thought he would be the governor's candidate against Kelly the following year. Courtney had been with the governor from the start of his march to power. But Horner was convinced (by Arvey, no doubt) that Courtney had acted selfishly against the best interests of the party. Horner the political leader, the political bookkeeper who made entries with an indelible pencil, scribbled a mark next to Courtney's name.

Horner's Standard Club campaign fund pipeline opened up for Lucas. Albert Lasker, the advertising executive who had two state policemen assigned to guard his Lake County home, gave $2,500. Despite his earlier split with the governor, Ben Lindheimer remained a major campaign benefactor. Lucas said later that Lindheimer "picked up" eight hundred billboards in the campaign.

Succumbing to the temptation, occasionally experienced by every politician, to snap back at a newspaper, the governor wrote Colonel McCormick at the end of the campaign: "It is too bad that your bitter partisanship in this campaign found it necessary for your malicious and unfair editorial of Tuesday of this week to insult my integrity and question my sincerity." The publisher answered with one of his characteristic retorts: "I regret the use of 'political sincerity and integrity.' A wider latitude in political conduct is tolerated and condoned than in other activities—just as we accept a freer morality among movie people than among others—

but there are people who might overlook the qualifying word 'political,' just as you, in your indignation, have chosen to do."

Horner found frequent cause to be disenchanted with the press and told associates that reporters made things up when they had nothing to write about. Nevertheless, in 1938, he criticized a bill introduced by Senator Sherman Minton of Indiana (later a Supreme Court justice) making it a felony for a publisher to print as fact what he knew to be false. Minton resented Horner's criticism and wrote that "lies deliberately printed in the news columns are not protected by the free press, and no one knows that better than you." Horner replied that civil remedies were available in such cases and made this comment:

> During the course of a long public career I have had a number of unpleasant experiences with newspapers. . . . However, I do not advocate that the freedom of the press be suppressed or that we do anything which tends in that direction. The principle of a free press is too fundamental, too basic and too priceless to be subjected to any impairment whatever. . . . The arbitrary exercise of such power as your bill would lead, in the hands of unscrupulous men . . . to a dictatorship of the press. . . . My personal judgment is that a newspaper which persists in misrepresenting facts falls quickly in public opinion.

Lucas won the election by a close 95,592 votes, receiving 51.3 per cent of the total. He lost downstate by 108,193 and dropped the Cook County suburbs by 51,492, but captured Chicago by 255,277—evidence that Arvey and Kelly had kept their word. Following the election, Arvey wrote the governor:

> About six weeks ago I told your sidekick Jim Slattery that I would never again be found fighting for any cause or person to which or to whom you were opposed—and that still goes. . . . It is a matter of great satisfaction to me that the Organization functioned beautifully and smoothly and that the Mayor, as well as P. A., were 100 per cent for the candidates in whom you were especially interested. . . . You have convinced every member of our party that you are a true loyal Democrat, and a fine friend. No power on earth can change that opinion of you.[8]

From his home in Havana, the senator-elect sent Horner a letter:

> No man in my life, except my deceased brother, has done more for me than you, and if I should live to be a hundred I should always remember your many kind and charitable acts.

> Your labor, your industry, your counsel, and your advice, together with your political strategy, could not have been more sincere and far-reaching had you been laboring for yourself.
>
> No one can gainsay that there was a definite trend toward the right . . . and we in Illinois should be happy and proud in our victory when we witness the demise of many of our political brothers. After you . . . are again back on the job, we should start to build for 1940.[9]

But the building would have to wait.

Two days before the election, a deadly tired Horner, gasping for breath, alternately pale and flushed, worn down by night after night of exhausting campaign traveling, lack of rest, and tons of sodden campaign cuisine, slumped in the back of the limousine while Captain Van Diver drove north from Kankakee to Chicago and the climax of the Lucas campaign.

Suddenly a sharp pain stabbed in the back of his neck, and the governor felt an odd sensation shoot through his body. Arriving at the hotel in Chicago, Van Diver noticed that Horner was stammering incoherently, beads of perspiration dotting his forehead. Dr. Rosen hastened to Chicago and was shocked to find the governor in tears. Horner tried to speak, but no words came out. Reporters were informed that he had taken a bad cold and would require several days of bed rest. In fact, it was easily discernible to the doctor that his patient had been stricken with cerebral thrombosis, a blood clot on the brain.

CHAPTER FIFTEEN

The Restless Reign of the Bedside Cabinet

The cortical lesions on the governor's brain would require much rest and ease of mind for him to fully recover. The Horner high command received this medical appraisal from Dr. Rosen at a secret meeting in Chicago after the election. A few days later, on Thanksgiving, the top aides were again summoned to the Congress Hotel. First, the governor, whose speaking ability had been partially restored, laid out a rather systematic plan for tending to the removal of Ed Kelly in the spring mayoral campaign. With Courtney removed from consideration, the only unknown quantity in this equation remained the choice of the right candidate. Then Horner announced that he would be leaving the state the next morning to recuperate at the Miami home of Colonel L. P. Bonfoey, chairman of the state aeronautics commission.

Under the Illinois Constitution, when the governor is out of the state the lieutenant governor takes his place. This requirement created some complications. "Keep an eye on Stelle," was the governor's parting admonition. To maintain surveillance, Horner designated a regency made up of the newly commissioned power elite—Jim Slattery, Lyn Smith, Sam Nudelman, and Charlie Schwartz.

His inability to return for the opening of the legislative session on January 9 required that Horner delegate the preparation of the governor's message to Stelle. Dr. Rosen brought back word from

Florida that Horner could not come home until April and needed at least six months more for full recovery from what was now described as a hypertensive heart condition.[1] The physician's public assurances did not prevent the spreading of rumors that the governor lay totally paralyzed, that he had cancer, that he was insane from neurosyphilis, or that he had been stricken by a coronary occlusion. The truth was that except for short walks on the sun porch, aided by a cane, Horner was bedridden. His weight had fallen from 203 to 173 pounds.

The conditions of his convalescence gave rise to journalistic speculation as well. On January 18 a headline appeared in the Chicago *Times*—"Horner Seen by Reporter"—over a story by Collis Jordan:

> I saw Governor Horner today. Bundled in a green bathrobe, wearing a gray hat and dark sunglasses, he sat on a beach chair on the porch of the palatial home of [Bonfoey]. It was the first time the ailing and closely guarded chief executive has been seen by newsmen since his arrival here Nov. 27. Our sight of him from a chartered speedboat cruising offshore from the estate dispelled a growing rumor Governor Horner had been removed from the Miami Beach retreat.

Dr. Rosen traveled to Florida periodically to examine his patient. He also had an opportunity to observe the regency in Springfield. During one of his stays in Miami, he recorded this passage in his diary:

> When they [the regents] got drunk, each was trying to outdo the other. They bragged about how they had made Horner Governor twice, instead of being thankful for what Horner had done for them. . . . I was irritated because the Governor's ailment meant so little to them. As my train pulled out [from Miami enroute to Chicago], their hilarious profanities were ringing in my ears. "What a regent, what a regent, what a regent," the train seemed to say. It brought memories from the history of the French revolution, and the fight for power of the Girondists, the Mountains, and the Jacobins when heads fell. With the wholesale butchery came down the heads of Danton, Marat, and finally Robespierre.

On April 8, "feeling fine except for my rubber legs," the governor returned to Illinois by train. He said he intended to resume his full duties, even though the doctor had ordered him to work only an hour or two a day at the office until he regained his strength.

Unfortunately, the reports from the regency of conflicts with Stelle worried him more than his blood pressure.

Slightly more than an hour after the governor's train crossed into Illinois, Senator James Hamilton Lewis died in a Washington hospital. By the space of one hour, Stelle had missed the opportunity to appoint a United States senator, a fatefully close call that seemed to tickle Horner immensely. Stelle said later that, had the governor's train been late, he would have named Pat Nash to the vacancy. But Horner filled the position with another Chicago Irishman, his commerce commission chairman James M. Slattery.

Mayor Kelly was in the greeting party when the governor arrived at the Polk Street station in Chicago. "Now I shall get strong rapidly," Horner predicted. "All I need is to get my feet in Illinois mud." A few days later he received a message from the president.

> Dear Henry: I was glad to hear at first hand today from Ed Kelly that you are safely back in Springfield and are daily regaining your strength. You must really take care of yourself, not only for the sake of your friends, among whom I count myself, but also because I am certain that if you do not hurry things too much you will be strong and well again soon. . . . I am glad you appointed Slattery, whom I hope to see in a few days. He has real ability and will make a name for himself and I am confident of his loyalty to your cause and mine.

The governor's incapacity forced a change of the earlier plans to challenge Kelly at the polls. Courtney ran anyhow and was swamped. His disappointment caused him to remark bitterly, according to some of those who were present, that "the Jew took a dive under the bed" during the mayoral campaign. The report of these slurring words was carried back to Horner and intensified his hatred of his onetime ally and friend. For a combination of reasons, Slattery arranged for the power of the leaderless Horner organization to assist Kelly against Courtney in the primary, a decision that was made before the governor resumed control. It has since been suggested privately by someone who was on hand at the time that Slattery was "a sly fox who always played ball secretly with Kelly." Jarecki, on the other hand, supported Courtney as a token of reciprocity for Courtney's help in 1938.

After his re-election to another four-year term, Kelly plotted in turn his overdue revenge in the legislature against the partially disabled governor. But he was dissuaded from most of this by Arvey, whose personal power in the party had continued to rise and who had now effected a *rapprochement* of sorts with Horner.

But a letter among the Horner Papers reveals that the governor had been angry because Roy Keehn, the commanding general of the 33d National Guard Division, gave Arvey a captaincy in the guard without clearing it with him in Florida. The letter dated November 21, 1939, from Keehn to Horner, said that Arvey had visited the National Guard encampment in 1937 and "evinced such an interest in the work of the Guard and National Defense that he expressed to me his hope that he might contribute something. . . . I myself secured the resignation of Captain Paul Jones to create a vacancy for Arvey, and I sent through the recommendation that his appointment be made. This did not reach Springfield until you had left for the South . . ."

Upon his return to Springfield the governor found affairs in a grand mess. The legislature was voting many hundreds of millions of dollars in excess of anticipated income for old-age pensions, relief, and school aid, prompting Horner to warn that his veto would be used to head off "a spending orgy as now seems in the offing." The chronic shortage of money for relief meant that in July the welfare allotment for a family of four had to be reduced from $47.50 to $31. Regardless of his infirmities, Horner mustered all his energy for the business at hand. He adopted Abe Marovitz, a new state senator and a graduate of the Twenty-fourth Ward, and tried to guide him around the pitfalls in Springfield. Horner told Marovitz to be mindful that he and the governor were among the few Jews in the government and must, above all, "reflect credit on our people." He took the Chicago senator to New Salem, lectured him on the principles of Lincoln, and instructed him not to become a "politician."

Actually, of course, Horner and Marovitz were not the only Jews in the Statehouse, a factor which must be faced in order to understand the bad feeling that grew more intense between the governor's forces and those of Stelle. Some of the men who were attracted to the southern Illinoisan during these years were unquestionably anti-Semitic. Congregating at the bar in one of the Springfield hotels, they would proclaim loudly that "we're going to have the bleacher concession in the Statehouse rotunda when we run those Jews out of there. Our day will come." The prime object of animosity for Stelle's cronies soon became Sam Nudelman, the clothing merchant who had been brought to Springfield by Lindheimer, placed in a $125-a-month clerk's job, and quickly elevated to finance director and a place in the regency. Nudelman was haughty, opportunistic, and ingratiating, although he was never able to charm Stelle, who disliked him enormously.

Stelle's Independence Day announcement that he definitely expected to be a candidate for governor in 1940 aroused Horner. "If anything will keep me alive," he informed his friends, "this, more than any medicine, is it." For a brief period after his return from Florida, the governor seemed to improve. But he would not follow medical instructions, and his underlings turned the mansion into a combination cafeteria, cocktail lounge, and poker casino. Dr. Rosen has spoken of a sickroom filled with cigar smoke; of his constant arguments with the "cheap politicians"; of his trying to stop them from annoying the governor; and of the "heartless profiteers who partied in the mansion while Horner lay gravely ill. Just when his condition picked up, he would be provoked to fury by some fresh incident of mismanagement or political friction, his blood pressure would rise, his face flushed, and his speech would again become scanning and inarticulate."

By the middle of 1939 he would lapse into a deep sleep for as long as four days at a time, taking only liquids for nourishment. The regency, joined now by Horner's public relations assistant, former reporter Milburn (Pete) Akers, assumed the role of a bedside cabinet. These men endeavored to keep Stelle and the public from knowing of the governor's prolonged periods of semiconsciousness when for all practical purposes the state of Illinois lacked a responsible chief executive. However, Horner would rally from such periods and, although physically exhausted, would be reasonably alert and capable of making decisions. "Watch out for people with black bags," he calmly instructed a new member of the commerce commission who had waited three days to catch the governor in a lucid moment and be officially advised of his appointment.

From time to time the governor's relatives and friends urged that he resign his office and give himself a reasonable chance to regain his health. "And turn the state over to Stelle? Never." This almost psychopathic hatred of the lieutenant governor was reinforced by Nudelman, who, more than the rest of the bedside cabinet, filled the governor's ear with dire warnings that Stelle would exploit the state.

Nevertheless, after the bill-signing period, the governor's doctors insisted that he get away from Springfield's untherapeutic atmosphere. Horner would not leave the state again, though, and he rented a house on a bluff overlooking Lake Michigan in Highland Park, north of Chicago. On the airplane trip from the capital, Dr. Rosen told his patient that his medical condition would never permit a third term campaign and that it was absurd for him even to think about it.

"Do you play poker, doctor? Do you know what an ace in the hole means? That's what I've got. I'm not committing myself. Then when the time comes I can choose my successor."

Three months later, on October 13, Horner returned again to Springfield and announced to reporters that "I'm going to run for re-election—there is no question about that. I can't stop in the middle of a job." His strength continued to ebb, though, and doctors prescribed twelve hours of sleep and a maximum of three hours' work daily. A pathetic mood closed in over the Governor's Mansion. During a dedication attended by Postmaster General Farley, reopening the United States Post Office in the restored Lincoln-Berry store at New Salem, the governor wept in his sick bed as he listened to the ceremonies on radio.

In one of the lucid intervals, a delegation led by Treasurer Louie Lewis and the state Democratic chairman, Harry Hershey, called to plead for executive clemency for the five young DuQuoin coal miners who had killed the fourteen-year-old daughter of a deputy sheriff during the mine wars in southern Illinois. Four had been sentenced to life imprisonment and the fifth to forty years. Horner studied the record of the case and then summoned Lewis to his bedroom. "This involved the death of an innocent little girl, Lou," he said. Then, pointing to the picture of his mother above his bed, he said, "She won't let me do it, I'm sorry." Then, overcome by melancholy, he tried to explain in stumbling, thick-tongued speech why he was still considering a third term. "Some people wonder why I want a third term. Well, all I've got in the world is this state. When Illinois is successful, I am pretty happy. When Illinois or any individual in it is unhappy, then I am unhappy too."

In bed, Horner mulled over the myriad of human burdens that the governor was expected to lift. A letter from Mary Jo White, age six, of Killen, Alabama . . . a car with Illinois license plates had hit her puppy on the highway . . . "It came like lightning and tore my puppy to pieces" . . . Could the governor do anything about it? . . . Nothing but extend sincere sympathies, which he did in a carefully composed letter to the child.[2]

Then in November of 1939 the first of two blows that would finish off Henry Horner landed with a thud.

II

Len Small had started his political career on the Board of Trustees of Kankakee State Hospital back in the days when each state institution was a political principality all its own. As governor, Small budgeted funds to begin construction of the first eight buildings of a second institution near the tiny village of Manteno in the midst of the cornfields of Kankakee County. Creviced limestone underlay the site, and engineers wondered how water would be supplied. Committed to the venture, succeeding governors had no choice but to enlarge Manteno hospital, and by 1939 its 6,200 patients made it one of the world's largest institutions for the mentally ill.

In Len Small's county of Kankakee, south of Chicago, the only politics that counted for much were Republican politics. By now the Small machine was being operated with the help of a local automobile dealer and state senator, Victor McBroom. Usually the only Democrats who got ahead in such surroundings were those who worked out an accommodation with the Small-McBroom organization. Patronage flowed, of course, from the Democratic state administration into the two huge mental institutions.

Though a Republican for many years, Horner's welfare director, Arch Bowen, had no more sympathy for the political demands of McBroom's cohorts than for those of Stelle or anyone else. By late 1939 this sore spot had been rubbed so raw that leaders in Kankakee County were anxious to inflict damage on both Bowen and the bedridden Horner. Unfortunately, an epidemic of typhoid fever had swept the one-hundred-building complex of Manteno hospital, bringing death to sixty patients and illness to four hundred and fifty others. When it was discovered that the state department of public health had sent a series of reports to Bowen's department warning that the water supply was contaminated and unsafe for drinking, the Democratic state's attorney of Kankakee County, Samuel H. Shapiro, impaneled a special grand jury to consider possible criminal negligence in the matter. As a young lawyer attending Horner's second inaugural almost three years before, Shapiro had been taken aside and told, "You're just starting your political career. I'm about at the end of mine. You have a brilliant future in front of you." In June of 1939 Horner, who admired the promising young Democrat, gave a wedding gift of silverware to Shapiro and his bride. Five months later, the grand jury indicted the hospital managing officer, his assistant, the dietician, and Director Bowen. The grand jury which considered the evidence consisted entirely of Republicans, among them precinct committeemen, an election judge, the wife of the former county assessor, a former mayor, and employees of Small's bank.

Archie Leonard Bowen was a taciturn puritan with such strict scruples that he would take a streetcar home rather than use his state automobile for personal affairs. After a full career as a newspaperman in his native Bloomington and in Springfield, Bowen worked for the state under five different governors over a span of twenty-five years. Horner prized the humanitarian instincts of his seventy-two-year-old welfare director and valued his friendship. While the Bowens were in Washington for the 1937 inauguration, Harriet Ela Bowen died of pneumonia. When the grief-stricken director returned to Springfield with his wife's body, one man met the train: Henry Horner.

Commenting on the malfeasance indictments, the governor stated at a press conference that he had looked into the facts of the case and that Bowen should not have been held personally responsible. Horner elaborated in a letter to a friend: "All of the facts [about Manteno] will one day be made public, and they will show that Mr. Bowen is in fact standing as a martyr for the errors of others. I am loath to see his health and energy dissipated fruitlessly in a long public trial of the issues." [3] The governor surprised Bowen with flowers on Thanksgiving and New Year's Day, accompanied by notes reaffirming his pride in Bowen's service to the state. "It has," Bowen replied, "racked me to the very foundation of my being to feel that possibly, somewhere along the line, I have been derelict or negligent or, perhaps, have failed in judgment." He thanked Horner for the flowers and said "they spoke to me of your kindness and thoughtfulness at a time when, I must admit, I was distressed."

The Bowen case is still subject to dispute.[4] A judge of the Circuit Court of Kankakee County ruled that Bowen was guilty of omission of duty for his "failure to exercise reasonable care to furnish reasonably safe drinking water" for the patients. Repeated inspection reports had mentioned the presence of bacteria in the well water, apparently due to seepage of sewage into the walls through the creviced limestone under the hospital. There is no doubt of Bowen's administrative insight, although it is questionable whether the director, who was neither doctor nor scientist, managing a department with 56,000 patients, inmates and prisoners in 25 institutions, and 10,000 employees, should have been held personally responsible. There is also reason to think that the prosecutor (Shapiro) was pressured into a political prosecution by the persistently harsh demands of the *Chicago Tribune* and by the dominant McBroom organization, with which he would have to deal for years to come in the standard bipartisan Kankakee pattern. This, of course, Shapiro denies. In any event, the old man was fined $1,000 and ordered removed from office in time for maximum Republican advantage in the 1940 state campaign. He exhausted his personal funds carrying his appeal to the state supreme court, which reversed the trial court. The supreme court pointed out that the evidence did not establish that the epidemic had even been water-borne and that, indeed, one woman patient could have been the carrier. The court made the further point that Bowen himself had been disabled for several weeks at Peoria Hospital during the height of the epidemic with a severe streptococcus infection and that during this crucial period he had had no firsthand knowledge of events at Manteno.

III

In January the governor's inner circle—and his doctors—gathered without him one Sunday morning at the Drake Hotel in Chicago to talk about what they had all been thinking but had not wanted to discuss individually for fear of being thought disloyal. The medical advice confirmed what they all now knew—that it would be senseless to give another thought to running this sick man for another four years in office. Electrocardiograms traced the lasting damage to his heart. He was fast losing what the doctors called the integrity of his motor center. He lapsed more frequently into deep sleep with Cheyne'-Stokes' breathing—cyclical changes in rapidity of breathing, followed by total cessation of breathing for almost a minute at a time. When he awoke he would stare silently for hours at the picture of his mother on the wall. The men at the Drake worked hard preparing a carefully worded statement of withdrawal. When Horner saw it the next morning, he read it, folded it up, and tore it into tiny pieces, saying "You damn fools, don't you know that's just what Kelly wants?"

At the beginning of February his long hours of mock political strategy-making with a room full of drinking, cigar-smoking politicians took their toll, and finally even the patient himself became alarmed. "My strength is leaving me," he whispered before falling asleep in the midst of a doctor's examination. Dr. Rosen minced no words telling both the governor and his associates that unless Horner withdrew promptly he would be courting calamity for himself and the party—because the party would find itself with a dead candidate in November.

Senator Slattery, who had a foot in both camps and wanted to keep the job to which he had been appointed, arranged for a meeting at the mansion attended by representatives of all factions but Stelle's. The man who had torn the party asunder lay dying in an upstairs bedroom. Downstairs, Kelly, Nash, Arvey, Slattery, and Nudelman tried to define their common ground. Pete Akers acted as messenger, running up and down the stairs with proposals and counterproposals. To pacify the governor at the outset, Kelly agreed that Stelle would not be considered for governor and that the popular auditor Eddie Barrett would be dumped. Horner demanded a "known progressive" in his place. Stelle and Barrett, meanwhile, held their own rump conference in the Abraham Lincoln Hotel a block away and burst out with the outright but premature declaration that Stelle would be a candidate for governor regardless of what Kelly and Horner decided. Horner would have preferred John Cassidy for governor, but the attorney general's attitudes about slot machines rendered him unacceptable to Kelly and Nash.

Negotiations dragged on into the next day. Horner got out of bed against his doctor's orders, dressed, and came down for lunch. He upset a tumbler of water, kidded Nash about his ignorance of Lincoln, and steered the conversation rather incoherently away from politics and towards Lincoln, to the embarrassment of the others. Finally the governor's strength gave out and he had to be led back to bed.

Kelly and Horner could both agree on former Attorney General Otto Kerner, then a federal judge, for governor. Cermak's old friend went to Springfield and was startled to hear of the proposal. He retired alone to an upstairs room to think about it. After a good deal of consideration, his answer was no. He told Horner, "If I were governor it wouldn't be long until I'd be in the same condition you are," referring to his own minor heart condition. It was also evident that he did not want to give up the security of his judgeship.

As their next choice the men settled on Harry Hershey, state Democratic chairman, Taylorville attorney for the United Mine Workers union, beneficiary of close ties with the Peabody Coal

Company. The fifty-four-year-old Hershey, a vigorous man with curly gray hair, was little known in Chicago, colorless, unaccomplished as an orator. But the hour was late, the Democratic bosses were tired, and this was the best compromise they could reach.

Whereupon Horner promptly issued his public announcement:

> After many weeks of calm deliberation I have come to the greatest personal decision of my life. I will not seek re-election as governor of Illinois. My physicians have made me resolve to avoid the ardors and demands of a vigorous campaign. I have every confidence that the leaders of our state Democracy will continue my fight for the physical and social betterment of the people. We are going into this 1940 fight stronger than ever in purpose and performance to guarantee that the horizons for humanity in Illinois will not be darkened by any cloud of reaction.

In his sick room the governor wept and told the man selected to succeed him that "I'm going to die. But I'll see that you're elected. They won't dare double-cross me. They won't dare." He said he wanted only one promise from Hershey: that he would see to it that the blind-deaf girl—Carol Sanders—would continue to be cared for with state funds after his departure. His biggest disappointment, the governor confided to Hershey, was not being able to see the sales tax—which had yielded $377,500,000 in six years—replaced with a tax that was more equitable.

Stelle, meanwhile, announced the formation of an opposition "rebel" slate: Stelle for governor; Barrett, who blamed the purge on "vicious undercover work by the Nudelman-Schwartz-Arvey clique," for auditor against John Martin; and the unpredictable Ben Adamowski, thirty-three years old and more impatient than ever, for senator against Slattery. For Adamowski, who had "bad paper" with the organization because of a ward committeeman squabble, the race was a calculated gamble. If Horner died before the primary, a distinct possibility, Stelle would grab the patronage power and the rebels would have an excellent chance of winning, or so thought this onetime organization regular.

The Chicago *Times* commented editorially that "the governor was not justified in risking his own life by running again. In 1933, when he took office, he faced chaotic conditions—finances exhausted, interest on bond issues overdue, the property tax pushed to the limit." After reciting Horner's accomplishments, Finnegan detailed some faults: inability to compromise, reluctance to delegate authority and accept advice. "Of him it may be truly said that he has worn himself out in zealous, perhaps over-zealous, service to his city and state."

IV

The Republicans picked Dwight H. Green, the dynamic young federal attorney in Chicago, to run for governor. A couple of days after his withdrawal notice, Horner received a copy of a telegram which Julius Klein (who had been bombarding him for eight years with advisory communications signed "Your Pal . . .") had dispatched to the Republican candidate. The message said that now that Horner had retired "there is nothing in the way for me to help you in this fight because I believe in you as I did in Horner. I shall devote all my time until you reach this goal. Your old friend and pal, Julius Klein."

The interlude of calm that was so essential if the governor was to regain his strength never came. The next crisis in the administration involved F. Lynden Smith, forty-four years old, who ran a prosperous lumberyard in Pontiac until his arrival on the political scene in 1936. After being rewarded for his help in the 1936 primary battle with the job of director of public works, he also assumed command of the Iroquois-Illinois League, a campaign slush fund supplied by the 2 per cent assessment on the paychecks of state employees, percentage "dues" from contractors, a dime-a-ton tribute on coal sales to the state, and similar sources. Started as an emergency campaign financing device in 1936, the league eventually accumulated large sums of money and attracted the attention of federal income tax investigators who were curious about where the dollars went.

Not unexpectedly, the control of this fund caused some dissension in Horner's bedside cabinet throughout the prolonged period of the governor's disability. Sam Nudelman, the finance director, for one, wanted a more important role in its custody. Smith and Nudelman thus had to contend for the governor's favor, and Smith eventually lost out. Receipts of the league were recorded by Smith in a little black book, which he regarded as an insurance policy. "I'm clean all the way through this thing and inside the covers of this book is the proof. As long as I keep it no one will be able to frame me."

Rumors of scandal nevertheless began circulating in Springfield. Suspicions of graft in government are always difficult to document, especially when many years have elapsed; hence, there is no specific imputation directed at any individual in this narrative. However, it is an essential element of the story that all who were there seem to agree that *some* of Horner's most trusted assistants were enriching themselves. The Smith-Nudelman feud damaged the morale of the leaders in the governor's administration and spread perniciously through his organization. Smith and Nudelman were also divided on their reaction to Stelle, Nudelman symbolizing the tough position and Smith representing a more moderate stand. The internal struggle with Nudelman affected Smith's emotional balance, and at the start of the 1940 primary campaign he was exiled on a leave of absence to Florida. Stelle, who was then running for governor against Hershey, arranged for Smith to endorse him later in the campaign. After his return to Springfield, Smith went to the basement of his home and burned a briefcase full of papers. The next day he appeared so agitated that his wife phoned a family friend, state police chief Walter Williams. In the police chief's presence, Smith yanked a butcher knife from a kitchen drawer and stabbed himself in the neck and over the heart. Entering St. John's Hospital under an assumed name for "observation of mental depression," Smith was treated for a four-inch gash in his throat and a wound near the heart that was held together with suture clamps. The next morning he had been scheduled to appear in court to answer a suit demanding an accounting of league funds. At 6 A.M. on that morning of March 9 he arose and went to the adjoining bathroom to shave with an electric razor. Five minutes later, a hospital orderly forced the locked door and found Smith's body in a tubful of water. The coroner never determined conclusively whether he had drowned in the tub or had been electrocuted by the shaver. In either case, the coroner decided Smith had committed suicide.

This unfortunate episode coincided with a sudden deterioration in the governor's condition. He was held incommunicado in the mansion for long stretches of time, encouraging rumors that he had died and that his followers were desperate to prevent Stelle from taking over. Were the truth known, Horner had now suffered a cerebral angiospasm. The slightest excitement would trigger a speechless semicoma which would hang on indefinitely.

Eventually, the lieutenant governor's supporters instituted quo warranto proceedings in court to challenge Horner's right to continue in office. Their suit cited the disability provisions of the

Illinois Constitution, alleging that the governor "has been incapacitated by reason of physical illness from exercising and performing any and all duties of governor." [5]

To counter this line of attack, Horner was dressed and propped up on a davenport for a Palm Sunday press conference. He wore a red lounging robe and held a cigar with considerable difficulty. The governor had trouble expressing himself coherently and criticized certain revisions that had been made in his prepared statement. For example, the word "inefficient" was substituted for "crooked." He accused Stelle of snide strategies and criticized the "truth twisting and desperate demogoguery of [Stelle] and his fellow conspirators."

His statement read:

> This last-minute conspiracy to disrupt party unity and coerce by confusion is beyond the limited vision of the present lieutenant governor. As a political pawn and malicious mouthpiece of a frantic and bitterly hostile anti-Roosevelt press, such as the Chicago *Tribune,* he is bartering his hypocrisy for headlines. The lieutenant governor's attitude on public service has always been "what about me?" and not "what about the people of Illinois?" . . . Many times in the past I have given utterance of my fears to the people of the state of Illinois about even leaving the state while governor—realizing that my administration would be subject to Stelle jeopardy—ruthless and without conscience. . . . The people of Illinois do not believe that a public official can serve the state government and the oil syndicate at the same time.

Horner said that he might campaign for Hershey. "They told me health was first, but who the hell cares about health. A year less or longer makes no difference. We have a record of when I came back from Florida. We found out a lot of things."

Stelle replied in an unexpected vein. "On Palm Sunday," he said, "the beginning of Holy Week, when all Christians of the world are earnestly centering their thoughts on God and His teachings, this selfish clique forces a broken man to issue a statement filled with invective and slanderous in its nature. I can only as a Christian man paraphrase what the greatest of all men once said, 'Excuse him, Father, for he knows not what he does.'" Stelle said he belonged to a syndicate having interests in nine oil wells, had $10,000 invested in a small refinery in Pana, and "like any other southern Illinois farmer I think I have oil under my property."

His campaign was planned to avoid a direct confrontation with Horner. He said traitors to the principles of Horner had seized control. He identified Nudelman and "Captain Jake Arvey, that great veteran of the battle of Grant Park last parade day," as men who were "around the governor like leeches." In a memorable speech at Herrin he said with a straight face that Illinois must have complete nonpolitical control of state institutions and "it is terrible to think such institutions have been made political footballs." On the larger scene, Legionnaire Stelle pleaded that the nation not draft one American boy to fight in "the European war."

Just before the election Horner issued a call for a special session to deal with increases in old-age pensions and a public aid deficiency appropriation. Stelle chose that time, however, to proclaim himself governor. He stormed into the governor's office, but the secretaries ignored him and kept typing away. After writing a letter to Nudelman removing him from office for "incompetence and neglect of duty and malfeasance in office," Stelle crossed the hall to the secretary of state's office just as the state seal was being affixed to Horner's special session call. "I'm going to bring in another one of those to be sealed in about five minutes," he declared. So the governor-pretender prepared his own call notice —adding a legislative investigation of Nudelman's slush fund activities for good measure. Returning, Stelle found the secretary of state's office abandoned. Tossing his rolled-up paper down on the counter, he announced, "I'm filing this call. I don't care about the seal. That doesn't mean anything anyway." The document lay untouched on the counter for days afterward.

Pete Akers, Horner's press aide, hit upon the perfect response to Stelle's tactics. The governor read a statement that Akers had prepared and which tickled the state's funny bone at precisely the wrong time for the lieutenant governor's purposes. "Stelle thinks he's governor," the statement ridiculed, "and there's a man over in Jacksonville [site of a state mental hospital] who thinks he's Napoleon."

Furthermore, Stelle wrote state employees that "it is my intention in the interests of the Democratic party to assume the duties of governor immediately after the primary election." Informed of this, Horner told reporters: "Why I'd like to invite him over here and punch him in the nose." Form letters over the governor's name were sent to state employees advising them not "to be intimidated by veiled threats that there may soon be a change in the governorship. I was elected by the people of Illinois to serve until next

January. Let there be no doubt. Henry Horner will fulfill that trust."

With Horner alive on primary election day, Adamowski lost his gamble and the election. Hershey swamped Stelle by 331,150 votes, carrying downstate by 76,098. The Hershey campaign is estimated to have cost $1,100,000. Barrett and Adamowski also lost.

Following the normal procedure, a legislative committee led by Republican Elmer Schnackenberg called on the governor to inquire if he had a message for the special session and to see for themselves how sick he was. Horner was seated in a straight-backed chair on the mansion sun porch, a dead cigar dangling from his emaciated hand, the other hand propped on the arm of the chair. Schnackenberg said he had read in the newspapers that an additional relief appropriation would be necessary. "They've got enough money," the governor rasped. "Don't give 'em any more money. See . . . what's that man's name, Artie? . . . Nudelman. That's it. See Nudelman. I'll have a printed message on the members' desks. That's my message." [6]

Intervals of clear thought became less frequent and of shorter duration. Radio news broadcasts came through to him as critiques of his administration. He sorrowed at the misfortunes that had afflicted his friendship with Dick Finnegan, whom he now regarded as "a mean man." And he harangued on and on about Tom Courtney. This prompted Ed Kelly, not ordinarily given to philosophic observation, to remark that "when we Irish are about to meet our Maker we usually want to patch up our quarrels and make up with our enemies. With you it's different. Your hatreds seem to be burrowing deeper."

In the meantime a House committee headed by Representative Clinton Searle initiated an investigation of state finances under Nudelman. Claiming knowledge of a "sales tax fix ring," the legislators asked to interview the governor. First, however, they subpoenaed Dr. Rosen for questioning. His testimony proceeded in this fashion: [7]

> Q. What is the physical and mental condition of the Governor?
>
> A. Satisfactory.
>
> Q. Have any additional complications followed the Governor's original illness?
>
> A. No, except for a cold or so. He has just been through a hard cold.

Q. Is the Governor able to discuss with the committee matters pertaining to the state?

A. He is being treated for high blood pressure and a hypertensive heart. The inquiries of the committee may raise his blood pressure.

Q. Has this illness been caused by some chronic infection of the blood?

A. If you mean syphilis, I deny it categorically. The Governor's condition has not been caused by that disease. I can go further to say that he never had syphilis, and can prove it by serologic and spinal fluid tests.

The governor became excited about the funds mismanagement investigation, Dr. Rosen recorded subsequently in his notes. "He called the director of finance and others to accounting. This was the blow which brought him down so completely. He now needed an oxygen tent at night. He was a pathetic figure. He felt drowsy and slept most of the time."

To prevent the Searle committee from forcing its way into the mansion and questioning the governor in person, Horner was loaded into an ambulance on the 2d of June and transported under as much secrecy as possible to another rented house, this one in Winnetka on the lake shore north of Chicago. For a moment, before the ambulance rolled down the mansion drive, the governor's pale eyes glowed and he wept softly, in complete possession of his wits. "These people, my friends, I know, I made them, and what have they done?" Then he lapsed just as quickly into a dream world, imagining that he was on the way to his wedding, his hallucinations interspersed with remarks to his mother.

Before leaving Springfield, Horner donated his Lincoln library to the state historical library. With it went this message to the library board consisting of Oliver Barrett, Lloyd Lewis, and Irving Dilliard:

> . . . This library will stand for all time as the shrine where pilgrims must come to learn just what kind of man and how great was the greatest son of Illinois. . . . For years I have had in mind to present to the library my own collection of books about Lincoln. Since I am . . . to leave my home that stands so close to the library, I wish to make this gift . . . of the greatest possible use to the people, whether they be the most scholarly of historical researchers or the humblest of school children.

By the autumn of 1940 the international situation had deteriorated. The president of the Republican Editorial Association of

Illinois urged that the governor return to the capital to supervise the creation of local Selective Service boards. "Inasmuch as you have been ill and in retirement for many months, many of our citizenry are doubtful as to whether or not you are actively performing the duties of governor," the letter said.[8] Throughout this period, Akers remained in Winnetka screening the papers that required the governor's signature and sometimes waiting days until Horner could write his name.

On October 5 the doctor issued a statement that "Governor Horner's illness took a sudden turn yesterday. His respirations are labored and his heart action rapid and feeble. His condition is most critical." Later the same day he said, "Governor Horner is getting weaker and weaker. His life hangs by a mere thread."

Finally, a formal certificate of disability was prepared, and Harry Hershey notified the lieutenant governor to go to Springfield and assume the duties of governor. "Because of the serious condition of the governor," the certificate read, "he is unable to exercise the powers and to perform the duties of the office of governor of the State of Illinois and by virtue of the provisions of Section 17, Article V, of the Constitution of the State of Illinois, such powers and duties devolve upon Honorable John Stelle, the lieutenant governor of the State of Illinois, during the residue of Governor Horner's term or until such disability shall be removed."

Even then, so long as a single heartbeat remained in the body of Henry Horner, Sam Nudelman protested the submission to the hated John Stelle.

A few hours later, at 2:30 A.M. on October 6, 1940, the governor died of cardio-vascular disease and inflammation of the kidneys. Clarence the butler, Van the chauffeur, and Ella, his secretary for thirty-seven years, were nearby at the end. He died hard, in painful throes and terrible agony for the last fourteen hours. The end came two days short of twenty-three months after he was first stricken in the car near Kankakee. Governor Horner had lost his desperate race with John Stelle to the end of his term by ninety-nine days.

CHAPTER SIXTEEN

Better He Woulda Lived

A driving rainstorm beat against the magnificent dome of the Statehouse on Sunday, October 6, as a small group of patient men crowded into the lieutenant governor's office to hear their chief, John Stelle, recite the oath of governor of Illinois. Anticlimactically, without any bleachers in the rotunda, their moment had finally arrived. Representative Paul Powell, who had remained steadfastly loyal to Horner against his fellow southern Illinoisan, walked across from the House side to the lieutenant governor's chamber and offered to make peace, fearful of a patronage purge. "But it [the change of governors] only cost me four jobs," he recalled many years later.

In Chicago the body of the dead governor was placed in a $500 bronze casket and moved from the Hyde Park funeral home to the National Guard armory housing the 122d field artillery on East Chicago Avenue. The move was preceded by a minor disagreement between Clarence the butler and Ella the secretary about whether or not the governor should be buried wearing his pince-nez. Clarence pointed out that Horner had not worn glasses when asleep, but he was overruled. Resting on an elevated bier in the middle of the huge sawdust floor the coffin was viewed during the next two days and nights by tens of thousands of mourners filing past on a long red carpet.

Bishop Griffin said in Springfield that "no governor in Illinois had more problems thrown into his lap because of the depression, and no governor could have been more conscientious, capable, and unselfish. May the Father of Mercies give to our late governor peace and happiness which were not his inheritance because of problems beyond his control."

Under the pseudonym of James Fox, Dick Finnegan wrote the obituary in the Chicago *Times:*

> . . . as governor Henry Horner found out that efficiency and honesty were more often battered about by the realities of practical politics than he had anticipated. His determination to keep his idealism unscratched led him to personal excesses of work, long hours, and insistence that his subordinates bring to his attention details of routine that got on his nerves. . . . [He] wasn't able to shed care with the ease that had marked his career as a Cook County jurist. His zeal for an administration without scandal had created in him an emotional turmoil which sapped his vitality to the danger point whenever he went through a crisis with the legislature or with the opposition within his own party.[1]

The *Tribune* added its editorial tribute: "He was a good governor from 1933 to 1938. He cannot be blamed for the subsequent conduct of the affairs of the state, for in these last years he has been an invalid, unequal to the task of guiding and restraining his subordinates. Indeed his value to the commonwealth can be measured by the deterioration in the quality of government which followed his removal from active life." [2]

II

On the mild and sunny morning of October 8, the governor was laid to rest. "The good earth of the state he loved so well that he wore himself out in her service today claims the body of Henry Horner, faithful servant," recorded the *Times.* For the military funeral in the armory, Kelly and Nash and Stelle and the men of the Democratic party donned their mourning clothes, frock coats, and silk top hats. About 7,500 people filled the armory, which had been draped in purple and black bunting. In front of the coffin, lifted now onto a gun carriage, the Reverend Dr. Gay C. White, superintendent of the Springfield district of the Methodist Church, and the Right Reverend Thomas V. Shannon, pastor of the Catholic St. Thomas the Apostle Church in Chicago, delivered prayers of lament.[3]

Speaking briefly, Senator Scott Lucas said Horner had given his life for "a cause I chanced, two years ago, to represent." He spoke of

> our departed friend—the careful scholar, the natural orator, the gentle humorist whose smile was like a morning sun, the genial philosopher, the inspiring optimist and humanist. And you were aware, too, of still another side—the fierce, though fair, antagonist when his high principles were challenged. You saw him as the vigorous warrior in the never-ending battle for social justice. For the usually gentle, genial Henry Horner could be a fighting lion when the occasion demanded. For he was among
>
> Men whom the lust of office does not kill;
> Men whom the spoils of office cannot buy;
> Men who possess opinions and a will;
> Men who have honor, men who will not lie.

In the front row, Ed Kelly squirmed a little and there were droplets of perspiration on his forehead.

The rabbi of the governor's own Sinai Congregation, Dr. Louis L. Mann, was chosen to deliver the principal eulogy.[4] A vigorous, learned man with a bushy mustache, it was Dr. Mann who had lectured Judge Horner in 1931 on his dislike for Tony Cermak; it was Dr. Mann who had hurried down to Springfield in 1933 to fight for the eyedrop bill.

He began in a solemn tone, staring into the distance, taking for his scriptural reading the words of Psalm 24:

> Who shall ascend into the hill of the Lord?
> Or shall stand in His holy place?
> He that hath clean hands, and a pure heart;
> Who hath not lifted up his soul unto vanity,
> nor sworn deceitfully.

Tracing Horner's career, Dr. Mann said he was

> thoroughly democratic and saw uncommon virtue in the common man. He numbered among his friends those in all walks and stations of life, among all creeds and classes, from the humble hod carrier and messenger boy, black and white, Catholic, Protestant, and Jew, native and foreign-born, to the leaders of industry, science and government, for, in the lines from Robert Burns that he quoted so often, "For a' that, an' a' that, . . . A man's a man for a' that."

At this point in the eulogy the rabbi turned to the frock coats in the front row and glared at Ed Kelly.

> Though modest and unassuming in all his ways, he felt that he was destined to uproot some of the unfortunate and sinister aspects of our political life—graft, corruption, dishonesty, and the spoils system—from the fair name of our state. When he was elected governor he set out to do this with the enthusiasm of a crusader and the consecration of a martyr. Certain it is that in trying to crush the machine and all that it stood for in 1938 he spent himself too lavishly and today he lies here before us a martyr to the cause of good government. His was a heroism as great as that of a soldier on a field of battle and for a cause equally worthy. In season and out of season Henry Horner bemoaned the fact that good men and women so frequently avoided the responsibility and the privilege of serving their fellow men through public office. Possibly his greatest disillusionment came when so many men and women who were willing to make financial contributions for a campaign were yet unwilling to uphold his hands for the cause of good government and civic righteousness. He was a statesman and not a politician. He did not, he would not and could not compromise. We must here resolve to carry on that which he so nobly began and which time and again was thwarted, frustrated, and blocked. To have made one soul better, to have struck one blow for truth, to have thrown in the face of men one thought that shall not die. To do this shall be immortality.

In the front row, the uncomfortable men in the frock coats stared back at the rabbi. Waiting for the procession to begin its march to the cemetery, Kelly told a reporter, "It's easy to talk now that it's all over. We must remember that we all make mistakes. I'm sure that if the governor made any mistakes they were honest ones."

The procession of eight hundred troops, including one unit of the Black Horse cavalry, moved down the Outer Drive. At North Avenue a battery of cannon fired a nineteen-gun salute out over Lake Michigan. At the grave in Mount Mayriv cemetery, a German Jewish cemetery on the Northwest Side of the city, Dr. Mann read Psalm 23. Then he plucked three flowers from a pillow of chrysanthemums that had been sent by President and Mrs. Roosevelt. "These flowers from the bouquet of President Roosevelt are symbolic," the rabbi said. "They go with Henry Horner as our hearts go with Henry Horner." One by one, he dropped the flowers into the open grave. Then the three churchmen walked away and workmen began shoveling earth into the grave alongside the resting place of Dilah Horner Levy in the family plot.

Pausing to watch the funeral procession pass, a Jewish cab driver removed his cap. "A swell funeral," he told his passenger, "but better he woulda lived."

CHAPTER SEVENTEEN

The Ninety-nine Days of John Stelle

For ninety-nine incredible days John Stelle governed Illinois. The new governor moved into the Executive Mansion with his wife and two sons, placed an initial order for thirty-five cases of beer, and directed that the bedrooms and the sun parlor that had housed the Lincoln library be redecorated for his three-month stay. From then until inauguration day in January the old building was lit up like a Christmas tree. Because the entertainment budget for the mansion had not been dented during Horner's illness, the new chief executive was able to invite his neighbors from southern Illinois in, on a round-robin basis, for dinner and an evening of "socializin'." Thirty or forty guests at a time were invited to partake of roast turkey and other delicacies. His new role did not, however, appear to turn the governor's head. He would arise early and read the newspapers in his pajamas in one of the several huge, nicely furnished downstairs sitting rooms, then eat breakfast in the kitchen with the help.[1]

Charlie Wheeler of the *Daily News* wrote of Stelle's first day in office: "There was a noticeable change in the atmosphere of the governor's office from that prevailing during Horner's regime when college professors were among his daily callers. The boys who man the polls and bring home the bacon were out in full force."

The smoke from the funeral cannon salute had barely cleared away when heads started to roll in the Statehouse. George

Schuppe, a heavy-jowled former Springfield reporter for the United Press, and Pete Rossiter, a Springfield coal dealer, manned the guillotine. Stelle took particular delight in having his cronies telephone a state official in the middle of the night to inform him of his departure from the payroll. Al Carter, a Murphysboro banker and American Legion officer, took Nudelman's place. Archie Bowen, who was still awaiting the final disposition of his appeal to the Supreme Court, was replaced, along with Dr. A. C. Baxter, the director of public health.

Possibly the most intriguing of Stelle's appointments was that of George Edward Day, a Springfield paint dealer and good friend, to the job of purchasing agent. The new governor had become bewitched by traffic safety and had hit upon the then novel idea of painting yellow lines on highways to designate areas of unsafe passing. At that time only Minnesota used yellow lines. Stelle, however, approaching the problem with great thoroughness, ordered two lines painted, one on either side of the center stripe, to denote danger from either direction. Purchasing agent Day bought vast quantities of yellow paint from paint dealer Day, and years later when the price of paint skyrocketed during World War II Illinois was fortunate enough still to have some of that yellow paint on hand.

With slightly more than a month remaining in his term, Stelle had the mansion repainted at a cost of $1,900. Criticism of such expenditures hurt the new governor's feelings. "All you can truly say about John Stelle," he asserted, "is that he changed a hell of a lot of positions and put his friends in." By December 5 he had more than four hundred of his supporters on the payroll and by the end of his term the number was beyond estimate. His patronage lieutenant for Chicago was Moe Rosenberg's brother Ed, a no-nonsense fellow who fired dozens of civil service employees before someone informed him that the "c. s." next to their names on the payroll lists didn't stand for Charlie Schwartz, who had been Horner's payroll dispenser.

From time to time the governor drove to Cairo, in one of the two new Cadillacs purchased for the chief executive, for a weekend of quail hunting. He established a reserve militia to take the place of the National Guard, which had been mobilized for federal service, handing out 468 honorary commissions to politicians and to his Legion buddies. Contracts were awarded for the purchase of 385,000 tons of coal, some of it at $1.22 a ton higher than the 1939 price. Newspaper reporters were dazzled by it all. *Tribune* reporter Hal Foust wrote that "millions are being spent amid confusion." He said things were happening so fast that even Stelle's aides could not keep up. "Among the few facts that are known," he noted, "is that millions are being spent and that there are still many more millions that can be spent before the end of the term."

Less than a month after the change of the guard, the supervisor of rules and regulations in the finance department resigned. The supervisor, Samuel Herman, charged that Stelle had issued a secret directive exempting contractors and materials suppliers from the sales tax. He said he had attended a meeting in the Morrison Hotel Democratic headquarters at which Stelle and an attorney for a materials supplier had consummated this agreement. Stelle insisted that the order had been intended only to force an early court decision on the tax liability of these groups. Attorney General Cassidy called the exemption order outrageous, though, pointing out that the suppliers stood to gain a refund of more than $700,000. The ruling was later voided by Circuit Judge Harry Fisher, who called Stelle's action "ill advised, indelicate, unfortunate, and unnecessary." The same materials company also succeeded in obtaining rights to gravel on state-owned land north of Stateville Penitentiary, a privilege previous governors had denied.

II

While all this was going on, of course, an election campaign was being waged. A few days after the Horner funeral, Dwight Green called on Rabbi Mann to thank him for "electing me governor of this state." Dr. Mann's attack upon the Democratic machine might have played some small part, but there were other more important forces at work. Word went out from Kelly headquarters the weekend before the election to "trim Hershey." And the precinct workers did. Kelly had had enough of a Democratic governor, and Green, the Republican candidate, beat Hershey by 256,954 votes. Hershey carried Chicago by only 41,703. The Peabody coal lawyer had made two serious mistakes: he had made some complimentary remarks about Tom Courtney in a speech; and he had promised to try to suppress gambling if elected. If any backbreaking straws were needed, Kelly found them here. Roosevelt carried Illinois, but only by 95,694, in his successful bid for a third term. However, Jim Slattery lost to C. Wayland Brooks, who had been Horner's 1936 opponent, by 20,827.

Stelle, who had told Green during the campaign that he had softened up Hershey for the kill, laid the defeat to "too much waistline on the Democrats in Cook County." His suggestion that he might like to be director of public works in Hershey's cabinet—and its prompt rejection by Hershey—might also have had something to do with Stelle's lack of interest in the campaign. He continued, nonetheless, to operate at whirling pace, paroling 187 convicts in November, 204 more on Christmas Eve, and pardoning many others. "It looks like a bad winter for the Chicago police department," moaned the chief of detectives, John L. Sullivan. On January 2d, Stelle fired 300 employees in the state highway department, explaining that he hadn't done it sooner "because I didn't want to be unkind to anyone before Christmas."

In the Chicago *Daily News,* Clem Lane wrote a whimsical column about the wisdom of a mythical character named Oxie O'Rourke. In one of the pieces Lane wrote during this period, O'Rourke turned his attention to Springfield:

> There are bright lights around the governor's mansion these nights and the sound of a duck being torn limb from limb, account the governor has shot some ducks and is having friends in these nights for a duck dinner.
>
> It also reminds me of Governor Horner because it's so different. They was some wild and hilarious times in the mansion when Henry was governor. He and a couple of friends would start a big evening with an argument as to whether Lincoln's speech was really lost and whether the speech which was pick up in the lost and found department is the genuine mekiah or an unreasonable facsimile thereof.
>
> This revelry would go maybe until 10 o'clock when the party would bust up and Henry would go up to his room to wrestle with an armful of legislative bills far into the A.M.
>
> But now! Why, Clarence, who is the Rochester of the executive mansion, is all wore out from excess butling, and Rufus, the assistant Rochester, is hoarse from announcing added starters for dinner.
>
> Governor Stelle start out by giving the mansion a coat of paint a couple of weeks ago. It is not customary to paint white houses except maybe in the spring or fall, but John he ain't gonna be in no governor's mansion come the spring or fall and so must be in November.
>
> They ain't no truth in the story that they is running bus

> excursions to the mansion from Stelle's old bailiwick in Hamilton County, but I hear that if all the people which eat in the mansion pays back John and the Mrs. with a dinner he ain't gonna worry about his grocery bills next year.
>
> The Mrs. she get a big bang out of showing the neighbors the new $759 (marked down from $800) French library suite where the Lincoln library used to be and I guess old Abe himself would of thought it hot stuff.
>
> Yes sir, these is great times for the old mansion and John is certainly a polite host. . . . They is a lot of muggs residing in the Big House at Stateville and they write John saying "Pardon me," and I hear he is so darn polite he is saying "why certainly."

On Christmas Eve the governor ordered that the five young miners from DuQuoin who had been imprisoned for the murder of a fourteen-year-old girl be brought to his Statehouse office. There, with the optimum holiday ballyhoo, Stelle pardoned them for their crimes. These were the men Horner had said his mother would not let him pardon. Stelle said he hoped it would improve relations between the UMW and the Progressive miners.

CHAPTER EIGHTEEN

The Real Goods

A bitter aftertaste of disillusion lingered. Horner had lived in an age of reform in America. His career had begun with the upsurge of Populism, continued during the era of the Progressive movement, and culminated with his service in the state's highest office during the period of the New Deal. Soon after his funeral, *The Advocate,* a Jewish weekly published in Chicago, commented that it would have been entirely appropriate for the epitaph on Horner's tomb to have come from the pen of Lincoln Steffens. Looking back, the magazine interpreted the story of Horner as "one of the more piercing critiques of democracy dormant that American life has yet produced." The editorial described how he had been swept into office and how, eight years later, he had "died a broken man, old before his time . . . victim of a broken heart." He had met, the magazine said,

> corruption in public office, machine politics of the most vicious character, the pork barrel of patronage in the sty of spoils, the vampire kiss of crime and politics. They anticipated that this genial jurist, this gentleman bibliophile, would relax in the executive mansion and pore over the first editions about the Prairie President while they, the machine men, would make merry with the rich plum which had fallen to them because their candidate was an honest man. If Henry Horner would not put in his thumb, they would. . . . Because he was a shrewd

> man he gathered around him men who could fight a ruthless political machine without fleeing back into an ivory tower of political aloofness. When he was well he could and did command these individuals as their leader. When illness came upon him, the subordinates became the henchmen. . . . We pose the very serious question of whether there is not a serious deficiency in the processes of democracy in this country when the common man must remark at the end of a career such as Henry Horner's—"he would have been all right if he had kept out of politics." [1]

This theme was repeated several years later in Rabbi Mann's recollections of his friend: "He suffered in office from overwork and from fear of betrayal. His disillusionment became a psychological fixation. He thought those who play the game of politics for their livelihood would change their coat of many colors into one that was all white. He was wrong."

Few Americans have ever been gifted with Carl Sandburg's genius of expression. During a conversation with the author in 1961, Sandburg offered this appraisal of Horner:

"He was the Real Goods. In the realm of politics there have been too few like him. He could collaborate with a Tony Cermak and at no time get sold down the river, which says something about Cermak too. He collaborated with men who were purchasable without becoming purchasable himself. He had thoroughgoing integrity. He got to high places without selling his soul."

Henry Horner was an exceptional man whose career was remarkable in many respects and whose story reflects the changing pattern of American life. In different words, the Jewish magazine, the rabbi, and Carl Sandburg each expressed attitudes that were prevalent during so much of Horner's life—disenchantment with the greed and the evil corruption of the big-city boss-led political machine; the striving for democracy in its purest unattainable form.

The provincial Populist tradition that relied on rural and small town values could be detected in the Illinois of Horner's youth. The farmers who delivered their produce by horse-drawn wagon to his grandfather's wholesale grocery mart considered the city a seat of moral decadence. It is only recently, moreover, that historians have given proper attention to the element of anti-Semitism in the Populist sentiments of the late nineteenth century. The "Jewish bankers" and the "international gold ring" were closely identified with the evils fought by the agrarian protest movement. It is ironically coincidental that one of John Stelle's ancestors—one John P. Stelle—was a leading southern Illinois agitator against the bankers and, for that matter, all "non-producers," an all-inclusive category that seemed to include all city dwellers who did not work with their hands. He deplored both the plight of the "toiling poor" and the "scheming politicians who used their positions to engage in public thievery." [2]

Near the turn of the century a British visitor to Chicago observed that "no one in America seems to realize that good government rests not merely on democratic institutions but on the growth of a new motive, that of social service combined with the selection of men for the work of government according to their capacity for that work." Former Governor Altgeld impressed the visitor as a dangerous ruler of men because of the complete absence of any tradition (inherited experience) and of science (present experience). "He is a metaphysician and not a statesman," the author suggested.[3]

At the start of his political career alongside Carter Harrison, the young Henry Horner offered the promise of precisely this kind of "new motive"—social service and the capacity to carry it out. Harrison was a reformer who realized he had to make alliances with the Kennas and Coughlins, an insight which did not escape Horner's attention. The Progressive movement unquestionably influenced Horner far more than a mere recitation of events might appear to indicate. In his first political campaign of 1914 it will be recalled that he sneered at the reformers. Many of his law school classmates already were becoming rich as "house counsel" for large banks, investment houses, and industrial firms. Ulysses S. Schwartz, who was appointed to the state appellate court, touched on this in a speech after his friend's death:

> His entire life was spent in the midst of the greatest industrial and commercial epoch the world has known. It was an age devoted to the making of money, to the enjoyment of comfort and luxury; an age which subordinated the business of government, despised politicians, gave the great statesman a position inferior to the industrialist. He could easily have adapted himself to this age. He had preeminent ability of the kind that would have made him a great business lawyer. . . . From that day 30 years ago when I first met Henry Horner at a political meeting, we often discussed the decline of political life because of the absorption of its more able citizens in industry and business.[4]

Thus, two threads of influence stand out in contrast—the businessmen's set with whom he dined at the Standard Club; and the powerful tide of progressive thought which prepared the way for social welfare measures, civil service reform, the direct primary election, and executive reorganization in Illinois. Horner was not a radical, certainly, and could never bring himself to the Progressive rejection of political bossism until he had suffered at its hands.

This gentle man carried to his office the "tradition" but not the "science." Nothing in his administrative or political experience had prepared him for the task ahead. His personal need for a father figure assumed additional importance after the death of Cermak, the leader he leaned upon and feared. When he became governor, he found the state treasury about empty, the government shattered, the people on the verge of civil insurrection. By acquiring the "science" quickly and by tapping a reservoir of strength and courage, he acted to restore fiscal integrity and as much stability as could be expected under the circumstances. The enormous problems of providing food and shelter for the unemployed and their families were compounded a thousand times by the sorry record of political pettiness and the greed of spoilsmen in his own party who saw the WPA as an adjunct of their organization and social welfare as an extension of patronage.

II

For many reasons, the years through which Horner served as governor marked the start of a turning point in Illinois political history. Early in this century, progressivism penetrated the power structure of Chicago and Illinois in only a very limited way. Power in the old Chicago was monopolized by self-made men—industrialists, grain merchants, department store owners, editors, and politicians—unburdened by any notable tradition of public responsibility. It will be recalled that Horner himself was reluctant about taking Finnegan's advice to strike hard at the Insull scandal. But the conscience of Illinois was disturbed by what happened to Horner. Although the Democratic organization would continue to be a boss-led party through the 1960's, its leader would never again be able to act in as arbitrary and blatantly disdainful a way as had Tony Cermak and Ed Kelly. Although the leader of the Democrats in the 1950's and 1960's, Mayor Richard J. Daley, does not enjoy a glittering national reputation, politics *is* several shades cleaner now in Illinois than it was then. Of course, it would be foolish to suggest that the Cash-Value School of Politics has disbanded altogether in the state. As Horner once put it, there are few saints on this earth, and politics is certainly the last place to look for them. But the machine is not monolithic, Daley *does* reflect a substantial segment of the community, and—by Chicago standards—he is, in some respects, almost semi-saintly. Moreover, in time of dire need the party has turned, albeit reluctantly and only occasionally, to distinguished Democrats like Adlai Stevenson and Paul Douglas. Almost certainly, the processes of change that began with the Horner-Kelly experiences and are being exacerbated by today's almost unmanageable urban social problems will produce the end of party bossism when Daley retires, and maybe sooner.

Many of the most enduring monuments to Horner's administration involved his role as middleman for the New Deal in Illinois. Kelly and Nash were not ideological New Dealers, and neither was John Stelle. Nor can it be said that Chicago, the capital of the conservative heartland of the nation, appeared initially receptive to the economic reforms. Horner stood out as an articulate spokesman for NRA, social security, unemployment insurance, and emergency relief, even though Roosevelt persisted in working with the big-city bosses and simply ignored whatever indiscretions they perpetrated. Horner's changing attitudes only reflected the shift in public opinion that has led to today's general acceptance of our version of the welfare state. Despite his Standard Club background, he had as instinctive a feeling for the victims of the depression as any radical. On his deathbed, Horner's last words to Arch Bowen were, "I am glad to know we have been able to do so much—you and I—for those who need help."

Crisis and federal assistance combined to strengthen the office of governor in the 1930's.[5] In Illinois a historical parallel can be drawn between Horner's experience and that of the Civil War governor Richard Yates. The war resulted in a significant enlargement of the scope of the office, just as the depression did later. Governors were called upon by the president to fulfill many direct obligations. In 1863 the Democratic-controlled legislature refused to appropriate funds, and the governor had to negotiate loans from private financial institutions to run the state. In the 1930's the Republican-controlled legislature came close to doing the same by refusing to appropriate funds for relief. Both Yates and Horner exploited the crisis situation and the demands of the federal government to enlarge the powers of the office. Although Horner clashed continuously with Harry Hopkins on one hand and Mayor Kelly's Chicago administration on the other, he used the twin levers of federalism and crisis to enhance the powers of the governor.

Always the skilled politician, Roosevelt mobilized his natural allies, labor leaders for instance, in his battles with his natural enemies in the business community. Horner could never untangle the coal mine union mess in Illinois. Although public opinion probably favored the Progressives, UMW leader John Lewis had access to the national administration, canceling out the governor's effectiveness. The back of the PMA was finally broken when thirty-three members were convicted in a bomb-throwing case. After the conviction, the special federal prosecutor attended a victory party in the UMW headquarters in Springfield. A few weeks later the same lawyer was retained by Lewis as special counsel for the UMW.

Through it all, Horner emerges as a superb politician. He projected simplicity, sincerity, and goodness. He would most likely have been a master at modern television campaigning because of those qualities and the force of his personality—attributes it is now fashionable to call *charisma.* Henry Horner—a Jew—bridged the cultural and emotional gap between metropolitan Chicago and rural downstate as no one else has done before or since.

If the message of this story is the effect of stress in high office upon a man with "thoroughgoing integrity," perhaps we should also devote a moment of reflection to the wonder of a system which could give Illinois at its moment of greatest civil peril a one-time precinct worker for Hinky Dink Kenna who a few eventful years later would be universally regarded as "the Real Goods."

CHAPTER NINETEEN

Epilogue

Long after a memorial portrait of Henry Horner had been hung in his beloved Standard Club, fate continued to work its frequently implausible magic on the others with whom his life had been entwined. Arch Bowen never recovered emotionally or financially from the ordeal of his Supreme Court appeal. In August of 1941 he wrote to a friend, "I do not know when I shall return to Springfield. All my efforts to secure employment have failed to date. There is nothing in the offing to give me any hope. Even a non-compensating job would be welcome. . . . I am terribly lonesome without some interest and some attachment, something to which I can hold and be assured that I have some place yet in the world." During his final illness Bowen had to be transferred from a Springfield hospital to the charitable institution he had once directed at Elgin. There he died soon after. Many years later, in 1963, the state of Illinois belatedly honored his memory. A new children's center was named for him at Harrisburg in southern Illinois, not far, as it happened, from John Stelle's former home.

Stelle was elected national commander of the American Legion in 1945, had a part in the preparation of the postwar G.I. Bill of Rights, and functioned as one of the national kingmakers of the legion. A ceramic tile plant that was defunct when he acquired it in Brazil, Indiana, became a multi-million dollar enterprise, thanks largely to government contracts. In company with his new ally, Paul Powell, Stelle continued to be a bipartisan political operator in southern Illinois. Governor Stevenson, who was elected in 1948, did not satisfy him for exactly the reasons Horner had not; and in 1952 Stelle supported Republican candidates for governor and for president. He would have endorsed Eddie Barrett, then the secretary of state, who wanted to replace Stevenson on the gubernatorial ballot in 1952 after the incumbent governor had been nominated for the presidency. But the Democratic state committee refused to slate Barrett.

Two days before his death from leukemia in 1962, Stelle told the author that he had no regrets about his life. He had helped his friends, he said, and they had helped him. After fifty years in politics Stelle boasted that he could still "get things done" in Chicago or Springfield. "There I was, three hundred miles south of Chicago," he explained in justification of his differences with Horner. "I had to have a foothold in Chicago. Without it I would have been dead as a mackerel." His break with Horner had been terrible, he recalled. In retrospect, he regarded the governor as "one of the finest, grandest persons you ever knew." Stelle insisted that he had no quarrel with Horner, "only those guys around him who could steal a hot stove in July." Horner was "a finished politician . . . the best governor Illinois ever had." But he had been surrounded by "a bunch of thieves." Be that as it may, John Stelle will surely never be duplicated in Illinois. It is interesting to note, however, that the John A. Logan heritage of rambunctious, two-fisted spoils politicians—so utterly scornful of reaction in the population centers—has lived on in southern Illinois, most recently in the person of Stelle's friend Powell, who was elected secretary of state.

Jake Arvey and Barnet Hodes formed a law partnership in Chicago. After the downfall of Ed Kelly, which started with the 1936 primary and reached a climax with his ouster by the machine in the early 1940's, Arvey reigned briefly as the boss. Looking back at the events of the 1930's, Arvey is now convinced that his decision in 1936 was the biggest blunder of his political career. Not only would supporting Horner against the organization have been the right thing to do, but his identification with the winner would also have increased his own power within the party. "But," Arvey now explains coolly, "I thought he would lose." Although the Irish regained leadership of the organization, and still have it, Arvey has served many years as Democratic national committeeman from Illinois. A young man he sponsored for United States district attorney in 1947 advanced to become governor of Illinois in 1961—Otto Kerner, Jr., whose father had been Cermak's protégé and Illinois attorney general and who had himself carefully considered the gubernatorial candidacy in 1940 in an upstairs bedroom of the Executive Mansion.

Ben Lindheimer died in 1960, leaving an estate valued at almost $7,000,000, including shares in Arlington Park race track, the Washington Park jockey club, and Hialeah race track in Miami. Horner's pen pal, Julius Klein, continued cultivating important people, dropping names, and operating as an international public relations counselor. Industrialists and politicians in West Germany, as well as government-subsidized West German trade associations, were among his principal clients after World War II. One of his highly placed friends, Senator Thomas Dodd of Connecticut, got into trouble when his Senate colleagues accused him in 1966 of having used his influence to try to save some of Klein's German accounts.

Scott Lucas was defeated for re-election by Everett McKinley Dirksen in 1950 and took up a successful career as a lobbyist in Washington. His health began failing after the death of his wife, and early in 1968 Lucas died on the way to a Florida vacation. Just as Horner had predicted, Bowen's prosecutor, Samuel Shapiro, did have a promising future in Democratic party affairs. As Kerner's running mate in 1960 he was elected lieutenant governor, the second Jew to attain state office in Illinois history. Kerner served two terms. But, due partly to the long illness of his wife Helena (who was Anton J. Cermak's daughter), he decided against trying for a third. Instead, he was appointed to the United States Court of Appeals in Chicago, where his father had sat before him.

Returning to Chicago in February of 1968 from the funeral of Scott Lucas in the Illinois River valley, the bosses of the Democratic organization met that afternoon to select their new candidate for governor. His name was Samuel H. Shapiro, and after Kerner resigned to take his position on the court Sam Shapiro finished his term—the second Jewish governor in Illinois history.

And what of Carol Sanders?

In his will, Horner bequeathed $5,000 to unspecified charities, $5,000 to his secretary Mrs. Cornwall, $500 each to nine nieces and nephews, a half-interest in Chicago real estate to his two brothers, and the remainder of the $50,000 estate to his cousins Robert and Henry Straus. The executors of his estate refused a request from Gault's institute at Northwestern University that some of the money willed for charity be used for the blind girl's support, on the grounds that the governor had not specifically mentioned such a bequest in his will.

Although Carol had made some progress, she retrogressed after Horner's death and became even more difficult to care for. As time passed, and as Gault's institute encountered further financial problems, it became evident that the child did not have the necessary intellectual capabilities to overcome her sensory handicaps. Allowing for her sensory deficiencies, a series of tests placed her IQ at only 33. Her learning potential was not considered sufficient to allow her to be placed in a state school for the blind. State welfare department funds for her support were discontinued. The Illinois Children's Home and Aid Society, a private agency, had to decide whether to continue investing its funds from voluntary contributions in a child who could never expect to lead anything like a normal life.

So it was reluctantly determined that Carol needed the protection that could only be provided by a state institution for the mentally deficient. On August 12, 1941, Carol Sanders was committed at age nine to the Dixon State School. Diagnosis: mental deficiency, idiopathis, severe.

Carol has been there ever since, blind, partially deaf, for more than a quarter of a century a resident of Cottage 13-B in the overcrowded and understaffed institution at Dixon. She is destructive, easily disturbed, biting and scratching others, noisy and untidy. Without the tiniest window to the world, she exists like an animal.

One can only surmise what the Restless Ash of Henry Horner thinks about that.

Chapter Notes

CHAPTER ONE

1. Letter to Horner, April 16, 1933. Horner Papers.
2. Letter to Horner, January 26, 1933. Horner Papers (Downstate correspondence files).
3. The statement attributed to Illinois District Eight of the Communist party is contained in a National Guard military intelligence report submitted to the governor by Colonel L. V. Regan. This and other military intelligence reports were kept in a special file in the Horner Papers (Subject files).
4. National Guard intelligence report dated January, 1934.
5. Carmen Welch to Horner, February 27, 1933. Horner Papers (Downstate correspondence files).
6. Colonel McCormick mailed a copy of his speech, dated April 26, 1933, to Horner. It is in the colonel's personal correspondence file in the Horner Papers.
7. Edgar Lee Masters, *The Sangamon* (New York: Holt, Rinehart & Winston, 1954), p. 168.
8. "In Memoriam: Henry Horner," *Chicago Bar Record*, Vol. XXII, No. 4 (January, 1941), p. 145.
9. Speech given by Horner, October 26, 1933. Horner Papers (Speech file).

CHAPTER TWO

1. Much of the information on the early life of Hannah Dernburg is from Carl Dernburg, *Memoirs of an American Pioneer, 1857–1943* (Chicago: privately published, 1943). Dernburg was a nephew of Hannah's.
2. Details of the development of Horner and Company are from Herman Eliassof, "The Jews of Illinois," *Reform Advocate*, May 4, 1901.
3. Chicago *Interocean*, February 21, 1902.
4. Letter to the author from Mrs. Hazel Yondorf Mannheimer, cousin of Henry Horner.
5. Most of the biographical data about Solomon Levy is from material in the Horner Papers sent by James Levy, Solomon Levy's

son, to Ella Cornwall, the governor's personal secretary, apparently at Horner's request.

6. Records in the Circuit Court of Cook County are the basic source for most of the details about the Levys' domestic difficulties. The transcript of the testimony and other records in the case of *Levy* v. *Levy* are still in the court clerk's office.
7. Letter from Mrs. Mannheimer.
8. Carter H. Harrison, *Stormy Years* (Indianapolis: Bobbs-Merrill Company, 1935), p. 79.
9. C. David Tompkins, "John Peter Altgeld as a Candidate for Mayor of Chicago in 1899." *Journal of the Illinois State Historical Society* (Winter, 1963), p. 41.

CHAPTER THREE

1. Horner speech, February 12, 1931, to the Abraham Lincoln Association of Springfield. Horner Papers (Speech file).
2. Horner speech, February 12, 1938, Lincoln, Illinois. Horner Papers (Speech file).
3. Interview, Paul Angle, January 22, 1961.
4. Throughout this chapter, descriptive material on Kenna and Coughlin is taken from that excellent work on Chicago political history, Lloyd Wendt and Herman Kogan, *Lords of the Levee* (Indianapolis: Bobbs-Merrill Company, 1943).
5. The remarks by Coughlin and Horner are in an undated transcript, evidently based on shorthand notes taken at a First Ward rally, in the 1914 campaign file in the Horner Papers.
6. Burial information about Solomon Levy is from letters to the author, dated October 17, 1961, and October 26, 1961, from Clarence F. Judah, executive director of the Conference of Jewish Organizations, Louisville, Kentucky.
7. Horner to Lew Sarett, September 5, 1934. Horner Papers.
8. Horner to Bessie McCartney of Sparland, Illinois, who was preparing a Mother's Day program for the women's club of Macon, April 22, 1933. Horner Papers.
9. Carter Harrison, *Stormy Years* (Indianapolis: Bobbs-Merrill Company, 1935), p. 296.

CHAPTER FOUR

1. A copy of this undated prepared speech is in the Horner Papers (1914 campaign file).
2. The Horner Papers are the source for most of the material about probate court operation.
3. Forrest Crissey, "Keeping Faith with the Veterans," *Saturday Evening Post*, February 14, 1925, p. 40.
4. Details of this case have been taken from a letter to the author from Edwin C. Austin.
5. The Horner Papers contain a thick file on the judge's activities in the Chicago Literary Club and his Restless Ash projects.
6. The Albert Horner will incident is documented by reports and

correspondence in the Horner Papers and by a letter written to the author by Maurice Horner, Jr.

7. From an interview with Carl Sandburg.
8. Burt Massee, a Skeeter member, was helpful with his reminiscences of the Skeeters.
9. Much of the inside story of Republican politics in Chicago in the 1920's, helpful throughout this and subsequent chapters, is told in William H. Stuart, *The Twenty Incredible Years* (Chicago: M. A. Donohue & Company, 1935).
10. Interview with Louie Lewis, August 28, 1961, Christopher, Illinois.
11. The October, 1928, letter on the "Catholic question" can be found in the Horner Papers.
12. The author has borrowed from Alex Gottfried, *Boss Cermak of Chicago* (Seattle: University of Washington Press, 1962) for biographical information about Cermak. As a reporter, John Dienhart had inside knowledge of Cermak's strategies and was a valuable additional source.
13. From Rosenberg's "confession," as described in Gottfried, *Boss Cermak of Chicago*, p. 180.
14. *Illinois State Journal*, Springfield, April 4, 1930.
15. From a letter dated June 8, 1931, which can be found in the Horner Papers.
16. Gottfried, *Boss Cermak of Chicago*, p. 205.
17. Horner's letter to Rabbi Mann is in the personal correspondence file in the Horner Papers.
18. Interview, Judge Ulysses S. Schwartz, September 11, 1961.
19. Fletcher Dobyns, *The Underworld of American Politics* (New York: Fletcher Dobyns, 1932), p. 117.

CHAPTER FIVE

1. Cermak's intention of seeking the governorship himself is recalled by Alex Gottfried, *Boss Cermak of Chicago* (Seattle: University of Washington Press, 1962), and has been corroborated by Dienhart and others.
2. Chicago *Times*, April 8, 1932.
3. Horner Papers (1932 primary campaign speech file).
4. Carter Harrison, *Growing Up with Chicago* (Chicago: R. F. Seymour, 1944), p. 322.
5. Philip, William Booth, *Chicago and the Downstate, A Study of Their Conflicts, 1870–1934* (Chicago: privately published 1944), p. 8.
6. Interview with John W. Allen, southern Illinois historian.
7. From the *History of Gallatin, Saline, Hamilton, Franklin, and Williamson Counties, Illinois* (Chicago: Goodspeed Publishing Company, 1887), p. 284.
8. Benjamin Thomas, *Lincoln's New Salem* (New York: Alfred A. Knopf, 1954), p. 26.
9. The Christian County dialogue on the Jewish Question is a composite of the recollections of several interviewees, but chiefly

Emil Davis, Marshall Wheeler, Louie Lewis, and Joseph Knight.

10. The journals are in the Horner Papers as a part of the 1932 primary campaign file.
11. Horner Papers (1932 campaign file).
12. Reports and newspaper clippings of Sullivan's remarks on October 28, 1932, are in the Horner Papers (1932 campaign file).
13. Horner to Finnegan, August 8, 1932. Horner Papers (in a special file for Finnegan correspondence). Much of the material about the Horner-Finnegan relationship has been taken from the following excellent works of Walter C. Meyers: *Chicago's Mister Finnegan, A Gentleman of the Press* (Ph.D. dissertation, Northwestern University, 1959); "Henry Horner and Richard Finnegan—Footnote to a Friendship," *Journal of the Illinois State Historical Society* (Winter, 1962).
14. Finnegan to Horner, September 22, 1932. Horner Papers (Finnegan file).
15. The Griffin and Sandburg post-election messages can be found in the special correspondence files labeled with their names in the Horner Papers. The Nudelman and Rossiter messages are in the 1932 campaign file.

CHAPTER SIX

1. Inaugural address of Henry Horner, January 9, 1933. This and the other published addresses of the governor's are on file in the Illinois Legislative Reference Bureau, Statehouse, Springfield.
2. Finnegan to Horner, January 10, 1933. Horner Papers (Finnegan file).
3. Fisher to Horner, January 16, 1933. Horner Papers (Correspondence file, Cook County).
4. This and all the other National Guard reports are in the Horner Papers in a special military file that was maintained for that purpose.
5. The bulk of the biographical material about John L. Lewis is from Saul Alinsky, *John L. Lewis, An Unauthorized Biography* (New York: Putnam's, 1949).
6. The governor's statement is in the Horner Papers, part of a general file devoted to the coal mine union controversy.
7. Montgomery Winning, an assistant Illinois attorney general at the time, recalled the governor's efforts to resolve the union conflict, in an interview with the author.
8. Most of the bank crisis details have been taken from Horner's letter to Ray Moley, November 15, 1939, Horner Papers; and from William Manchester's article, "Great Bank Holiday," *Holiday*, February, 1960, p. 60.
9. Richberg's statement on the Illinois situation, dated October 17, 1933, is in the Horner Papers as part of the mine union files.

CHAPTER SEVEN

1. Horner to Wilfred S. Reynolds, executive secretary, Illinois Emergency Relief Commission, July 24, 1933. Horner Papers (Relief file).

2. As has been indicated previously, the National Guard intelligence reports, referred to often in this chapter, are in the Horner Papers.
3. Letter dated May 1, 1933. Horner Papers.
4. Arthur M. Schlesinger, Jr., *The Coming of the New Deal* (Boston: Houghton Mifflin Company, 1961), p. 274.
5. This and Horner's other addresses to the legislature are in the Horner Papers and the Illinois Legislative Reference Bureau.
6. Decatur *Herald,* October 27, 1933.
7. Correspondence to and from Bishop Griffin was kept in a separate file in the governor's office, a large one that is evidently intact in the Horner Papers.
8. Chase to Horner, July 8, 1933. Horner Papers (University of Illinois file).
9. Memoranda and other documents in two files in the Horner Papers, one labeled "Relief and unemployment" and the other "Relief, misc.," are the sources of much of the detailed material in this chapter.
10. Harold L. Ickes, *The Secret Diary of Harold L. Ickes,* 3 vols. (New York: Simon & Schuster, 1953), I, 439.
11. Monmouth *Daily Review Atlas,* November 16, 1934.
12. The nurse who was pursued about the mansion by the governor described the experience in an interview but is deserving of the feminine privilege of anonymity.

CHAPTER EIGHT

1. The conversation and incident surrounding the eyedrop bill are largely as reconstructed by Rabbi Mann. All conversations in this book are derived from a composite of recollections, some written, others repeated in the course of interviews.
2. The details are from the Horner Papers; a letter to the author from Dr. Gault; records of the Illinois Department of Public Welfare (now the Department of Mental Health) and the Dixon State School; an interview with Louie Lewis, the former speaker of the Illinois House of Representatives and state treasurer; and a letter from the Illinois Children's Home and Aid Society.

CHAPTER NINE

1. Horner to Oliver Barrett, October 30, 1937. Horner Papers (Correspondence file, Cook County).
2. From Dr. Rosen's notes, made available to the author.
3. Mrs. Franklin D. Roosevelt to Horner, September 6, 1938. Horner Papers.
4. Horner to Bobby Breen, October 8, 1937. Horner Papers.

CHAPTER TEN

1. Chicago *Times,* December 20, 1933. Quoted in Walter Meyers, "Henry Horner and Richard Finnegan—Footnote to a Friendship," *Journal of the Illinois State Historical Society* (Winter, 1962).

2. Horner to Finnegan, December 20, 1933. Horner Papers (Finnegan file).
3. Finnegan to Horner, December 23, 1933. Horner Papers (Finnegan file).
4. Chicago *Times*, May 10, 1934.
5. Jennie Purvin to Horner, November 10, 1933. Horner Papers (Correspondence file, Cook County).
6. A thorough report of the meeting of Jewish precinct captains in October of 1934 was submitted to the governor by Stillman Frankland and is in the Horner Papers.
7. Whitman to Horner, April 29, 1936. Horner Papers (Whitman file).
8. The Chicago Democrat involved in the road joint company correspondence is purposely not identified. Although the letters and other documents in the file appear fully incriminating, the individual involved is dead and presumably might have been able to cite mitigating circumstances were he available for interviewing.
9. There is a fat file in the Horner Papers abundantly filled with correspondence to and from Mr. Klein.
10. Horner to McIntyre, October 6, 1937. Horner Papers (FDR file).
11. Finnegan to Horner, April 22, 1935. Horner Papers (Finnegan file). The original of the letter shows that Finnegan scratched out the formal "Dear Governor" greeting referred to by Meyers (who had access to Finnegan's carbon copy) and substituted "Dear Henry."

CHAPTER ELEVEN

1. See *Veto Messages,* 59th General Assembly, House Bill 1045, July 11, 1935.
2. The Young Jewish Lawyers' Association resolution was dated August 21, 1935, and is in the Horner Papers.
3. The baby book episode is recounted in the Horner Papers through correspondence from Bundesen, Hodes, and Jirka, in a file on the matter.
4. Scott Lucas said in an interview that Kelly made this mid-autumn, 1935, remark in his presence at an American Legion convention in St. Louis.
5. State policeman Van Diver witnessed the conversation among Kelly, Nash, and Horner in the governor's car on December 9, 1935.
6. Decatur *Herald,* December 12, 1935.

CHAPTER TWELVE

1. From Armand de Caulaincourt, *With Napoleon in Russia* (New York: William Morrow & Company, 1935), pp. 353, 367, 369.
2. Harry Fisher to Horner, February 25, 1936. Horner Papers.
3. Robert S. Hunt to Horner, January 25, 1936. Horner Papers.
4. Farley to Bonfoey (copy in Horner Papers), January 23, 1936.
5. Horner to Bonfoey, February 13, 1936. Horner Papers.
6. Horner to J. Hamilton Lewis, March 12, 1936. Horner Papers.

7. Julius Klein's letter, written on February 20, 1936, was made available by him to the author.
8. An undated copy of Rabbi Feinberg's sermon is in the 1936 primary campaign file in the Horner Papers.
9. *Report of the Board of Managers of the Chicago Bar Association Concerning an Inquiry Conducted by It in Reference to the Activities of Judges in Partisan Politics,* June 11, 1936.
10. Newspaper stories and the author's interviews with Spike Hennessey and a number of others who were associated with Bundesen's campaign are the sources of the details of that campaign in this chapter.
11. Harold L. Ickes, *The Secret Diary of Harold L. Ickes,* 3 vols. (New York: Simon & Schuster, 1953), II, 458.

CHAPTER THIRTEEN

1. The story about the old man at the synagogue was related by Arvey.
2. "Kelly-Nash Political Machine," *Fortune,* August, 1936, p. 46.
3. Conclusions on the correlation between the neighborhood relief load and the Jewish vote for Horner have been based on the author's analysis of demographic data. See Edward L. Burchard, *District Factbook for 75 Chicago Local Communities* (Chicago Board of Education, 1935).
4. Arvey's letter is in the Horner Papers. It is assumed by the author that the business to which he referred was state business.
5. Horner to Farley, July 21, 1936. Horner Papers.

CHAPTER FOURTEEN

1. Roosevelt to Horner, November 21, 1936. Horner Papers.
2. Horner to Lewis, April 22, 1937, April 26, 1937, and June 25, 1937. Horner Papers.
3. Horner to Claude Bowers, undated. Horner Papers.
4. Interview, J. R. Fitzpatrick, December 15, 1961.
5. Horner to Finnegan, December 15, 1939. Horner Papers.
6. J. T. Flynn, "These Our Rulers: Kelly-Nash Machine," *Collier's,* July 20, 1940, p. 18.
7. Oliver Barrett to Horner, May 25, 1937. Horner Papers.
8. Arvey to Horner, November 11, 1938. Horner Papers.
9. Lucas to Horner, November 15, 1938. Horner Papers.

CHAPTER FIFTEEN

1. Dr. Rosen's notes are the source for this and most of the other medical details in this chapter.
2. Mary Jo White to Horner, March 6, 1940. Horner Papers (Out-of-state correspondence file).
3. Horner to a friend, January 15, 1940. Horner Papers.
4. Most of the technical material about the Manteno epidemic is taken from the 1945 report of the State Department of Public Health.

5. The subject of the constitutional disability issue during Horner's protracted illness is reviewed in Clyde F. Snider, "Gubernatorial Disability," *University of Chicago Law Review* (April, 1941).
6. Interview, Judge Elmer Schnackenberg, September 15, 1961.
7. The transcript of the testimony, dated May 23, 1940, was supplied by Dr. Rosen from his records.
8. Republican Editorial Association of Illinois to Horner, September 18, 1940. Horner Papers.

CHAPTER SIXTEEN

1. Chicago *Times,* October 6, 7, 1940.
2. Chicago *Tribune,* October 7, 1940.
3. The funeral orations were published in Lloyd Lewis, *Henry Horner, Governor of Illinois, a Tribute* (Chicago: Lakeside Press, private printing, 1949).
4. Many of the details of the funeral have been taken from conversations with Dr. Mann.

CHAPTER SEVENTEEN

1. The Stelle material is abstracted from daily newspaper accounts, particularly those in the Chicago *Tribune,* Chicago *Daily News,* and Chicago *Times;* and from interviews with Executive Mansion staff and other contemporaries.

CHAPTER EIGHTEEN

1. *The Advocate,* October 11, 1940.
2. For a good article on John Patterson Stelle, see Roy V. Scott, "John Patterson Stelle: Agrarian Crusader from Southern Illinois," *Journal of the Illinois State Historical Society* (Autumn, 1962).
3. From David Shannon (ed.), *Beatrice Webb's American Diary: 1898* (Madison, Wis.: University of Wisconsin Press, 1963).
4. Judge Schwartz's remarks are from his address at a Standard Club dedication of a Horner portrait donated by James Levy.
5. The theme developed here is adapted from Daniel Elazar's perceptive paper on "The Office of Governor in Illinois: 1818–1933," Institute of Government and Public Affairs, University of Illinois, 1962.

Sources

By far the most important source for this biography has been the official Horner Papers, which are preserved in the Illinois State Historical Library in Springfield. One hundred and forty-four file drawers of correspondence, reports, and personal documents were turned over to the state of Illinois by the governor's heirs with the understanding that they remain locked up until 1962. Unsorted and unclassified, the files were made available then for the author's examination. Since that time, the curator of manuscripts for the library has classified the papers in eleven general categories. But the library does not have a name index for the correspondence, nor is the collection alphabetically arranged. It has not been possible, therefore, to devise a systematic reference system for the papers that would direct anyone to a certain source document. These are the general classification groups:

1. Political, with separate sets of files for the 1932, 1936, and 1938 campaigns.

2. Departmental files, based generally on the appropriate state department or agency.

3. Subject files, with about 270 subject titles.

4. Correspondence files, downstate, filed by county and then alphabetically by the name of the correspondent.

5. Correspondence files, Cook County, filed alphabetically by the name of the correspondent. There are about 600 folders in the downstate and Cook County files.

6. Business papers.

7. Correspondence files from out of state, approximately 200 folders.

8. Correspondence files, personal, filed alphabetically by name of the writer.

9. Correspondence files, subjects, filed alphabetically by subject headings.

10. Scrapbooks.

11. Miscellaneous subject files, containing letters, copies of speeches, published material, newspapers, memorabilia, pictures, and a great variety of miscellany. There are about 520 subject folders in this group.

Because the author examined the papers before they were placed in their present arrangement, the staff of the library advises that an exhaustive search is the only practical way to locate a particular item. It is hoped, of course, that a cataloguing system will be devised in the future to assist scholars of the depression era.

Other valuable sources were fifty volumes of Horner scrapbooks maintained by the governor's office staff and now on file in the Chicago Historical Society Library in Chicago; notes compiled from Dr. Nathan Rosen's diaries and other records; and personal interviews.

Interviews were conducted with seventy-eight persons. Some are still actively practicing politicians who supplied information on the condition that they not be quoted. Whenever possible, specific important statements are attributed to their sources in the notes to each chapter. Information obtained in the off-the-record interviews was cross-checked against the available documents and the versions of others in an effort to weigh the evidence. The interviews were all helpful, but the following persons deserve special mention and gratitude: Carl Sandburg, Louie Lewis, Mrs. Edith Steinbrecher Downs, Joseph Knight, Benjamin Adamowski, Everett Van Diver, Milburn Akers, Burt Massee, Dr. Robert Bowen, Harry Barnard, John Dienhart, John Cassidy, Barnet Hodes, Paul Angle, Donald Chamberlain, George Schuppe, Marshall Wheeler, Clarence Liggins, Malden Jones, U. S. Schwartz, Edward J. Barrett, Percy Wood, William Stuart, Dr. Louis Mann, Jacob Arvey, Maurice Horner, Jr., Elmer Schnackenberg, Robert Perbohner, Montgomery Winning, Baxter Richardson, Emil Davis, John Weigel, Scott Lucas, J. R. Fitzpatrick, Abraham Marovitz, Adolph Belval, Sr., Michael Igoe, Edward Low, George Eisenberg, Simeon Leland, Ernest Palmer, Blanche Fritz, Harry Hershey, Mrs. Otto Kerner, Sr., Hallie Holt, Grace Jacobs, John Stelle, Mary Odbert, Henry Straus, and Henry McCarthy.

Selected Bibliography

Alinsky, Saul. *John L. Lewis, An Unauthorized Biography.* New York: Putnam's, 1949.

Allen, John W. *Legends and Lore of Southern Illinois*. Binghamton, N. Y.: Vail-Ballou Press, 1963.

Bregstone, Philip P. *Chicago and Its Jews*. Chicago: privately published, 1933.

Brownell, Baker. *The Other Illinois*. New York: Duell, Sloan & Pearce, 1958.

Burchard, Edward L. *District Fact Book for 75 Chicago Local Communities*. Chicago: Chicago Board of Education, 1935.

Chicago Bar Association. "In Memoriam: Henry Horner." *Chicago Bar Record,* Vol. XXII, No. 4 (January, 1941), p. 145.

———. *Report of the Board of Managers Concerning an Inquiry Conducted by It in Reference to the Activities of Judges in Partisan Politics,* June 11, 1936.

Crissey, Forrest. "Keeping Faith with Veterans." *Saturday Evening Post,* February 14, 1925, p. 40.

Dedmon, Emmett. *Fabulous Chicago*. New York: Random House, 1953.

Dernburg, Carl. *Memoirs of an American Pioneer, 1857–1943*. Chicago: privately published, 1943.

Dobyns, Fletcher. *The Underworld of American Politics*. New York: Fletcher Dobyns, 1932.

Elazar, Daniel J. "The Office of Governor in Illinois: 1818–1933." Background paper, Assembly on the Office of Governor, December, 1962, sponsored by the Institute of Government and Public Affairs, University of Illinois, Allerton Park, Illinois.

———. *The American Partnership*. Chicago: University of Chicago Press, 1962.

Eliassof, Herman. "The Jews of Illinois." *Reform Advocate,* May 4, 1901.

Flynn, J. T. "These Our Rulers: Kelly-Nash Machine." *Collier's,* July 20, 1940, p. 18.

Fortune. "Kelly-Nash Political Machine," August, 1936, p. 46.

Garvey, Neil F. *The Government and Administration of Illinois*. American Commonwealth Series. New York: Crowell, 1958.

Gosnell, Harold F. *Machine Politics: Chicago Model*. Chicago: University of Chicago Press, 1937.

Gottfried, Alex. *Boss Cermak of Chicago*. Seattle: University of Washington Press, 1962.

Harrison, Carter H. *Stormy Years*. Indianapolis: Bobbs-Merrill Company, 1935.

———. *Growing Up with Chicago*. Chicago: R. F. Seymour, 1944.

History of Gallatin, Saline, Hamilton, Franklin, and Williamson

Counties, Illinois. Chicago: Goodspeed Publishing Company, 1887.

Hofstadter, Richard. *The Age of Reform—Bryan to FDR*. New York: Alfred A. Knopf, 1955.

Ickes, Harold L. *The Secret Diary of Harold L. Ickes*. 3 vols. New York: Simon & Schuster, 1953.

Illinois Department of Public Health. *A Report on the Typhoid Epidemic at Manteno State Hospital in 1939*. 1945.

Journals of the Illinois Senate and House of Representatives, 1931–1940.

Kohn, Walter S. G. "Illinois' Convention Ratifies the Twenty-First Amendment." *Journal of the Illinois State Historical Society* (Winter, 1963).

Korshak, Max M. "A Lawyer's World." Unpublished personal memoirs of a Chicago lawyer and politician.

Lewis, Lloyd. *Henry Horner, Governor of Illinois, a Tribute*. Chicago: Lakeside Press, private printing, 1949.

Lipson, Leslie. *The American Governor: From Figurehead to Leader*. Chicago: University of Chicago Press, 1939.

Long, Patricia Lee. "The Banking Holiday in Gillespie, Illinois." Unpublished thesis, Blackburn College, Carlinville, Illinois, 1961.

Manchester, William. "Great Bank Holiday." *Holiday*, February, 1960, p. 60.

Masters, Edgar Lee. *The Sangamon*. New York: Holt, Rinehart & Winston, 1954.

Meites, Hyman L. *History of the Jews in Chicago*. Chicago: Jewish Historical Society of Illinois, 1924.

Merriam, Charles E. *Chicago: A More Intimate View of Urban Politics*. New York: Macmillan Company, 1929.

Meyers, Walter Cameron. *Chicago's Mister Finnegan, a Gentleman of the Press*. Ph.D. dissertation, Northwestern University, 1959.

———. "Henry Horner and Richard Finnegan—Footnote to a Friendship." *Journal of the Illinois State Historical Society* (Winter, 1962).

Pease, Theodore Calvin. *The Story of Illinois*. Chicago: University of Chicago Press, 1939.

Philip, William Booth. *Chicago and the Downstate, A Study of Their Conflicts, 1870–1934*. Chicago: privately published, 1944.

Pratt, Harry E. "Famous Lincoln Collections." *Abraham Lincoln Quarterly* (June, 1940).

Schlesinger, Arthur M., Jr. *The Coming of the New Deal.* Boston: Houghton Mifflin Company, 1959.

Scott, Roy V. "John Patterson Stelle: Agrarian Crusader from Southern Illinois." *Journal of the Illinois State Historical Society* (Autumn, 1962).

The Sentinel's History of Chicago Jewry, 1911–1961. Chicago: Sentinel Publishing Company, 1961.

Shannon, David (ed.). *Beatrice Webb's American Diary: 1898.* Madison, Wis.: University of Wisconsin Press, 1963.

Snider, Clyde F. "Gubernatorial Disability." *University of Chicago Law Review* (April, 1941).

Steiner, Gilbert Y., and Gove, Samuel K. "Governors, Issues and Styles: 1933–1960." *University of Illinois Bulletin* (1963).

Stelle, J. P. and E. E. *Family Souvenir, John P. and Eliza E. Stelle.* Dahlgren, Illinois: privately printed, 1910.

Stuart, William H. *The Twenty Incredible Years.* Chicago: M. A. Donohue & Company, 1935.

Survey Graphic. Special Chicago issue (October, 1934).

Thomas, Benjamin P. *Lincoln's New Salem.* New York: Alfred A. Knopf, 1954.

Tompkins, C. David. "John Peter Altgeld as a Candidate for Mayor of Chicago in 1899." *Journal of the Illinois State Historical Society* (Winter, 1963).

Wade, Louise C. *Graham Taylor, Pioneer for Social Justice, 1851–1938.* Chicago: University of Chicago Press, 1964.

Wendt, Lloyd, and Kogan, Herman. *Lords of the Levee.* Indianapolis: Bobbs-Merrill Company, 1943.

Williams, Elmer Lynn. *The Fix-It Boys.* Chicago: privately printed, 1940.

Index